MEMOIRS TO ILLUSTRATE ⌐
TIME: VOLUME 1
BY
François Guizot

MEMOIRS TO ILLUSTRATE THE HISTORY OF MY TIME: VOLUME 1

Published by Wallachia Publishers

New York City, NY

First published circa 1874

Copyright © Wallachia Publishers, 2015

All rights reserved

ABOUT WALLACHIA PUBLISHERS

Wallachia Publishers mission is to publish the world's finest European history texts. More information on our recent publications and catalog can be found on our website.

CHAPTER I.: FRANCE BEFORE THE RESTORATION.: 1807-1814.

MY REASONS FOR PUBLISHING THESE MEMOIRS DURING MY LIFE.—MY INTRODUCTION INTO SOCIETY.—MY FIRST ACQUAINTANCE WITH M. DE CHÂTEAUBRIAND, M. SUARD, MADAME DE STAEL, M. DE FONTANES, M. ROYER-COLLARD.—PROPOSAL TO APPOINT ME AUDITOR IN THE IMPERIAL STATE COUNCIL.—WHY THE APPOINTMENT DID NOT TAKE PLACE.—I ENTER THE UNIVERSITY, AND BEGIN MY COURSE OF LECTURES ON MODERN HISTORY.—LIBERAL AND ROYALIST PARTIES.—CHARACTERS OF THE DIFFERENT OPPOSITIONS TOWARDS THE CLOSE OF THE EMPIRE.—ATTEMPTED RESISTANCE OF THE LEGISLATIVE BODY.—MM. , GALLOIS, MAINE-BIRAN, RAYNOUARD, AND FLAUGERGUES.—I LEAVE PARIS FOR NISMES.—STATE OF PARIS AND FRANCE IN MARCH, 1814.—THE RESTORATION TAKES PLACE.—I RETURN TO PARIS, AND AM APPOINTED SECRETARY-GENERAL TO THE MINISTRY OF THE INTERIOR.

I adopt a course different from that recently pursued by several of my contemporaries; I publish my memoirs while I am still here to answer for what I write. I am not prompted to this by the weariness of inaction, or by any desire to re-open a limited field for old contentions, in place of the grand arena at present closed. I have struggled much and ardently during my life; age and retirement, as far as my own feelings are concerned, have expanded their peaceful influence over the past. From a sky profoundly serene, I look back towards an horizon pregnant with many storms. I have deeply probed my own heart, and I cannot find there any feeling which envenoms my recollections. The absence of gall permits extreme candour. Personality alters or deteriorates truth. Being desirous to speak of my own life, and of the times in which I have lived, I prefer doing so on the brink, rather than from the depths of the tomb. This appears to me more dignified as regards myself, while, with reference to others, it will lead me to be more scrupulous in my words and opinions. If objections arise, which I can scarcely hope to escape, at least it shall not be said that I was unwilling to hear them, and that I have removed myself from the responsibility of what I have done.

Other reasons, also, have induced this decision. Memoirs, in general, are either published too soon or too late. If too soon, they are indiscreet or unimportant; we either reveal what would be better held back for the present, or suppress details which it would be both profitable and curious to relate at once. If too late, they lose much of their opportunity and interest; contemporaries have passed away, and can no longer profit by the truths which are imparted, or participate in their recital with personal enjoyment. Such memoirs retain only a moral and literary value, and excite no feeling beyond idle curiosity. Although I well know how much experience evaporates in passing from one generation to another, I cannot believe that it becomes altogether extinct, or that a correct knowledge of the mistakes of our fathers, and of the causes of their failures, can be totally profitless to their descendants. I wish to transmit to those who may succeed me, and who also will have their trials to undergo, a little of the light I have derived from mine. I have, alternately, defended liberty against absolute power, and order against the spirit of revolution,—

two leading causes which, in fact, constitute but one, for their disconnection leads to the ruin of both. Until liberty boldly separates itself from the spirit of revolution, and order from absolute power, so long will France continue to be tossed about from crisis to crisis, and from error to error. In this is truly comprised the cause of the nation. I am grieved, but not dismayed, at its reverses. I neither renounce its service, nor despair of its triumph. Under the severest disappointments, it has ever been my natural tendency, and for which I thank God as for a blessing, to preserve great desires, however uncertain or distant might be the hopes of their accomplishment.

In ancient and in modern times, the greatest of great historians, Thucydides, Xenophon, Sallust, Cæsar, Tacitus, Macchiavelli, and Clarendon, have written, and some have themselves published, the annals of the passing age and of the events in which they participated. I do not venture on such an ambitious work; the day of history has not yet arrived for us, of complete, free, and unreserved history, either as relates to facts or men. But my own personal and inward history; what I have thought, felt, and wished in my connection with the public affairs of my country; the thoughts, feelings, and wishes of my political friends and associates, our minds reflected in our actions,—on these points I can speak freely, and on these I am most desirous to record my sentiments, that I may be, if not always approved, at least correctly known and understood. On this foundation, others will hereafter assign to us our proper places in the history of the age.

I only commenced public life in the year 1814. I had neither served under the Revolution nor the Empire: a stranger to the first from youth, and to the second from disposition. Since I have had some share in the government of men, I have learned to do justice to the Emperor Napoleon. He was endowed with a genius incomparably active and powerful, much to be admired for his antipathy to disorder, for his profound instincts in ruling, and for his energetic rapidity in reconstructing the social framework. But this genius had no check, acknowledged no limit to its desires or will, either emanating from Heaven or man, and thus remained revolutionary while combating revolution: thoroughly acquainted with the general conditions of society, but imperfectly, or rather, coarsely understanding the moral necessities of human nature; sometimes satisfying them with the soundest judgment, and at others depreciating and insulting them with impious pride. Who could have believed that the same man who had established the Concordat, and re-opened the churches in France, would have carried off the Pope from Rome, and kept him a prisoner at Fontainebleau?

It is going too far to apply the same ill-treatment to philosophers and Christians, to reason and faith. Amongst the great men of his class, Napoleon was by far the most necessary for the times. None but himself could have so quickly and effectually substituted order in place of anarchy; but no one was so chimerical as to the future, for after having been master of France and Europe, he suffered Europe to drive him even from France. His name is greater and more enduring than his actions, the most brilliant of which, his conquests, disappeared suddenly and for ever, with himself. In rendering homage to his exalted qualities, I feel no regret at not having appreciated them until after his death. For me, under the Empire, there was too much of the arrogance of power, too much contempt of right, too much revolution, and too little liberty.

It is not that at that period I was much engaged in politics, or over-impatient for the freedom that should open to me the road I desired. I associated myself with the Opposition, but it was an Opposition bearing little resemblance to that which we have seen and created during the last thirty years. It was formed from the relics of the philosophic world and liberal aristocracy of the eighteenth century, the last representatives of the saloons in which all subjects whatever had been freely proposed and discussed, through the impulse of inclination, and the gratification of mental indulgence, rather than from any distinct object of interest or ambition. The errors and disasters of the Revolution had not led the survivors of that active generation to renounce their convictions or desires; they remained sincerely liberal, but without practical or urgent pretension, and with the reserve of men who had suffered much and succeeded little in their attempts at legislative reform. They still held to freedom of thought and speech, but had no aspirations after power. They detested and warmly criticized despotism, but without any open attempt to repress or overthrow existing authority. It was the opposition of enlightened and independent lookers-on, who had neither the opportunity nor inclination to interfere as actors.

After a long life of fierce contention, I recur with pleasure to the remembrance of this enchanting society. M. de Talleyrand once said to me, "Those who were not living in and about the year 1789, know little of the enjoyments of life." In fact, nothing could exceed the pleasure of a great intellectual and social movement, which, at that epoch, far from suspending or disturbing the arrangements of the world, animated and ennobled them by mingling serious thoughts with frivolous recreations, and as yet called for no suffering, or no sacrifice, while it opened to the eyes of men a dazzling and delightful perspective. The eighteenth century was, beyond all question, the most tempting and seductive of ages, for it promised to satisfy at once the strength and weakness of human nature; elevating and enervating the mind at the same time; flattering alternately the noblest sentiments and the most grovelling propensities; intoxicating with exalted hopes, and nursing with effeminate concessions. Thus it has produced, in pellmell confusion, utopians and egotists, sceptics and fanatics, enthusiasts and incredulous scoffers, different offspring of the same period, but all enraptured with the age and with themselves, indulging together in one common drunkenness on the eve of the approaching chaos.

When I first mixed with the world in 1807, the storm had for a long time burst; the infatuation of 1789 had completely disappeared. Society, entirely occupied with its own re-establishment, no longer dreamed of elevating itself in the midst of mere amusement; exhibitions of force had superseded impulses towards liberty. Coldness, absence of fellow-feeling, isolation of sentiment and interests,—in these are comprised the ordinary course and weary vexations of the world. France, worn out with errors and strange excesses, eager once more for order and common sense, fell back into the old track. In the midst of this general reaction, the faithful inheritors of the literary saloons of the eighteenth century held themselves aloof from its influence; they alone preserved two of the noblest and most amiable propensities of their age—a disinterested taste for pleasures of the mind, and that readiness of sympathy, that warmth and ardour of curiosity, that necessity for moral improvement and free discussion, which embellish the social relations with so much variety and sweetness.

In my own case, I drew from these sources a profitable experience. Led into the circle I have named, by an incident in my private life, I entered amongst them very young, perfectly unknown, with no other title than a little presumed ability, some education, and an ardent taste for refined pleasures, letters, and good company. I carried with me no ideas harmonizing with those I found there. I had been brought up at Geneva, with extremely liberal notions, but in austere habits and religious convictions entirely opposed to the philosophy of the eighteenth century, rather than in coincidence with or in admiration of its works and tendencies. During my residence in Paris, German metaphysics and literature had been my favourite study; I read Kant and Klopstock, Herder and Schiller, much more frequently than Condillac and Voltaire. M. Suard, the Abbé Morellet, the Marquis de Boufflers, the frequenters of the drawing-rooms of Madame d'Houdetot and of Madame de Rumford, who received me with extreme complaisance, smiled, and sometimes grew tired of my Christian traditions and Germanic enthusiasm; but, after all, this difference of opinion established for me, in their circle, a plea of interest and favour instead of producing any feeling of illwill or even of indifference. They knew that I was as sincerely attached to liberty and the privileges of human intelligence as they were themselves, and they discovered something novel and independent in my turn of thought, which inspired both esteem and attraction. At this period, they constantly supported me with their friendship and interest, without ever attempting to press or control me on the points on which we disagreed. From them especially, I have learned to exercise in practical life, that expanded equity, joined to respect for the freedom of others, which constitute the character and duty of a truly liberal mind.

This generous disposition manifested itself on every opportunity. In 1809, M. de Châteaubriand published 'The Martyrs.' The success of this work was at first slow, and strongly disputed. Amongst the disciples of the eighteenth century and of Voltaire, a great majority treated M. de Châteaubriand as an enemy, while the more moderate section looked on him with little favour. They rejected his ideas even when they felt that they were not called upon to contest them. His style of writing offended their taste, which was divested of all imagination, and more refined than grand. My own disposition was entirely opposed to theirs. I passionately admired M. de Châteaubriand in his ideas and language: that beautiful compound of religious sentiment and romantic imagination, of poetry and moral polemics, had so powerfully moved and subdued me, that, soon after my arrival at Paris in 1806, one of my first literary fantasies was to address an epistle, in very indifferent verse, to M. de Châteaubriand, who immediately thanked me in prose, artistically polished and unassuming. His letter flattered my youth, and 'The Martyrs' redoubled my zeal. Seeing them so violently attacked, I resolved to defend them in the 'Publicist,' in which I occasionally wrote. M. Suard, who conducted that journal, although far from coinciding with the opinions I had adopted, lent himself most obligingly to my desire. I have met with very few men of a natural temperament so gentle and liberal, and with a mind at the same time scrupulously refined and fastidious. He was much more disposed to criticize than to admire the talent of M. de Châteaubriand; but he admitted the great extent of his ability, and on that ground dealt with him gently, although with delicate irony. Besides which, the talent was full of independence, and exerted in opposition to the formidable tendencies of Imperial power. These qualities won largely upon the esteem of M. Suard, who, in consequence, allowed me an unfettered course in the 'Publicist,' of which I availed myself to espouse the cause of 'The Martyrs' against their detractors.

M. de Châteaubriand was deeply affected by this, and hastened to express his acknowledgments. My articles became the subject of a correspondence between us, which I still refer to with pleasure. He explained to me his intentions and motives in the composition of his poem, discussed with susceptibility and even with some degree of temper concealed under his gratitude, the strictures mixed with my eulogiums, and finished by saying: "In conclusion, Sir, you know the tempests raised against my work, and from whence they proceed. There is another wound, not exhibited, which is the real source of all this rage. It is that Hierocles massacres the Christians in the name of philosophy and liberty. Time will do me justice, if my work deserves it, and you will greatly accelerate this justice by the publication of your articles, provided you could be induced to change and modify them to a certain point. Show me my faults, and I will correct them. I only despise those critics who are as base in their language as in the secret motives which induce them to speak. I can find neither reason nor principle in the mouths of those literary mountebanks hired by the police, who dance in the gutters for the amusement of lacqueys.... I do not give up the hope of calling to see you, or of receiving you in my hermitage. Honest men should, particularly at present, unite for mutual consolation; generous feelings and exalted sentiments become every day so rare, that we ought to consider ourselves too happy when we encounter them.... Accept, I entreat you, once more, the assurance of my high consideration, of my sincere devotion, and if you will permit, of a friendship which we commence under the auspices of frankness and honour."

Between M. de Châteaubriand and myself, frankness and honour, most certainly, have never been disturbed throughout our political controversies; but friendship has not been able to survive them. The word is too rare and valuable to be hastily pronounced.

When we have lived under a system of real and serious liberty, we feel both an inclination and a right to smile when we consider what, in other times, has been classed as factious opposition by the one side, and courageous resistance by the other. In August, 1807, eighteen months before the publication of 'The Martyrs,' I stopped some days in Switzerland, on my way to visit my mother at Nismes; and with the confident enthusiasm of youth, as anxious to become acquainted with living celebrities as I was myself unknown, I addressed a letter to Madame de Staël, requesting the honour of calling upon her. She invited me to dinner at Ouchy, near Lausanne, where she then resided. I was placed next to her; I came from Paris; she questioned me as to what was passing there, how the public were occupied, and what were the topics of conversation in the saloons. I spoke of an article by M. de Châteaubriand, in the 'Mercury,' which was making some noise at the moment of my departure. A particular passage had struck me, which I quoted according to the text, as it had strongly impressed itself on my memory. "When, in the silence of abject submission, we hear only the chains of the slave and the voice of the informer, when all tremble before the tyrant, and it is as dangerous to incur favour as to merit disgrace, the historian appears to be charged with the vengeance of nations. It is in vain that Nero triumphs. Tacitus has been born in the Empire; he grows up unnoticed near the ashes of Germanicus, and already uncompromising Providence has handed over to an obscure child the glory of the master of the world." My tone of voice was undoubtedly excited and striking, as I was myself deeply moved and arrested by the words. Madame de Staël, seizing me by the arm, exclaimed, "I am sure you would make an excellent tragedian; remain with us and take a part in the 'Andromache.'" Theatricals were at that time the prevailing taste and amusement in her house. I excused myself from her kind conjecture and proposal, and the conversation returned to M. de Châteaubriand and his article, which was greatly admired, while at the same time it excited some apprehension. The admiration was just, for the passage was really eloquent; neither was the alarm without grounds, for the 'Mercury' was suppressed precisely on account of this identical paragraph. Thus, the Emperor Napoleon, conqueror of Europe and absolute master of France, believed that he could not suffer it to be written that his future historian might perhaps be born under his reign, and held himself compelled to take the honour of Nero under his shield. It was a heavy penalty attached to greatness, to have such apprehensions to exhibit, and such clients to protect!

Exalted minds, who felt a little for the dignity of human nature, had sound reason for being discontented with the existing system; they saw that it could neither establish the happiness nor the permanent prosperity of France; but it seemed then so firmly established in general opinion, its power was so universally admitted, and so little was any change anticipated for the future, that even within the haughty and narrow circle in which the spirit of opposition prevailed, it appeared quite natural that young men should enter the service of Government, the only public career that remained open to them. A lady of distinguished talent and noble sentiments, who had conceived a certain degree of friendship for me, Madame de Rémusat, was desirous that I should be named Auditor in the State Council. Her cousin, M. Pasquier, Prefect of Police, whom I sometimes met at her house, interested himself in this matter with much cordiality, and, under the advice of my most intimate friends, I acceded to the proposition, although, at the bottom of my heart, it occasioned me some uneasiness. It was intended that I should be attached to the Ministry of Foreign Affairs. M. Pasquier named me to the Duke of Bassano, then at the head of the department, and to Count d'Hauterive, Comptroller of the Archives. The Duke sent for me. I also had an interview with M. d'Hauterive, who possessed a fertile and ingenious mind, and was kindly disposed towards young men of studious habits. As a trial of ability, they ordered me to draw up a memorial on a question respecting which, the Emperor either was, or wished to appear, deeply interested—the mutual exchange of French and English prisoners. Many documents on the subject were placed in my hands. I completed the memorial; and, believing that the Emperor was sincere, carefully set forward those principles of the law of nations which rendered the measure desirable, and the mutual concessions necessary for its accomplishment. My work was duly submitted to the Duke of Bassano. I have reason to conclude that I had mistaken his object; and that the Emperor, looking upon the English detained in France as of more importance than the French confined in England, and believing also that the number of the latter pressed inconveniently on the English Government, had no serious intention of carrying out the proposed exchange. Whatever might be the cause, I heard nothing more either of my memorial or nomination, a result which caused me little regret.

Another career soon opened to me, more suitable to my views, as being less connected with the Government. My first attempts at writing, particularly my Critical Notes on Gibbon's 'History of the Decline and Fall of the Roman Empire,' and the 'Annals of Education,' a periodical miscellany in which I had touched upon some leading questions of public and private instruction, obtained for me the notice of literary men. With gratuitous kindness, M. de Fontanes, Grand Master of the University, appointed me Assistant Professor to the Chair of History, occupied by M. de Lacretelle, in the Faculty of Letters in the Academy of Paris. In a very short time, and before I had commenced my class, as if he thought he had not done enough to evince his esteem and to attach me strongly to the University, he divided the Chair, and named me Titular Professor of Modern History, with a dispensation on account of age, as I had not yet completed my twenty-fifth year. I began my lectures at the College of Plessis, in presence of the pupils of the Normal School, and of a public audience few in number but anxious for instruction, and with whom modern history, traced up to its remote sources, the barbarous conquerors of the Roman Empire, presented itself with an urgent and almost contemporaneous interest. In his conduct towards me, M. de Fontanes was not entirely actuated by some pages of mine he had read, or by a few friendly opinions he had heard expressed. This learned Epicurean, become powerful, and the intellectual favourite of the most potent Sovereign in Europe, loved literature for itself with a sincere and disinterested attachment. The truly beautiful touched him as sensibly as in the days of his early youth and poetical inspirations. What was still more extraordinary, this refined courtier of a despot, this official orator, who felt satisfied when he had embellished flattery with noble eloquence, never failed to acknowledge, and render due homage to independence. Soon after my appointment, he invited me to dinner at his country-house at Courbevoie. Seated near him at table, we talked of studies, of the different modes of teaching, of ancient and modern classics, with the freedom of old acquaintances, and almost with the association of fellow-labourers. The conversation turned upon the Latin poets and their commentators. I spoke with warm praise of the great edition of Virgil by Heyne, the celebrated professor of the University of Göttingen, and of the merit of his annotations. M. de Fontanes fiercely attacked the German scholars. According to him, they had neither discovered nor added anything to the earlier commentaries, and Heyne was no better acquainted with Virgil and the ancients than Père La Rue. He fulminated against German literature in the mass, philosophers, poets, historians, or philologists, and pronounced them all unworthy of attention. I defended them with the confidence of conviction and youth; when M. de Fontanes, turning to his neighbour on the other side, said to him, with a smile, "We can never make these Protestants give in." But, instead of taking offence at my obstinacy, he was cordially pleased with the frankness of this little debate. His toleration of my independence was, not long after, subjected to a more delicate trial.

When I was about to commence my course, in December, 1812, he spoke to me of my opening address, and insinuated that I ought to insert in it a sentence or two in praise of the Emperor. It was the custom, he said, particularly on the establishment of a new professorship, and the

Emperor sometimes demanded from him an account of these proceedings. I felt unwilling to comply, and told him, I thought this proposal scarcely consistent. I had to deal exclusively with science, before an audience of students; how then could I be expected to introduce politics, and, above all, politics in opposition to my own views? "Do as you please," replied M. de Fontanes, with an evident mixture of regard and embarrassment; "if you are complained of, it will fall upon me, and I must defend you and myself as well as I can."

He displayed as much clear penetration and good sense as generosity, in so quickly and gracefully renouncing the proposition he had suggested. In regard to the master he served, the opposition of the society in which I lived had in it nothing of practical or immediate importance. It was purely an opposition of ideas and conversation, without defined plan or effective influence, earnest in philosophic inquiry, but passive in political action; disposed to be satisfied with tranquil life, in the unshackled indulgence of thought and speech.

On entering the University, I found myself in contact with another opposition, less apparent but more serious, without being, at the moment, of a more active character. M. Royer-Collard, at that time Professor of the History of Philosophy, and Dean of the Faculty of Letters, attached himself to me with warm friendship. We had no previous acquaintanceship; I was much the younger man; he lived quite out of the world, within a small circle of selected associates; we were new to each other, and mutually attractive. He was a man, not of the old system, but of the old times, whose character had been developed, though not controlled, by the Revolution, the principles, transactions, and leading promoters of which he judged with rigid independence, without losing sight of the primary and national cause. His mind, eminently liberal, highly cultivated, and supported by solid good sense, was more original than inventive, profound rather than expanded, more given to sift thoroughly a single idea than to combine many; too much absorbed within himself, but exercising a singular power over others by the commanding weight of his reason, and by an aptitude of imparting, with a certain solemnity of manner, the unexpected brilliancy of a strong imagination, continually under the excitement of very lively impressions. Before being called to teach philosophy, he had never made this particular branch of science the object or end of his special study, and throughout our political vicissitudes between 1789 and 1814 he had never taken an important position, or connected himself prominently with any party. But, in youth, under the influence of the traditions of Port-Royal, he had received a sound classical and Christian education; and after the Reign of Terror, under the government of the Directory, he joined the small section of Royalists who corresponded with Louis XVIII., less to conspire, than to enlighten the exiled Prince on the true state of the country, and to furnish him with suggestions equally advantageous for France and the House of Bourbon, if it were destined that the House of Bourbon and France should be re-united on some future day. He was therefore decidedly a spiritualist in philosophy, and a royalist in politics. To restore independence of mind to man, and right to government, formed the prevailing desire of his unobtrusive life. "You cannot believe," he wrote to me in 1823, "that I have ever adopted the word Restoration in the restricted sense of an individual fact; but I have always regarded, and still look upon this fact as the expression of a certain system of society and government, and as the condition on which, under the circumstances of France, we are to look for order, justice, and liberty; while, without this condition, disorder, violence, and irremediable despotism, springing from things and not from men, will be the necessary consequence of the spirit and doctrines of the Revolution." Passionately imbued with this conviction, an aggressive philosopher and an expectant politician, he fought successfully in his chair against the materialistic school of the eighteenth century, and watched from the retirement of his study, with anxiety but not without hope, the chances of the perilous game on which Napoleon daily staked his empire.

By his lofty and intuitive instincts, Napoleon was a spiritualist: men of his order have flashes of light and impulses of thought, which open to them the sphere of the most exalted truths. In his hours of better reflection, spiritualism, reviving under his reign, and sapping the materialism of the last century, was sympathetic with and agreeable to his own nature. But the principle of despotism quickly reminded him that the soul cannot be elevated without enfranchisement, and the spiritualistic philosophy of M. Royer-Collard then confused him as much as the sensual ideology of M. de Tracy. It was, moreover, one of the peculiarities of Napoleon's mind, that his thoughts constantly reverted to the forgotten Bourbons, well knowing that he had no other competitors for the throne of France. At the summit of his power he more than once gave utterance to this impression, which recurred to him with increased force when he felt the approach of danger. On this ground, M. Royer-Collard and his friends, with whose opinions and connections he was fully acquainted, became to him objects of extreme suspicion and disquietude. Not that their opposition (as he was also aware) was either active or influential; events were not produced through such agencies; but therein lay the best-founded presentiments of the future; and amongst its members were included the most rational partisans of the prospective Government.

Hitherto they had ventured nothing beyond vague and half-indulged conversations, when the Emperor himself advanced their views to a consistence and publicity which they were far from assuming. On the 19th of December, 1813, he convened together the Senate and the Legislative Body, and ordered several documents to be laid before them relative to his negotiations with the Allied Powers, demanding their opinions on the subject. If he had then really intended to make peace, or felt seriously anxious to convince France, that the continuance of the war would not spring from the obstinacy of his own domineering will, there can be no doubt that he would have found in these two Bodies, enervated as they were, a strong and popular support. I often saw and talked confidentially with three of the five members of the Commission of the Legislative Body, MM. Maine-Biran, Gallois, and Raynouard, and through them I obtained a correct knowledge of the dispositions of the two others, MM. Lainé and Flaugergues. M. Maine-Biran, who, with M. Royer-Collard and myself formed a small philosophical association, in which we conversed freely on all topics, kept us fully informed as to what passed in the Commission, and even in the Legislative Assembly itself. Although originally a Royalist (in his youth he had been enrolled amongst the bodyguards of Louis XVI.), he was unconnected with any party or intrigue, scrupulously conscientious, even timid when conviction did not call for the exercise of courage, little inclined to politics by taste, and, under any circumstances, one of the last men to form an extreme resolution, or take the initiative in action. M. Gallois, a man of the world and of letters, a moderate liberal of the philosophic school of the eighteenth century, occupied himself much more with his library than with public affairs. He wished to discharge his duty to his country respectably, without disturbing the peaceful tenor of his life. M. Raynouard, a native of Provence and a poet, had more vivacity of manner and language, without being of an adventurous temperament. It was said that his loud complaints against the tyrannical abuses of the Imperial Government, would not have prevented him from being contented with those moderate concessions which satisfy honour for the present, and excite hope for the future. M. Flaugergues, an honest Republican, who had put on mourning for the death of Louis XVI., uncompromising in temper and character, was capable of energetic but solitary resolutions, and possessed little influence over his colleagues, although he talked much. M. Lainé, on the contrary, had a warm and sympathetic heart under a gloomy exterior, and an elevated mind, without much vigour or originality. He spoke imposingly and convincingly when moved by his subject; formerly a Republican, he had paused as a simple partisan of liberal tendencies, and being promptly acknowledged as the head of the Commission, consented without hesitation to become its organ. But, like his colleagues, he had no premeditated hostility or concealed engagement against the Emperor. All were desirous of conveying to him a true impression of the desires of France; externally for a pacific policy, and internally for a respect for public rights and the legal exercise of power. Their Report contained nothing beyond a guarded expression of these moderate sentiments.

With such men, animated by such views, a perfect understanding was anything but difficult. Napoleon would not even listen to them. It is well known how he suddenly suppressed the Report and adjourned the Legislative Body, and with what rude but intentional violence he received the Deputies and their Commissioners on the 1st of January, 1814. "Who are you who address me thus? I am the sole representative of the nation. We are one and inseparable. I have a title, but you have none.... M. Lainé, your mouthpiece, is a dishonest man who corresponds with England through the Advocate Desèze. I shall keep my eye upon him. M. Raynouard is a liar." In communicating to the Commission the papers connected with the negotiation, Napoleon had forbidden his Minister of Foreign Affairs, the Duke of Vicenza, to include that which specified the conditions on which the Allied Powers were prepared to treat, not wishing to pledge himself to any recognized basis. His Minister of Police, the Duke of Rovigo, took upon himself to carry to extremity the indiscretion of his anger. "Your words are most imprudent," said he to the members of the Commission, "when there is a Bourbon in the field." Thus, in the very crisis of his difficulties, under the most emphatic warnings from heaven and man, the despot at bay made an empty parade of absolute power; the vanquished conqueror displayed to the world that the ostensible negotiations were only a pretext for still trying the chances of war; the tottering head of the new dynasty proclaimed himself that the old line was there, ready to supplant him.

The day had arrived when glory could no longer repair the faults which it still covers. The campaign of 1814, that uninterrupted masterpiece of skill and heroism, as well on the part of the leader as of his followers, bore, nevertheless, the ineffaceable stamp of the false calculations and false position of the Emperor. He wavered continually between the necessity of protecting Paris, and the passion of reconquering Europe; anxious to save his throne without sacrificing his ambition, and changing his tactics at every moment, as a fatal danger or a favourable change alternately presented itself. God vindicated reason and justice, by condemning the genius which had so recklessly braved both, to sink in hesitation and uncertainty, under the weight of its own incompatible objects and impracticable desires.

While Napoleon in this closing struggle wasted the last remnants of his fortune and power, he encountered no disappointment or obstacle from any quarter of France, either from Paris or the departments, the party in opposition, or the public in general. There was no enthusiasm in his cause, and little confidence in his success, but no one rose openly against him; all hostility was comprised in a few unfavourable expressions, some preparatory announcements, and here and there a change of side as people began to catch a glimpse of the approaching issue. The Emperor acted in full liberty, with all the strength that still pertained to his isolated position, and the moral and physical exhaustion of the country. Such general apathy was never before exhibited in the midst of so much national anxiety, or so many disaffected persons abstaining from action under similar circumstances, with such numerous partisans ready to renounce the master they still served with implicit docility. It was an entire nation of wearied spectators who had long given up all interference in their own fate, and knew not what catastrophe they were to hope or fear to the terrible game of which they were the stake.

I grew impatient of remaining a motionless beholder of the shifting spectacle; and not foreseeing when or how it would terminate, I determined, towards the middle of March, to repair to Nismes, and pass some weeks with my mother, whom I had not seen for a considerable time. I have still before my eyes the aspect of Paris, particularly of the Rue de Rivoli (then in progress of construction), as I passed along on the morning of my departure. There were no workmen and no activity; materials heaped together without being used, deserted scaffoldings, buildings abandoned for want of money, hands, or confidence, and in ruins before completion. Everywhere, amongst the people, a discontented air of uneasy idleness, as if they were equally in want of labour and repose. Throughout my journey, on the highways, in the towns, and in the fields, I noticed the same appearance of inactivity and agitation, the same visible impoverishment of the country; there were more women and children than men, many young conscripts marching mournfully to their battalions, sick and wounded soldiers returning to the interior; in fact, a mutilated and exhausted nation. Side by side with this physical suffering, I also remarked a great moral perplexity, the uneasiness of opposing sentiments, an ardent longing for peace, a deadly hatred of foreign invaders, with alternating feelings, as regarded Napoleon, of anger and sympathy. By some he was denounced as the author of all their calamities; by others he was hailed as the bulwark of the country, and the avenger of her injuries. What struck me as a serious evil, although I was then far from being able to estimate its full extent, was the marked inequality of these different expressions amongst the divided classes of the population. With the affluent and educated, the prominent feeling was evidently a strong desire for peace, a dislike of the exigencies and hazards of the Imperial despotism, a calculated foreshadowing of its fall, and the dawning perspective of another system of government. The lower orders, on the contrary, only roused themselves up from lassitude to give way to a momentary burst of patriotic rage, or to their reminiscences of the Revolution. The Imperial rule had given them discipline without reform. Appearances were tranquil, but in truth it might be said of the popular masses as of the emigrants, that they had forgotten nothing, and learned nothing. There was no moral unity throughout the land, no common thought or passion, notwithstanding the common misfortunes and experience. The nation was almost as blindly and completely divided in its apathy, as it had lately been in its excitement. I recognized these unwholesome symptoms; but I was young, and much more disposed to dwell on the hopes than on the perils of the future. While at Nismes, I soon became acquainted with the events that had taken place in Paris. M. Royer-Collard wrote to press my return. I set out on the instant, and a few days after my arrival, I was appointed Secretary-General to the Ministry of the Interior, which department the King had just confided to the Abbé de Montesquiou.

CHAPTER II.: THE RESTORATION.: 1814-1815.

SENTIMENTS WITH WHICH I COMMENCED PUBLIC LIFE.—TRUE CAUSE AND CHARACTER OF THE RESTORATION.—CAPITAL ERROR OF THE IMPERIAL SENATE.—THE CHARTER SUFFERS FROM IT.—VARIOUS OBJECTIONS TO THE CHARTER.—WHY THEY WERE FUTILE.—CABINET OF KING LOUIS XVIII.— UNFITNESS OF THE PRINCIPAL MINISTERS FOR CONSTITUTIONAL GOVERNMENT.—M. DE TALLEYRAND.—THE DE MONTESQUIOU.—M. DE BLACAS.—LOUIS XVIII.—PRINCIPAL AFFAIRS IN WHICH I WAS CONCERNED AT THAT EPOCH.—ACCOUNT OF THE STATE OF THE KINGDOM LAID BEFORE THE CHAMBERS.—BILL RESPECTING THE PRESS.—DECREE FOR THE REFORM OF PUBLIC INSTRUCTION.—STATE OF THE GOVERNMENT AND THE COUNTRY.— THEIR COMMON INEXPERIENCE.—EFFECTS OF THE LIBERAL SYSTEM.— ESTIMATE OF PUBLIC DISCONTENT AND CONSPIRACIES.—SAYING OF NAPOLEON ON THE FACILITY OF HIS RETURN.

Under these auspices, I entered, without hesitation, on public life. I had no previous tie, no personal motive to connect me with the Restoration; I sprang from those who had been raised up by the impulse of 1789, and were little disposed to fall back again. But if I was not bound to the former system by any specific interest, I felt no bitterness towards the old Government of France. Born a citizen and a Protestant, I have ever been unswervingly devoted to liberty of conscience, equality in the eye of the law, and all the acquired privileges of social order. My confidence in these acquisitions is ample and confirmed; but, in support of their cause, I do not feel myself called upon to consider the House of Bourbon, the aristocracy of France, and the Catholic clergy, in the light of enemies. At present, none but madmen exclaim, "Down with the nobility! Down with the priests!" Nevertheless, many well-meaning and sensible persons, who are sincerely desirous that revolutions should cease, still cherish in their hearts some relics of the sentiments to which these cries respond. Let them beware of such feelings. They are essentially revolutionary and antisocial; order can never be thoroughly re-established as long as honourable minds encourage them with secret complaisance. I mean, that real and enduring order which every extended society requires for its prosperity and permanence. The interests and acquired rights of the present day have taken rank in France, and constitute henceforward the strength and vitality of the country; but because our social system is filled with new elements, it is not therefore new in itself; it can no more deny what it has been, than it can renounce what it has become; it would establish perpetual confusion and decline within itself, if it remained hostile to its true history. History is the nation, the country, viewed through ages. For myself, I have always maintained an affectionate respect for the great names and actions which have held such a conspicuous place in our destinies; and being as I am, a man of yesterday, when the King, Louis XVIII., presented himself with the Charter in his hand, I neither felt angry nor humiliated that I was compelled to enjoy or defend our liberties under the ancient dynasty of the Sovereigns of France, and in common with all Frenchmen, whether noble or plebeian, even though their old rivalries might sometimes prove a source of mistrust and agitation.

It was the remembrance of foreign intervention that constituted the wound and nightmare of France under the Government of the Restoration. The feeling was legitimate in itself. The jealous passion of national independence and glory doubles the strength of a people in prosperity, and saves their pride under reverses. If it had pleased Heaven to throw me into the ranks of Napoleon's soldiers, in all probability that single passion would also have governed my soul. But, placed as I was, in civil life, other ideas and instincts have taught me to look elsewhere than to predominance in war for the greatness and security of my country. I have ever prized, above all other considerations, just policy, and liberty restrained by law. I despaired of both under the Empire; I hoped for them from the Restoration. I have been sometimes reproached with not sufficiently associating myself with general impressions. Whenever I meet them sincerely and strongly manifested, I respect and hold them in account, but I cannot feel that I am called upon to abdicate my reason for their adoption, or to desert the real and permanent interest of the country for the sake of according with them. It is truly an absurd injustice to charge the Restoration with the presence of those foreigners which the mad ambition of Napoleon alone brought upon our soil, and which the Bourbons only could remove by a prompt and certain peace. The enemies of the Restoration, in their haste to condemn it from the very first hour, have plunged into strange contradictions. If we are to put faith in their assertions, at one time they tell us that it was imposed on France by foreign bayonets; at another, that in 1814, no one, either in France or Europe, bestowed a thought upon the subject; and again, that a few old adherences, a few sudden defections, and a few egotistical intrigues alone enabled it to prevail. Puerile blindness of party spirit! The more it is attempted to prove that no general desire, no prevailing force, from within or without, either suggested or produced the Restoration, the more its inherent strength will be brought to light, and the controlling necessity which determined the event. I have ever been surprised that free and superior minds should thus fetter themselves within the subtleties and credulities of prejudice, and not feel the necessity of looking facts in the face, and of viewing them as they really exist. In the formidable crisis of 1814, the restoration of the House of Bourbon was the only natural and solid solution that presented itself; the only measure that could be reconciled to principles not dependent on the influence of force and the caprices of human will. Some alarm might thence be excited for the new interests of French society; but with the aid of institutions mutually accepted, the two benefits of which France stood most in need, and of which for twenty-five years she had been utterly deprived, peace and liberty, might also be confidently looked for. Under the influence of this double hope, the Restoration was accomplished, not only without effort, but in despite of revolutionary remembrances, and was received throughout France with alacrity and cheerfulness. And France did wisely in this adoption, for the Restoration, in fact, came accompanied by peace and liberty.

Peace had never been more talked of in France than during the last quarter of a century. The Constituent Assembly had proclaimed, "No more conquests;" the National Convention had celebrated the union of nations; the Emperor Napoleon had concluded, in fifteen years, more pacific negotiations than any preceding monarch. Never had war so frequently ended and recommenced; never had peace proved such a transient illusion; a treaty was nothing but a truce, during which preparations were making for fresh combats.

It was the same with liberty as with peace. Celebrated and promised, at first, with enthusiasm, it had quickly disappeared under civil discord, even before the celebration and the promise had ceased; thus, to extinguish discord, liberty had also been abolished. At one moment people became maddened with the word, without caring for the reality of the fact; at another, to escape a fatal intoxication, the fact and the word were equally proscribed and forgotten.

True peace and liberty returned with the Restoration. War was not with the Bourbons a necessity or a passion; they could reign without having recourse every day to some new development of force, some fresh shock to the fixed principles of nations. Treating with them, foreign Governments could and did believe in a sincere and lasting peace. Neither was the liberty which France recovered in 1814, the triumph of any particular school in philosophy or party in politics. Turbulent propensities, obstinate theories and imaginations, at the same time ardent and idle, were unable to find in it the gratification of their irregular and unbounded appetites. It was, in truth, social liberty, the practical and legalized enjoyment of rights, equally essential to the active life of the citizens and to the moral dignity of the nation.

What were to be the guarantees of liberty, and consequently of all the interests which liberty itself was intended to guarantee? By what institutions could the control and influence of the nation in its government be exercised? In these questions lay the great problem which the Imperial Senate attempted to solve by its project of a Constitution in April, 1814, and which, on the 4th of June following, the King, Louis XVIII., effectually decided by the Charter.

The Senators of 1814 have been much and justly reproached for the selfishness with which, on overthrowing the Empire, they preserved for themselves, not only the integrity, but the perpetuity of the material advantages with which the Empire had endowed them;—a cynical error, and one of those which most depreciate existing authorities in the estimation of the people, for they are offensive, at the same time, to honest feelings and envious passions. The Senate committed another mistake less palpable, and more consistent with the prejudices of the country, but in my judgment more weighty, both as a political blunder, and as to the consequences involved. At the same moment when it proclaimed the return of the ancient Royal House, it blazoned forth the pretension of electing the King, disavowing the monarchical right, the supremacy of which it accepted, and thus exercising the privilege of republicanism in re-establishing the monarchy:—a glaring contradiction between principles and acts, a childish bravado against the great fact to which it was rendering homage, and a lamentable confounding of rights and ideas. It was from necessity, and not by choice, on account of his hereditary title, and not as the chosen candidate of the day, that Louis XVIII. was called to the throne of France. There was neither truth, dignity, nor prudence, but in one line of conduct,—to recognize openly the royal claim in the House of Bourbon, and to demand as openly in return the national privileges which the state of the country and the spirit of the time required. Such a candid avowal and mutual respect for mutual rights, form the very essence of free government. It is by this steady union that elsewhere monarchy and liberty have developed and strengthened themselves together; and by frank co-operation, kings and nations have extinguished those internal wars which are denominated revolutions. Instead of adopting this course, the Senate, at once obstinate and timid, while wishing to place the restored monarchy under the standard of republican election, succeeded only in evoking the despotic in face of the revolutionary principle, and in raising up as a rival to the absolute right of the people, the uncontrolled authority of the King.

The Charter bore the impress of this impolitic conduct; timid and obstinate in its turn, and seeking to cover the retreat of royalty, as the Revolution had sought to protect its own, it replied to the pretensions of the revolutionary system by the pretensions of the ancient form, and presented itself as purely a royal concession, instead of proclaiming its true character, such as it really was, a treaty of peace after a protracted war, a series of new articles added by common accord to the old compact of union between the nation and the King.

In this point lay the complaint of the Liberals of the Revolution against the Charter, as soon as it appeared. Their adversaries, the supporters of the old rule, assailed it with other reproaches. The most fiery, such as the disciples of M. de Maistre, could scarcely tolerate its existence. According to them, absolute power, legitimate in itself alone, was the only form of government that suited France. The moderates, amongst whom were M. de Villèle in the reply he published at Toulouse to the declaration of Saint-Ouen, accused this plan for a constitution, which became the Charter, of being an importation from England, foreign to the history, the ideas, and the manners of France; and which, they said, "would cost more to establish than the ancient organization would require for repairs."

I do not here propose to enter upon any discussion of principles, with the apostles of absolute power; as applied to France and our own time, experience, and a very overwhelming experience, has supplied an answer. Absolute power, amongst us, can only belong to the Revolution and its representatives, for they alone can (I do not say for how long) retain the masses in their interest, by withholding from them the securities of liberty.

For the House of Bourbon and its supporters, absolute power is impossible; under them France must be free; it only accepts their government by supplying it with the eye and the hand.

The objections of the moderate party were more specious. It must be admitted that the government established by the Charter had, in its forms at least, something of a foreign aspect. Perhaps too there was reason for saying that it assumed the existence of a stronger aristocratic element in France, and of a more trained and disciplined spirit of policy, than could, in reality, be found there. Another difficulty, less palpable but substantial, awaited it; the Charter was not alone the triumph of 1789 over the old institutions, but it was the victory of one of the Liberal sections of 1789 over its rivals as well as its enemies, a victory of the partisans of the English Constitution over the framers of the Constitution of 1791, and over the republicans as well as the supporters of the ancient monarchy,—a source teeming with offences to the self-love of many, and a somewhat narrow basis for the re-settlement of an old and extensive country.

But these objections had little weight in 1814. The position of affairs was urgent and imperative; it was necessary that the old monarchy should be reformed when restored. Of all the measures of improvement proposed or attempted since 1789, the Charter comprised that which was the most generally recognized and admitted by the public at large, as well as by professed politicians. At such moments controversy subsides; the resolutions adopted by men of action, present an epitome of the ideas common to men of thought. A republic would be to revive the Revolution; the Constitution of 1791 would be government without power; the old French Constitution, if the name were applicable, had been found ineffective in 1789, equally incapable of self-maintenance or amelioration. All that it had once possessed of greatness or utility, the Parliaments, the different Orders, the various local institutions, were so evidently beyond the possibility of re-establishment, that no one thought seriously of such a proposition. The Charter was already written in the experience and reflection of the country. It emanated as naturally from the mind of Louis XVIII., returning from England, as from the deliberations of the Senate, intent on renouncing the yoke of the Empire. It was the produce of the necessities and convictions of the hour. Judged by itself, notwithstanding its inherent defects and the objections of opponents, the Charter was a very practicable political implement. Power and liberty found ample scope there for exercise and defence; the workmen were much less adapted to the machine than the machine to the work.

Thoroughly distinguished from each other in ideas and character, and extremely unequal in mind and merit, the three leading Ministers of Louis XVIII. at that epoch, M. de Talleyrand, the Abbé de Montesquiou, and M. de Blacas, were all specially unsuited to the government they were called on to found.

I say only what I truly think; yet I do not feel myself compelled, in speaking of those with whom I have come in contact, to say all that I think. I owe nothing to M. de Talleyrand; in my public career he thwarted rather than assisted me; but when we have been much associated with an eminent man, and have long reciprocated amicable intercourse, self-respect renders it imperative to speak of him with a certain degree of reserve. At the crisis of the Restoration, M. de Talleyrand displayed, in a very superior manner, the qualities of sagacity, cool determination, and preponderating influence. Not long after, at Vienna, he manifested the same endowments, and others even more rare and apposite, when representing the House of Bourbon and the European interests of France. But except in a crisis or a congress, he was neither able nor powerful. A courtier and a politician, no advocate upon conviction, for any particular form of government, and less for representative government than for any other, he excelled in negotiating with insulated individuals, by the power of conversation, by the charm and skilful employment of social relations; but in authority of character, in fertility of mental resources, in promptitude of resolution, in command of language, in the sympathetic association of general ideas with public passions,—in all these great sources of influence upon collected assemblies, he was absolutely deficient. Besides which, he had neither the inclination nor habit of sustained, systematic labour, another important condition of internal government. He was at once ambitious and indolent, a flatterer and a scoffer, a consummate courtier in the art of pleasing and of serving without the appearance of servility; ready for everything, and capable of any pliability that might assist his fortune, preserving always the mien, and recurring at need to the attractions of independence; a diplomatist without scruples, indifferent as to means, and almost equally careless as to the end, provided only that the end advanced his personal interest. More bold than profound in his views, calmly courageous in danger, well suited to the great enterprises of absolute government, but insensible to the true atmosphere and light of liberty, in which he felt himself lost and incapable of action. He was too glad to escape from the Chambers and from France, to find once more at Vienna a congenial sphere and associations.

As completely a courtier as M. de Talleyrand, and more thoroughly belonging to the old system, the Abbé de Montesquiou was better suited to hold his ground under a constitutional government, and occupied a more favourable position for such a purpose, at this period of uncertainty. He stood high in the estimation of the King and the Royalists, having ever remained immovably faithful to his cause, his order, his friends, and his sovereign. He was in no danger of being taxed as a revolutionist, or of having his name associated with unpleasant reminiscences. Through a rare disinterestedness, and the consistent simplicity of his life, he had won the confidence of all honest men. His character was open, his disposition frank, his mind richly cultivated, and his conversation unreserved, without being exceptious as to those with whom he might be conversing. He could render himself acceptable to the middle classes, although indications of pride and aristocratic haughtiness might be occasionally detected in his words and manner. These symptoms were only perceptible to delicate investigators; by the great majority he was considered affable and unassuming. In the Chambers he spoke with ease and animation, if not with eloquence, and often indulged in an attractive play of fancy. He could have rendered good service to the constitutional government, had he either loved or trusted it; but he joined it without faith or preference, as a measure of necessity, to be evaded or restrained even during the term of endurance. Through habit, and deference for his party, or rather for his immediate coterie, he was perpetually recurring to the traditions and tendencies of the old system, and endeavouring to carry his listeners with him by shallow subtleties and weak arguments, which were sometimes retorted upon himself. One day, partly in jest, and partly in earnest, he proposed to M. Royer-Collard to obtain for him from the King the title of Count. "Count?" replied M. Royer-Collard, in the same tone, "make yourself a Count?" The Abbé de Montesquieu smiled, with a slight expression of disappointment, at this freak of citizen pride. He believed the old aristocracy to be beaten down, but he wished to revive and strengthen it by an infusion with the new orders. He miscalculated in supposing that none amongst the latter class would, from certain instinctive tendencies, think lightly of a title which flattered their interests, or that they could be won over by conciliation without sympathy. He was a thoroughly honourable man, with a heart more liberal than his ideas, of an enlightened and accomplished mind, naturally elegant, but volatile, inconsiderate, and absent; little suited for long and bitter contentions, formed to please rather than to control, and incapable of leading his party or himself in the course in which reason suggested that they should follow.

In the character of M. de Blacas there were no such apparent inconsistencies. Not that he was either an ardent, or a decided and stirring partisan of the contra-revolutionary reaction; he was moderate through coldness of temperament, and a fear of compromising the King, to whom he was sincerely devoted, rather than from clear penetration. But neither his moderation nor his loyalty gave him any insight into the true state of the country, or any desire to occupy himself with the subject. He remained at the Tuileries what he had been at Hartwell, a country gentleman, an emigrant, a courtier, and a steady and courageous favourite, not deficient in personal dignity or domestic tact, but with no political genius, no ambition, no statesmanlike activity, and almost as entirely a stranger to France as before his return. He impeded the Government more than he pretended to govern, taking a larger share in the quarrels and intrigues of the palace, than in the deliberations of the Council, and doing much more injury to public affairs by utter neglect, than by direct interference.

I do not think it would have been impossible for an active, determined monarch to employ these three ministers profitably, and at the same time, however much they differed from one another. Neither of them aspired to the helm, and each, in his proper sphere, could have rendered good service. M. de Talleyrand desired nothing better than to negotiate with Europe; the Abbé de Montesquiou had no desire to rule at court, and M. de Blacas, calm, prudent, and faithful, might have been found a valuable confidant in opposition to the pretensions and secret intrigues of courtiers and princes. But Louis XVIII. was not in the least capable of governing his ministers. As a King he possessed great negative or promissory qualities, but few that were active and immediate. Outwardly imposing, judicious, acute, and circumspect, he could reconcile, restrain, and defeat; but he could neither inspire, direct, nor give the impulse while he held the reins. He had few ideas, and no passion. Persevering application to business was as little suited to him, as active movement. He sufficiently maintained his rank, his rights, and his power, and seldom committed a glaring mistake; but when once his dignity and prudence were vindicated, he allowed things to take their own course; with too little energy of mind and body to control men, and force them to act in concert for the accomplishment of his wishes.

From my inexperience, and the nature of my secondary post in a special department, I was far from perceiving the full mischief of this absence of unity and supreme direction in the Government. The Abbé de Montesquiou sometimes mentioned it to me with impatience and regret. He was amongst the few who had sufficient sense and honesty not to deceive themselves as to their own defects. He reposed great confidence in me, although even within his most intimate circle of associates, efforts had been made to check this disposition. With generous irony, he replied to those who objected to me as a Protestant, "Do you think I intend to make him Pope?" With his habitual unrestraint, he communicated to me his vexations at the Court, his differences with M. de Blacas, his impotence to do what he thought good, or to prevent what he considered evil. He went far beyond this freedom of conversation, by consigning to me, in his department, many matters beyond the duties of my specific office, and would have allowed me to assume a considerable portion of his power. Thus I became associated, during his administration, with three important circumstances, the only ones I shall dwell on, for I am not writing the history of the time; I merely relate what I did, saw, and thought myself, in the general course of events.

The Charter being promulgated, and the Government settled, I suggested to the Abbé de Montesquiou that it would be well for the King to place before the Chambers a summary of the internal condition of France, as he had found it, showing the results of the preceding system, and explaining the spirit of that which he proposed to establish. The Minister was pleased with the idea, the King adopted it, and I immediately applied myself to the work. The Abbé de Montesquiou also assisted; for he wrote well, and took personal pleasure in the task. On the 12th of July, the statement was presented to the two Chambers, who thanked the King by separate addresses. It contained, without exaggeration or concealment, a true picture of the miseries which unlimited and incessant war had inflicted on France, and the moral and physical wounds which it had left to be healed,—a strange portrait, when considered with reference to those which Napoleon, under the Consulate and the dawning Empire, had also given to the world; and which eulogized, with good reason at the time, the restoration of order, the establishment of rule, the revival of prosperity, with all the excellent effects of strong, able, and rational power. The descriptions were equally true, although immeasurably different; and precisely in this contrast lay the startling moral with which the history of the Imperial despotism had just concluded. The Abbé de Montesquiou ought to have placed the glorious edifices of the Consulate side by side with the deserved ruins of the Empire. Instead of losing by this course, he would have added to the impression he intended to produce; but men are seldom disposed to praise their enemies, even though the effect should be to injure them. By alluding only to the disasters of Napoleon, and their fatal consequences, the exposition of the state of the kingdom in 1814 was undignified, and appeared to be unjust. The points in which it reflected honour on the authority from whence it emanated, were the moral tone, the liberal spirit, and the absence of all quackery, which were its leading features. These recommendations had their weight with right-minded, sensible people; but they passed for little with a public accustomed to the dazzling noise and bustle of the power which had recently been extinguished.

Another exposition, more special, but of greater urgency, was presented a few days after, by the Minister of Finance, to the Chamber of Deputies. This included the amount of debt bequeathed by the Empire to the Restoration, with the Ministerial plan for meeting the arrear, as well as providing for the exigencies of 1814 and 1815. Amongst all the Government officials of my time, I have never been acquainted with any one more completely a public servant, or more passionately devoted to the public interest, than the Baron Louis. Ever resolved to cast aside all other considerations, he cared neither for personal risk nor labour, in promoting the success of what that interest demanded. It was not only the carrying out of his financial measures that he so ardently desired; he made these subservient to the general policy of which they were a portion. In 1830, in the midst of the disturbances occasioned by the Revolution of July, I one day, as Minister of the Interior, demanded from the Council, in which the Baron Louis also had a seat as Minister of Finance, the allocation of a large sum. Objections were made by several of our colleagues, on account of the embarrassed state of the treasury. "Govern well," said the Baron Louis to me, "and you will never spend as much money as I shall be able to supply." A judicious speech, worthy of a frank, uncompromising disposition, controlled by a firm and consistent judgment. The Baron Louis's financial scheme was founded on a double basis,—constitutional order in the State, and probity in the Government. With these two conditions, he reckoned confidently on public prosperity and credit, without being dismayed by debts to be paid, or expenses incurred. His assertions as to the closing state of the finances under the Empire, drew from the Count Mollien, the last Minister of the Imperial treasury, a man as able as he was honest, some well-founded remonstrances, and his measures were in consequence severely opposed in the Chambers. He had to contend with dishonest traditions, the passions of the old system, and the narrow views of little minds. The Baron Louis maintained the struggle with equal enthusiasm and perseverance. It was fortunate for him that M. de Talleyrand and the Abbé de Montesquiou had been his associates in the Church in early youth, and had always maintained a close intimacy with him. Both having enlightened views on political economy, they supported him strongly in the Council and in the Chambers. The Prince de Talleyrand even undertook to present his bill to the Chamber of Peers, adopting boldly the responsibility and the principles. This sound policy was well carried through by the whole cabinet, and justly met with complete success, in spite of prejudiced or ignorant opposition.

It was not exactly the same with another measure in which I took a more active part,—the bill relating to the press, presented to the Chamber of Deputies on the 5th of July by the Abbé de Montesquiou, and which passed into law on the 21st of the following October, after having undergone, in both assemblies, animated debates and important amendments.

In its first conception, this bill was reasonable and sincere. The object was to consecrate by legislative enactment the liberty of the press, both as a public right and as a general and permanent institution of the country; and at the same time, on the morrow of a great revolution and a long despotism, and on the advent of a free government, to impose some temporary and limited restrictions. The two persons who had taken the most active part in framing this bill, M. Royer-Collard and myself, were actuated simply and solely by this double end. I may refer the reader to a short work which I published at the time, a little before the introduction of the bill, and in which its spirit and intention are stated without reserve.

It must be evident that the King and the two Chambers had the right of prescribing in concert, temporarily, and from the pressure of circumstances, certain limitations to one of the privileges recognized by the Charter. This cannot be denied without repudiating constitutional government itself, and its habitual practice in those countries in which it is developed with the greatest vigour. Provisional enactments have frequently modified or suspended, in England, the leading constitutional privileges; and with regard to the liberty of the press in particular, it was not until five years after the Revolution of 1688 that, under the reign of William III. in 1693, it was relieved from the censorship.

I recognize no greater danger to free institutions than that blind tyranny which the habitual fanaticism of partisanship, whether of a faction or a small segment, pretends to exercise in the name of liberal ideas. Are you a staunch advocate for constitutional government and political guarantees? Do you wish to live and act in co-operation with the party which hoists this standard? Renounce at once your judgment and your independence. In that party you will find upon all questions and under all circumstances, opinions ready formed, and resolutions settled beforehand, which assume the right of your entire control. Self-evident facts are in open contradiction to these opinions—you are forbidden to see them. Powerful obstacles oppose these resolutions—you are not allowed to think of them. Equity and prudence suggest circumspection—you must cast it aside. You are in presence of a superstitious Credo, and a popular passion. Do not argue—you would no longer be a Liberal. Do not oppose—you would be looked upon as a mutineer. Obey, advance—no matter at what pace you are urged, or on what road. If you cease to be a slave, you instantly become a deserter!

My clear judgment and a little natural pride revolted invincibly against this yoke. I never imagined that even the best system of institutions could be at once imposed on a country without some remembrance of recent events and actual facts, both as regarded the dispositions of a considerable portion of the country itself and of its necessary rulers. I saw not only the King, his family, and a great number of the old Royalists, but even in new France, a crowd of well-meaning citizens and enlightened minds—perhaps a majority of the middle and substantial classes—extremely uneasy at the idea of the unrestricted liberty of the press, and at the dangers to which it might expose public peace, as well as moral and political order. Without participating to the same extent in their apprehensions, I was myself struck by the excesses in which the press had already begun to indulge; by the deluge of recriminations, accusations, surmises, predictions, animated invectives, or frivolous sarcasms, which threatened to rouse into hostility all parties, with all their respective errors, falsehoods, fears, and antipathies. With these feelings and facts before me, I should have considered myself a madman to have treated them lightly, and therefore I decided at once that a temporary limitation of liberty, in respect to journals and pamphlets alone, was not too great a sacrifice for the removal of such perils and fears, or at least to give the country time to overcome by becoming accustomed to them.

But to ensure the success of a sound measure, open honesty is indispensable. Whether in the proposition or the debate, Government itself was called upon to proclaim the general right, as well as the limits and reasons for the partial restriction which it was about to introduce. It ought not to have evaded the principle of the liberty or the character of the restraining law. This course was not adopted. Neither the King nor his advisers had formed any fixed design against the freedom of the press; but they were more disposed to control it in fact than to acknowledge it in right, and wished rather that the new law, instead of giving additional sanction to the principle recorded in the Charter, should leave it in rather a vague state of doubt and hesitation. When the bill was introduced, its true intent and bearing were not clearly indicated. Weak himself, and yielding still more to the weaknesses of others, the Abbé de Montesquiou endeavoured to give the debate a moral and literary, rather than a political turn. According to his view, the question before them was the protection of literature and science, of good taste and manners, and not the exercise and guarantee of an acknowledged public right. An amendment in the Chamber of Peers was necessary to invest the measure with the political and temporary character which it ought to have borne from the beginning, and which alone confined it to its real objects and within its legitimate limits. The Government accepted the amendment without hesitation, but its position had become embarrassed. Mistrust, the most credulous of all passions, spread rapidly amongst the Liberals. Those who were not enemies to the Restoration had, like it, their foibles. The love of popularity had seized them, but they had not yet acquired foresight. They gladly embraced this opportunity of making themselves, with some display, the champions of a Constitutional principle which in fact was in no danger, but which power had assumed the air of eluding or disavowing. Three of the five honourable members who had been the first to restrain the Imperial despotism—Messrs. Raynouard, Gallois, and Flaugergues—were the declared adversaries of the bill; and in consequence of not having been boldly presented, from the opening, under its real and legitimate aspect, the measure entailed more discredit on the Government than it afforded them security.

The liberty of the press, that stormy guarantee of modern civilization, has already been, is, and will continue to be the roughest trial of free governments, and consequently of free people, who are greatly compromised in the struggles of their rulers; for in the event of defeat, they have no alternative but anarchy or tyranny. Free nations and governments have but one honourable and effective method of dealing with the liberty of the press,—to adopt it frankly, without undue complaisance. Let them not make it a martyr or an idol, but leave it in its proper place, without elevating it beyond its natural rank. The liberty of the press is neither a power in the State, nor the representative of the public mind, nor the supreme judge of the executive authorities; it is simply the right of all citizens to give their opinions upon public affairs and the conduct of Government,—a powerful and respectable privilege, but one naturally overbearing, and which, to be made salutary, requires that the constituted authorities should never humiliate themselves before it, and that they should impose on it that serious and constant responsibility which ought to weigh upon all rights, to prevent them from becoming at first seditious, and afterwards tyrannical.

The third measure of importance in which I was concerned at this epoch, the reform of the general system of public instruction, by a Royal ordinance of the 17th of February, 1815, created much less sensation than the Law of the Press, and produced even less effect than noise; for its execution was entirely suspended by the catastrophe of the 20th of March, and not resumed after the Hundred Days. There were more important matters then under consideration. This measure was what is now called the de-centralization of the University. Seventeen separate Universities, established in the principal cities of the kingdom, were to be substituted for the one general University of the Empire. Each of these local colleges was to have a complete and separate organization, both as regarded the different degrees of instruction and the various scholastic establishments within its jurisdiction. Over the seventeen Universities a Royal Council and a great Normal School were appointed, one to superintend the general course of public teaching, and the other to train up for professors the chosen scholars who had prepared themselves for that career, and who were to be supplied from the local Universities. There were two motives for this reform. The first was a desire to establish, in the departments, and quite independent of Paris, leading centres of learning and intellectual activity; the second, a wish to abolish the absolute power which, in the Imperial University, held sole control over the establishments and the masters, and to bring the former under a closer and more immediate authority, by giving the latter more permanence, dignity, and independence in their respective positions. These were sound ideas, to carry out which the decree of the 17th of February, 1815, was but a timid rather than an extended and powerful application. The local Universities were too numerous. France does not supply seventeen natural centres of high learning. Four or five would have sufficed, and more could not have been rendered successful or productive. The forgotten reform which I am here recalling had yet another fault. It was introduced too soon, and was the result, at once systematic and incomplete, of the meditations of certain men long impressed with the deficiencies of the University system, and not really the fruit of public impulse and opinion. Another influence also appeared in it, that of the clergy, who silently commenced at that time their struggle with the University, and adroitly looked for the extension of their personal power in the progress of general liberty. The decree of the 17th of February, 1815, opened this arena, which has since been so fiercely agitated. The Abbé de Montesquiou hastened to bestow on the clergy an early gratification, that of seeing one of their most justly esteemed members, M. de Beausset, formerly Bishop of Alais, at the head of the Royal Council. The Liberals of the University gladly seized this occasion of increasing their action and independence; and the King, Louis XVIII., voluntarily charged his civil list with an additional million for the immediate abolition of the University tax, until a new law, contained in the preamble of the decree, should come into operation to complete the reform, and provide from the public funds for all the requirements of the new system.

It becomes my duty here to express my regret for an error which I ought to have endeavoured more urgently to prevent. In this reform, the opinion and situation of M. de Fontanes were not sufficiently estimated. As head of the Imperial University, he had rendered such eminent services to public instruction, that the title of Grand Officer of the Legion of Honour was far from being a sufficient compensation for the retirement which the new system rendered, in his case, desirable and almost necessary.

But neither reform in public education, nor any other reform, excited much interest at that moment, when France was entirely given up to different considerations. Having scarcely entered on the new system, a sudden impression of alarm and mistrust began to rise and expand from day to day. This system was liberty, with its uncertainties, its contests, and its perils. No one was accustomed to liberty, and liberty contented no one. From the Restoration, the men of old France promised themselves the ascendency; from the Charter, new France expected security. Both were dissatisfied. They found themselves drawn up in presence of each other, with their opposing passions and pretensions. It was a sad disappointment for the Royalists to find the King victorious without their being included in the triumph; and it was a bitter necessity which reduced the men of the Revolution to the defensive after they had so long domineered. Both parties felt surprised and irritated at their position, as equally an insult to their dignity and an attack upon their rights. In their irritation, they gave themselves up, in words and projects, to all the fantasies and transports of their wishes and apprehensions. Amongst the rich and powerful of the old classes, many indulged, towards the influential members of the new, in menaces and insults. At the Court, in the drawing-rooms of Paris, and much more in the provinces, by newspapers, pamphlets, and conversation, and in the daily conduct of their private lives, the nobles and the citizens, the clergy and the laity, the emigrants and the purchasers of national property, allowed their animosities, their ill humour, their dreams of hope and fear, to exhibit themselves without disguise. This was nothing more than the natural and inevitable consequence of the extreme novelty of the system which the Charter, seriously interpreted and exercised, had suddenly introduced into France. During the Revolution there was contest; under the Empire silence; but the Restoration introduced liberty into the bosom of peace. In the general inexperience and susceptibility, the excitement and stir of freedom amounted to civil war on the eve of re-commencement.

To meet the difficulties of such a state of things, to preserve at the same time liberty and peace, to cure the wounds without restraining the blows, no Government could have been too strong or too able. Louis XVIII. and his advisers were unequal to the task. With regard to a liberal system, they were neither more experienced nor inured than France herself. Their acts appeared to be regulated by no steady conviction: they believed that the Charter would check the birth of discontent; but when discontent manifested itself rather vehemently, they hastened to calm it down by abandoning or modifying the measures through which it had been excited. The celebrated rescript of Count Beugnot, on the observance of Sundays and religious festivals, ended in an abortive law which never came into operation. The offensive expressions of Count Ferrand, on introducing to the Chamber of Deputies the bill for the restitution of unsold estates to their old proprietors, was loudly disavowed, not only in the speeches, but in the resolutions and conduct of the Government in that matter. In reality, the interests which imagined themselves threatened were in no danger whatever; and in the midst of the alarms and remonstrances of France, the King and his principal ministers were much more inclined to yield than to contend. But having performed this act of constitutional wisdom, they believed themselves emancipated from all care, and relapsed back into their old tastes and habits, desirous also to live in peace with their ancient and familiar friends. It was indeed but a modified power, which attached importance to its oaths, and conceived no formidable designs against the new rights and interests of the country; but it was also an authority without leading vigour, isolated and a stranger in its own kingdom, divided and embarrassed within itself, weak with its enemies, weak with its friends, seeking only for personal security in repose, and called upon hourly to deal with a stubborn and restless people, who had suddenly passed from the rugged shocks of revolution and war to the difficult exercise of liberty.

Under the prolonged influence of this liberty, such a Government, without obstinate prejudices, and disposed to follow public opinion when clearly expressed, might have corrected while strengthening itself, and from day to day have become more competent to its task. But this required time and the concurrence of the country. The country, discontented and unsettled, neither knew how to wait nor assist. Of all the knowledge necessary to a free people, the most essential point is to learn how to bear what displeases them, that they may preserve the advantages they possess, and acquire those they desire.

There has been much discussion as to what plots and conspirators overthrew the Bourbons, and brought back Napoleon, on the 20th of March, 1815,—a question of inferior importance, and interesting only as an historical curiosity. It is certain that from 1814 to 1815 there existed in the army and with the remnants of the Revolution, amongst generals and conventionalists, many plans and secret practices against the Restoration, and in favour of a new Government,—either the Empire, a regency, the Duke of Orleans, or a republic. Marshal Davoust promised his support to the Imperial party, and Fouché offered his to all. But if Napoleon had remained motionless at the island of Elba, these revolutionary projects would, in all probability, have successively failed, as did those of the Generals d'Erlon, Lallemand, and Lefèvre Desnouettes, even so late as the month of March. The fatuity of the contrivers of conspiracy is incalculable; and when the event seems to justify them, they attribute to themselves the result which has been achieved by mightier and much more complicated causes than their machinations. It was Napoleon alone who dethroned the Bourbons in 1815, by calling up, in his own person, the fanatical devotion of the army, and the revolutionary instincts of the popular masses.

However tottering might be the monarchy lately restored, it required that great man and a combination of these great social powers to subvert it. Stupefied and intimidated, France left events to their course, without opposition or confidence. Napoleon adopted this opinion, with his admirable penetration:—"They allowed me to arrive," he said to Count Mollien, "as they permitted the others to depart."

Four times in less than half a century we have seen kings traverse their realms as fugitives. Different enemies have described, with evident pleasure, their helplessness and destitution in flight,—a mean and senseless gratification, which no one, in the present day, has a right to indulge. The retreats of Napoleon in 1814 and 1815 were neither more brilliant nor less bitter than those of Louis XVIII. on the 20th of March, 1815, of Charles X. in 1830, and of Louis Philippe in 1848. Each state of greatness endured the same degradation; every party has the same need of modesty and mutual respect. I myself, as much as any participator, was impressed, on the 20th of March, 1815, with the blindness, the hesitation, the imbecility, the misery of every description, to which that terrible explosion gave birth. It would afford me no pleasure, and would lead to no advantage, to repeat them. People are too much inclined at present to conceal their own weaknesses under a display of the deficiencies of royalty. I prefer recording that neither royal nor national dignity were wanting at that epoch in noble representatives. The Duchess d'Angoulême, at Bordeaux, evinced courage equal to her misfortunes, and M. Lainé, as president of the Chamber of Deputies, protested fearlessly on the 28th of March, in the name of justice and liberty, against the event at that time fully accomplished, and which no longer encountered, through the wide extent of France, any resistance beyond the solitary accents of his voice.

CHAPTER III.: THE HUNDRED DAYS.: 1815.

I IMMEDIATELY LEAVE THE MINISTRY OF THE INTERIOR, TO RESUME MY
LECTURES.—UNSETTLED FEELING OF THE MIDDLE CLASSES ON THE RETURN OF
NAPOLEON.—ITS REAL CAUSES.—SENTIMENTS OF FOREIGN NATIONS AND
GOVERNMENTS TOWARDS NAPOLEON.—APPARENT RECONCILIATION, BUT REAL
STRUGGLE, BETWEEN NAPOLEON AND THE LIBERALS.—THE FEDERATES.—
CARNOT AND FOUCHÉ.—DEMONSTRATION OF LIBERTY DURING THE HUNDRED
DAYS, EVEN IN THE IMPERIAL PALACE.—LOUIS XVIII. AND HIS COUNCIL AT
GHENT.—THE CONGRESS AND M. DE TALLEYRAND AT VIENNA.—I GO TO GHENT
ON THE PART OF THE CONSTITUTIONAL ROYALIST COMMITTEE AT PARIS.—MY
MOTIONS AND OPINIONS DURING THIS JOURNEY.—STATE OF PARTIES AT
GHENT.—MY CONVERSATION WITH LOUIS XVIII.—M. DE BLACAS.—
M. DE CHÂTEAUBRIAND.—M. DE TALLEYRAND RETURNS FROM VIENNA.—LOUIS
XVIII. RE-ENTERS FRANCE.—INTRIGUE PLANNED AT MONS AND DEFEATED AT
CAMBRAY.—BLINDNESS AND IMBECILITY OF THE CHAMBER OF
REPRESENTATIVES.—MY OPINION RESPECTING THE ADMISSION OF FOUCHÉ
INTO THE KING'S CABINET.

The King having quitted, and the Emperor having re-entered Paris, I resumed my literary
pursuits, determined to keep aloof from all secret intrigue, all useless agitation, and to occupy
myself with my historical labours and studies, not without a lively regret that the political career
which had scarcely opened to me, should be so suddenly closed. It is true I did not believe that I
was excluded beyond the possibility of return. Not but that the miraculous success of Napoleon
had convinced me there was a power within him which, after witnessing his fall, I was far from
believing. Never was personal greatness displayed with more astounding splendour; never had an
act more audacious, or better calculated in its audacity, arrested the imagination of nations.
Neither was external support wanting to the man who relied so much on himself, and on himself
alone.

The army identified itself with him, with an enthusiastic and blind devotion. Amongst the
popular masses, a revolutionary and warlike spirit, hatred of the old system and national pride,
rose up at his appearance and rushed madly to his aid. Accompanied by fervent worshippers, he
re-ascended a throne abandoned to him on his approach. But by the side of this overwhelming
power, there appeared almost simultaneously a proportionate weakness. He who had traversed
France in triumph, and who by personal influence had swept all with him, friends and enemies,
re-entered Paris at night, exactly as Louis XVIII. had quitted that capital, his carriage surrounded
by dragoons, and only encountering on his passage a scanty and moody populace. Enthusiasm
had accompanied him throughout his journey; but at its termination he found coldness, doubt,
widely disseminated mistrust, and cautious reserve; France divided, and Europe irrevocably
hostile.

The upper, and particularly the middle classes, have often been reproached with their indifference and selfishness. It has been said that they think only of their personal interests, and are incapable of public principle and patriotism. I am amongst those who believe that nations, and the different classes that constitute nations—and, above all, nations that desire to be free— can only live in security and credit under a condition of moral perseverance and energy; with feelings of devotion to their cause, and with the power of opposing courage and self-sacrifice to danger. But devotion does not exclude sound sense, nor courage intelligence. It would be too convenient for ambitious pretenders, to have blind and fearless attachment ever ready at their command. It is often the case with popular feeling, that the multitude, army or people, ignorant, unreflecting, and short-sighted, become too frequently, from generous impulse, the instruments and dupes of individual selfishness, much more perverse and more indifferent to their fate than that of which the wealthy and enlightened orders are so readily accused. Napoleon, perhaps more than any other eminent leader of his class, has exacted from military and civil devotion the most trying proofs; and when, on the 21st of June, 1815, his brother Lucien, in the Chamber of Representatives, reproached France with not having upheld him with sufficient ardour and constancy, M. de la Fayette exclaimed, with justice: "By what right is the nation accused of want of devotion and energy towards the Emperor Napoleon? It has followed him to the burning sands of Egypt, and the icy deserts of Moscow; in fifty battle-fields, in disaster as well as in triumph, in the course of ten years, three millions of Frenchmen have perished in his service. We have done enough for him!"

Great and small, nobility, citizens, and peasants, rich and poor, learned and ignorant, generals and private soldiers, the French people in a mass had, at least, done and suffered enough in Napoleon's cause to give them the right of refusing to follow him blindly, without first examining whether he was leading them, to safety or to ruin.

The unsettled feeling of the middle classes in 1815 was a legitimate and patriotic disquietude. What they wanted, and what they had a right to demand, for the advantage of the entire nation as well as for their own peculiar interests, was that peace and liberty should be secured to them; but they had good reason to question the power of Napoleon to accomplish these objects.

Their doubts materially increased when they ascertained the Manifesto of the Allied Powers assembled at the Congress of Vienna, their declaration of March 13th, and their treaty of the 25th. Every reflecting mind of the present day must see, that unless the nation had obstinately closed its eyes, it could not delude itself as to the actual situation of the Emperor Napoleon, and his prospects for the future. Not only did the Allied Powers, in proclaiming him the enemy and disturber of the peace of the whole world, declare war against him to the last extremity, and engage themselves to unite their strength in this common cause, but they professed themselves ready to afford to the King of France and the French nation the assistance necessary to re-establish public tranquillity; and they expressly invited Louis XVIII. to give his adhesion to their treaty of March 25th. They laid it down also as a principle, that the work of general pacification and reconstruction accomplished in Paris by the treaty of the 30th of May, 1814, between the King of France and confederated Europe, was in no degree nullified by the violent outbreak which had recently burst forth; and that they should maintain it against Napoleon, whose return and sudden success—the fruit of military and revolutionary excitement—could establish no European right whatever, and could never be considered by them as the prevailing and true desire of France:—a solemn instance of the implacable judgments that, assisted by God and time, great errors draw down upon their authors!

The partisans of Napoleon might dispute the opinion of the Allied Powers as to the wishes of France; they might believe that, for the honour of her independence, she owed him her support; but they could not pretend that foreign nations should not also have their independence at heart, nor persuade them that, with Napoleon master of France, they could ever be secure. No promises, no treaties, no embarrassments, no reverses, could give them confidence in his future moderation. His character and his history deprived his word of all credit.

It was not alone governments, kings, and ministers who showed themselves thus firmly determined to oppose Napoleon's return; foreign nations were even more distrustful and more violent against him. He had not alone overwhelmed them with wars, taxes, invasions, and dismemberments; he had insulted as much as he had oppressed them. The Germans, especially, bore him undying hatred. They burned to revenge the injuries of the Queen of Prussia, and the contempt with which their entire race had been treated. The bitter taunts in which he had often indulged when speaking of them were repeated in every quarter, spread abroad and commented on, probably with exaggeration readily credited. After the campaign in Russia, the Emperor was conversing, one day, on the loss sustained by the French army during that terrible struggle. The Duke of Vicenza estimated it at 200,000 men. "No, no," interrupted Napoleon, "you are mistaken; it was not so much." But, after considering a moment, he continued, "And yet you can scarcely be wrong; but there were a great many Germans amongst them." The Duke of Vicenza himself related this contemptuous remark to me; and the Emperor Napoleon must have been pleased both with the calculation and reply, for on the 28th of June, 1813, at Dresden, in a conversation which has since become celebrated, he held the same language to the Prime Minister of the first of the German Powers, to M. de Metternich himself. Who can estimate the extent of indignation roused by such words and actions, in the souls not only of the heads of the government and army—— amongst the Steins, Gneisenaus, Blüchers, and Müfflings—but in those of the entire nation? The universal feeling of the people of Germany was as fully displayed at the Congress of Vienna as the foresight of their diplomatists and the will of their sovereigns.

Napoleon, in quitting Elba, deceived himself as to the disposition of Europe towards him. Did he entertain the hope of treating with and dividing the Coalition? This has been often asserted, and it may be true; for the strongest minds seldom recognize all the difficulties of their situation. But, once arrived at Paris, and informed of the proceedings of the Congress, he beheld his position in its true light, and his clear and comprehensive judgment at once grappled with it in all its bearings. His conversations with the thinking men who were then about him, M. Molé and the Duke of Vicenza, confirm this opinion. He sought still to keep the public in the uncertainty that he himself no longer felt. The Manifesto of the Congress of the 13th of March was not published in the 'Moniteur' until the 5th of April, and the treaty of the 25th of March only on the 3rd of May. Napoleon added long commentaries to these documents, to prove that it was impossible they could express the final intentions of Europe. At Vienna, both by solemnly official letters and secret emissaries, he made several attempts to renew former relations with the Emperor Francis, his father-in-law, to obtain the return of his wife and son, to promote disunion, or at least mistrust, between the Emperor Alexander and the sovereigns of England and Austria, and to bring back to his side Prince Metternich, and even M. de Talleyrand himself. He probably did not expect much from these advances, and felt little surprise at not finding, in family ties and feelings, a support against political interests and pledges. He understood and accepted without a sentiment of anger against any one, and perhaps without self-reproach, the situation to which the events of his past life had reduced him. It was that of a desperate gamester, who, though completely ruined, still plays on, alone, against a host of combined adversaries, a desperate game, with no other chance of success than one of those unforeseen strokes that the most consummate talent could never achieve, but that Fortune sometimes bestows upon her favourites.

It has been, pretended, even by some of his warmest admirers, that at this period the genius and energy of Napoleon had declined; and they sought in his tendency to corpulence, in his attacks of languor, in his long slumbers, the explanation of his ill fortune. I believe the reproach to be unfounded, and the pretext frivolous. I can discover in the mind or actions of Napoleon during the hundred days, no symptoms of infirmity; I find, in both, his accustomed superiority. The causes of his ultimate failure were of a deeper cast: he was not then, as he had long been, upheld and backed by general opinion, and the necessity of security and order felt throughout a great nation; he attempted, on the contrary, a mischievous work, a work inspired only by his own passions and personal wants, rejected by the morality and good sense, as well as by the true interests of France. He engaged in this utterly egotistical enterprise with contradictory means, and in an impossible position. From thence came the reverses he suffered, and the evil he produced.

It presented a strange spectacle to intelligent spectators, and one slightly tinged with the ridiculous, on both sides, to see Napoleon and the heads of the Liberal party arranged against each other, not to quarrel openly, but mutually to persuade, seduce, and control. A superficial glance sufficed to convince that there was little sincerity either in their dispute or reconciliation. Both well knew that the real struggle lay in other quarters, and that the question upon which their fate depended would be settled elsewhere than in these discussions.

If Napoleon had triumphed over Europe, assuredly he would not long have remained the rival of M. de La Fayette and the disciple of Benjamin Constant; but when he lost the day of Waterloo, M. de La Fayette and his friends set themselves to work to complete his overthrow.

From necessity and calculation, the true thoughts and passions of men are sometimes buried in the recesses of their hearts; but they quickly mount to the surface as soon as an opportunity occurs for their reappearing with success. Frequently did Napoleon resign himself, with infinite pliability, shrewdness, and perception, to the farce that he and the Liberals were playing together; at one moment gently, though obstinately, defending his old policy and real convictions; and at another yielding them up with good grace, but without positive renunciation, as if out of complaisance to opinions which he hesitated to acknowledge. But now and then, whether from premeditation or impatience, he violently resumed his natural character; and the despot, who was at once the child and conqueror of the Revolution, reappeared in complete individuality.

When an attempt was made to induce him to insert, in the Additional Act to the Constitutions of the Empire, the abolition of the confiscation proclaimed by the Charter of Louis XVIII., he exclaimed passionately, "They drive me into a path that is not my own; they enfeeble and enchain me. France will seek, and find me no longer. Her opinion of me was once excellent; it is now execrable. France demands what has become of the old arm of the Emperor, the arm which she requires to control Europe. Why talk to me of innate virtue, of abstract justice, of natural laws? The first law is necessity; the first principle of justice is public safety ... Every day has its evil, every circumstance its law, every man his own nature; mine is not that of an angel. When peace is made, we shall see." On another occasion, on this same question of preparing the Additional Act, and with reference to the institution of an hereditary peerage, he yielded to the excursive rapidity of his mind, taking the subject by turns under different aspects, and giving unlimited vent to contradictory observations and opinions. "Hereditary peerage," said he, "is opposed to the present state of public opinion; it will wound the pride of the army, deceive the expectations of the partisans of equality, and raise against myself a thousand individual claims. Where do you wish me to look for the elements of that aristocracy which the peerage demands?... Nevertheless a constitution without an aristocracy resembles a balloon lost in the air. A ship is guided because there are two powers which balance each other; the helm finds a fulcrum. But a balloon is the sport of a single power; it has no fulcrum. The wind carries it where it will, and control is impossible."

When the question of principle was decided, and the nomination of his hereditary house of peers came under consideration, Napoleon was anxious to include many names from amongst the old Royalists; but after mature reflection, he renounced this idea, "not," says Benjamin Constant, "without regret," and exclaimed, "We must have them sooner or later; but memories are too recent. Let us wait until after the battle—they will be with me if I prove the strongest."

He would thus willingly have deferred all questions, and have done nothing until he came back a conqueror; but with the Restoration liberty once more re-entered France, and he himself had again woke up the Revolution. He found himself in conflict with these two forces, constrained to tolerate, and endeavouring to make use of them, until the moment should arrive when he might conquer both.

He had no sooner adopted all the pledges of liberty that the Additional Act borrowed from the Charter, than he found he had still to deal with another ardent desire, another article of faith, of the Liberals, still more repugnant to his nature. They demanded an entirely new constitution, which should confer on him the Imperial crown by the will of the nation, and on the conditions which that will prescribed. This was, in fact, an attempt to remodel, in the name of the sovereign people, the entire form of government, institutional and dynastic; an arrogant and chimerical mania which, a year before, had possessed the Imperial Senate when they recalled Louis XVIII., and which has vitiated in their source nearly all the political theories of our time.

Napoleon, while incessantly proclaiming the supremacy of the people, viewed it in a totally different light. "You want to deprive me of my past," said he, to his physicians; "I desire to preserve it. What becomes then of my reign of eleven years? I think I have some right to call it mine; and Europe knows that I have. The new constitution must be joined to the old one; it will thus acquire the sanction of many years of glory and success."

He was right: the abdication demanded of him was more humiliating than that of Fontainebleau; for, in restoring the throne to him, they at the same time compelled him to deny himself and his immortal history. By refusing this, he performed an act of rational pride; and in the preamble as well as in the name of the Additional Act, he upheld the old Empire, while he consented to modified reforms. When the day of promulgation arrived, on the 1st of June, at the Champ de Mai, his fidelity to the Imperial traditions was less impressive and less dignified. He chose to appear before the people with all the outward pomp of royalty, surrounded by the princes of his family arrayed in garments of white taffeta, by the great dignitaries, in orange-coloured mantles, by his chamberlains and pages:—a childish attachment to palatial splendour, which accorded ill with the state of public affairs, and deeply disgusted public feeling, when, in the midst of this glittering pageant, twenty thousand soldiers were seen to march past and salute the Emperor, on their road to death.

A few days before, a very different ceremony had revealed another embarrassing inconsistency in the revived Empire. While discussing with the Liberal aristocracy his new constitution, Napoleon endeavoured to win over and subdue, while he flattered, the revolutionary democrats. The population of the Faubourgs St. Antoine and St. Marceau became excited, and conceived the idea of forming themselves into a federation, as their fathers had done, and of demanding from the Emperor leaders and arms. They obtained their desire; but they were no longer Federates, as in 1792; they were now called Confederates, in the hope that, by a small alteration of name, earlier reminiscences might be effaced. A police regulation minutely settled the order of their progress through the streets, provided against confusion, and arranged the ceremonial of their introduction to the Emperor, in the courtyard of the Tuileries. They presented an address, which was long and heavy to extreme tediousness. He thanked them by the name of "federated soldiers" (soldats fédérés), carefully impressing upon them, himself, the character in which it suited him to regard them. The next morning, the 'Journal de l'Empire' contained the following paragraph:— "The most perfect order was maintained, from the departure of the Confederates until their return; but in several places we heard with pain the Emperor's name mingled with songs which recall a too memorable epoch." This was being rather severely scrupulous on such an occasion.

Some days later, I happened to pass through the garden of the Tuileries. A hundred of these Federates, shabby enough in appearance, had assembled under one of the balconies of the palace, shouting, "Long live the Emperor!" and trying to induce him to show himself. It was long before he complied; but at length a window opened, the Emperor came forward, and waved his hand to them; but almost instantly the window was re-closed, and I distinctly saw Napoleon retire, shrugging his shoulders; vexed, no doubt, at being obliged to lend himself to demonstrations so repugnant in their nature, and so unsatisfactory in their limited extent.

He was desirous of giving more than one pledge to the revolutionary party. Before reviewing their battalions in the court of his palace, he had taken into council the oldest and most celebrated of their leaders; but I scarcely think he expected from them any warm co-operation. Carnot, an able officer, a sincere republican, and as honest a man as an idle fanatic can possibly be, could not fail to make a bad Minister of the Interior; for he possessed neither of the two qualities essential to this important post,—knowledge of men, and the power of inspiring and directing them otherwise than by general maxims and routine.

Napoleon knew better than anybody else how Fouché regulated the police,—for himself first, and for his own personal power; next for the authority that employed him, and just as long as he found greater security or advantage in serving than in betraying that authority. I only met the Duke of Otranto twice, and had but two short conversations with him. No man ever so thoroughly gave me the idea of fearless, ironical, cynical indifference, of imperturbable self-possession combined with an inordinate love of action and prominence, and of a fixed resolution to stop at nothing that might promote success, not from any settled design, but according to the plan or chance of the moment. He had acquired from his long associations as a Jacobin proconsul, a kind of audacious independence; and remained a hardened pupil of the Revolution, while, at the same time, he became an unscrupulous implement of the Government and the Court. Napoleon assuredly placed no confidence in such a man, and knew well that, in selecting him as a minister, he would have to watch more than he could employ him. But it was necessary that the revolutionary flag should float clearly over the Empire under its proper name; and he therefore preferred to endure the presence of Carnot and Fouché in his cabinet, rather than to leave them without, to murmur or conspire with certain sections of his enemies. At the moment of his return, and during the first weeks of the resuscitated Empire, he probably reaped from this double selection the advantage that he anticipated; but when the dangers and difficulties of his situation manifested themselves, when he came to action with the distrustful Liberals within, and with Europe without,—Carnot and Fouché became additional dangers and difficulties in his path. Carnot, without absolute treachery, served him clumsily and coldly; for in nearly all emergencies and questions he inclined much more to the Opposition than to the Emperor; but Fouché betrayed him indefinitely, whispering and arguing in an under tone, of his approaching downfall, with all who might by any possible chance happen to be his successors; just as an indifferent physician discourses by the bedside of a patient who has been given over.

Even amongst his most trusted and most devoted adherents, Napoleon no longer found, as formerly, implicit faith and obedient temperaments, ready to act when and how he might please to direct. Independence of mind and a feeling of personal responsibility had resumed, even in his nearest circle, their scruples and their predominance. Fifteen days after his arrival in Paris, he summoned his Grand Marshal, General Bertrand, and presented to him, for his counter-signature, the decree dated from Lyons, in which he ordered the trials and sequestration of property of the Prince de Talleyrand, the Duke of Ragusa, the Abbé de Montesquiou, M. Bellard, and nine other persons, who in 1814, before the abdication, had contributed to his fall. General Bertrand refused. "I am astonished," said the Emperor, "at your making such objections; this severity is necessary for the good of the State." "I do not believe it, Sire." "But I do, and I alone have the right to judge. I have not asked your concurrence, but your signature, which is a mere matter of form, and cannot compromise you in the least." "Sire, a minister who countersigns the decree of his sovereign becomes morally responsible. Your Majesty has declared by proclamation that you granted a general amnesty. I countersigned that with all my heart; I will not countersign the decree which revokes it."

Napoleon urged and cajoled in vain; Bertrand remained inflexible, the decree appeared without his signature: and Napoleon might, even on the instant, have convinced himself that the Grand Marshal was not the only dissentient; for, as he crossed the apartment in which his aides-de-camp were assembled, M. de La Bédoyère said, loud enough to be overheard, "If the reign of proscriptions and sequestrations recommences, all will soon be at an end."

When liberty reaches this point in the interior of the palace, it may be presumed that it reigns predominantly without. After several weeks of stupor, it became, in fact, singularly bold and universal. Not only did civil war spring up in the western departments, not only were flagrant acts of resistance or hostility committed in several parts of the country, and in important towns, by men of consequence,—but everywhere, and particularly in Paris, people thought, and uttered their thoughts without reserve; in public places as well as in private drawing-rooms, they went to and fro, expressing hopes and engaging in hostile plots, as if they were lawful and certain of success; journals and pamphlets, increased daily in number and virulence, and were circulated almost without opposition or restraint. The warm friends and attached servants of the Emperor testified their surprise and indignation.

Fouché pointed out the mischief, in his official reports to Napoleon, and requested his concurrence in taking measures of repression. The 'Moniteur' published these reports; and the measures were decreed. Several arrests and prosecutions took place, but without vigour or efficacy. From high to low, the greater portion of the agents of government had neither zeal in their cause, nor confidence in their strength. Napoleon was aware of this, and submitted, as to a necessity of the moment, to the unlicensed freedom of his opponents, maintaining, without doubt, in his own heart, the opinion he had declared aloud on a previous occasion,—"I shall have them all with me if I prove the strongest."

I question whether he appreciated justly, and at its true value, one of the causes, a hidden but powerful one, of the feebleness that immediately succeeded his great success. Notwithstanding the widely-spread discontent, uneasiness, mistrust, and anger that the Government of the Restoration had excited, a universal feeling soon sprang up, that there was not enough to justify a revolution, the opposition of an armed force against authority legally established, or the involvement of the country in the dangers to which it was exposed. The army had been drawn towards its old chief by a strong sentiment of attachment and generous devotion, rather than from views of personal interest; the army, too, was national and popular; but nothing could change the nature of acts or the meaning of words. The violation of an oath, desertion with arms in their hands, the sudden passing over from one camp to another, have always been condemned by honour as well as duty, civil or military, and denominated treason. Individuals, nations, or armies, men under the influence of a controlling passion, may contemn, at the first moment, or perhaps do not feel the moral impression which naturally attaches itself to their deeds; but it never fails to present itself, and, when seconded by the warnings of prudence or the blows of misfortune, it soon regains its empire.

It was the evil destiny of the Government of the Hundred Days that the influence of moral opinion ranged itself on the side of its adversaries the Royalists; and that the conscience of the nation, clearly or obscurely, spontaneously or reluctantly, justified the severe judgments to which its origin had given rise.

I and my friends attentively watched the progress of the Emperor's affairs and of the public temper. We soon satisfied ourselves that Napoleon would fall, and that Louis XVIII. would re-ascend the throne. While this was our impression of the future, we felt hourly more convinced that, from the deplorable state into which the enterprise of the Hundred Days had plunged France, abroad and at home, the return of Louis XVIII. would afford her the best prospect of restoring a regular government within, peace without, and the reassumption of her proper rank in Europe. In public life, duty and reason equally dictate to us to encourage no self-delusion as to what produces evil; but to adopt the remedy firmly, however bitter it may be, and at whatever sacrifice it may demand. I had taken no active part in the first Restoration; but I concurred, without hesitation, in the attempts of my friends to establish the second under the most favourable conditions for preserving the dignity, liberty, and repose of France.

Our tidings from Ghent gave us much uneasiness. Acts and institutions, all the problems of principle or expediency which we flattered ourselves had been solved in 1814, were again brought forward. The struggle had recommenced between the Constitutional Royalists and the partisans of absolute power, between the Charter and the old system. We often smile ourselves, and seek to make others smile, when we revert to the discussions, rival pretensions, projects, hopes, and fears which agitated this small knot of exiles, gathered round an impotent and throneless monarch. Such an indulgence is neither rational nor dignified. What matters it whether the theatre be great or small, whether the actors fail or succeed, or whether the casualties of human life are displayed with imposing grandeur or contemptible meanness? The true measurement lies in the subjects discussed and the future destinies prepared. The question in debate at Ghent was how France should be governed when this aged King, without state or army, should be called on a second time to interpose between her and Europe. The problem and the solution in perspective were sufficiently important to occupy the minds of reflecting men and honest citizens.

The intelligence from Vienna was no less momentous. Not that in reality there was either doubt or hesitation in the plans or union of the Allied Powers. Fouché, who had for some time been in friendly correspondence with Prince Metternich, made many overtures to him which the Chancellor of Austria did not absolutely reject. Every possible modification which promised a government to France was permitted to suggest itself. All were discussed in the cabinets or drawing-rooms of the Ministers, and even in the conferences of the Congress. In these questions were included, Napoleon II. and a Regency, the Duke of Orleans, and the Prince of Orange. The

English Ministry, speaking with the authority of Parliament, announced that they had no intention of carrying on war merely for the purpose of imposing any particular form of government or dynasty on France; and the Austrian Cabinet seconded this declaration. But these were only personal reserves, or an apparent compliance with circumstances, or methods of obtaining correct knowledge, or mere topics of conversation, or the anticipation of extreme cases to which the leaders of European politics never expected to be reduced. Diplomacy abounds in acts and propositions of little moment or value, which it neither denies nor acknowledges; but they exercise no real influence on the true convictions, intents, and labours of the directors of government.

Without wishing to proclaim it aloud, or to commit themselves by formal and public declarations, the leading kingdoms of Europe, from principle, interest, or honour, looked upon their cause at this period as allied, in France, with that of the House of Bourbon. It was near Louis XVIII. in his exile, that their ambassadors continued to reside; and with all the European Governments, the diplomatic agents of Louis XVIII. represented France. By the example and under the guidance of M. de Talleyrand, all these agents, in 1815, remained firm to the Royal cause, either from fidelity or foresight, and satisfied themselves, with him, that in that cause lay final success.

But, side by side with this general disposition of Europe in favour of the House of Bourbon, a balancing danger presented itself,—an apprehension that the sovereigns and diplomatists assembled at Vienna had become convinced that the Bourbons were incapable of governing France. They had all, for twenty years, treated with and known France such as the Revolution and the Empire had made her. They still feared her, and deeply pondered over her position. The more uneasy they became at her leaning towards anarchy and war, the more they judged it indispensable that the ruling power should be placed in the hands of considerate, able, and prudent men, capable of understanding their functions, and of making themselves understood in their turn. For a considerable time they had ceased to retain any confidence in the companions of exile and courtiers of Louis XVIII.; and late experience had redoubled their mistrust. They looked upon the old Royalist party as infinitely more capable of ruining kings than of governing states.

A personal witness to these conflicting doubts of the foreign Powers as to the future they were tracing themselves, M. de Talleyrand, at Vienna, had also his own misgivings. Amidst all the varied transformations of his life and politics, and although the last change had made him the representative of the ancient royalty, he did not desire, and never had desired, to separate himself entirely from the Revolution; he was linked to it by too many decided acts, and had acknowledged and served it under too many different forms, not to feel himself defeated when the Revolution was subdued. Without being revolutionary either by nature or inclination, it was in that camp that he had grown up and prospered, and he could not desert it with safety. There are certain defections which skilful egotism takes care to avoid; but the existing state of public affairs, and his own particular position, pressed conjointly and weightily upon him at this juncture. What would become of the revolutionary cause and its partisans under the second

Restoration, now imminently approaching? What would even be the fate of this second Restoration if it could not govern and uphold itself better than its predecessor? Under the second, as under the first, M. de Talleyrand played a distinguished part, and rendered important services to the Royal cause. What would be the fruit of this as regarded himself? Would his advice be taken, and his co-operation be accepted? Would the Abbé de Montesquiou and M. de Blacas still be his rivals? I do not believe he would have hesitated, at this epoch, as to which cause he should espouse; but feeling his own power, and knowing that the Bourbons could scarcely dispense with him, he allowed his predilections for the past and his doubts for the future to betray themselves.

Well informed of all these facts, and of the dispositions of the principal actors, the Constitutional Royalists who were then gathered round M. Royer-Collard, considered it their duty to lay before Louis XVIII., without reserve, their opinions of the state of affairs, and of the line of conduct it behoved him to adopt. It was not only desirable to impress on him the necessity of perseverance in a system of constitutional government, and in the frank acknowledgment of the state of social feeling in France, such as the new times had made it; but it was also essential to enter into the question of persons, and to tell the King that the presence of M. de Blacas near him would militate strongly against his cause; to request the dismissal of that favourite, and to call for some explicit act or public declaration, clearly indicating the intentions of the monarch on the eve of re-assuming possession of his kingdom; and finally to induce him to attach much weight to the opinions and influence of M. de Talleyrand, with whom it must be observed that, at this period, none of those who gave this advice had any personal connection, and to the greater part of whom he was decidedly objectionable.

Being the youngest and most available of this small assembly, I was called on to undertake a mission not very agreeable in itself. I accepted the duty without hesitation. Although I had then little experience of political animosities and their blind extremes, I could not avoid perceiving which party of opponents would one day be likely to turn on me for taking this step; but I should feel ashamed of myself if fear of responsibility and apprehensions for the future could hold me back when circumstances call upon me to act, within the limits of duty and conviction, as the good of my country demands.

I left Paris on the 23rd of May. One circumstance alone is worthy of notice in my journey—the facility with which I accomplished it. It is true there were many police restrictions on the roads and along the frontier; but the greater part of the agents were neither zealous nor particular in enforcing them. Their speech, their silence, and their looks, implied a kind of understood permission and tacit connivance. More than one official face appeared to say to the unknown traveller, "Pass on quickly," as if they dreaded making a mistake, or damaging a useful work by interfering with its supposed design. Having arrived at Ghent, I called first on the men I knew, and whose views corresponded with my own, MM. de Jaucourt, Louis, Beugnot, de Lally-Tolendal, and Mounier. I found them all faithful to the cause of the Constitution, but sad as exiles, and anxious as advisers without repose in banishment; for they had to combat incessantly with the odious or absurd passions and plans of the spirit of reaction.

The same facts furnish to different parties the most opposite conclusions and arguments; the catastrophe, which again attached some more firmly than ever to the principles and politics of the Charter, was to others the sentence of the Charter; and a convincing proof that nothing but a return to the old system could save the monarchy. I need not repeat the details, given to me by my friends, of the advice with which the counter-revolutionists and partisans of absolutism beset the King; for in the idleness that succeeds misfortune, men give themselves up to dreams, and helpless passion engenders folly. The King stood firm, and agreed with his constitutional advisers. The Report on the state of France presented to him by M. de Châteaubriand a few days before we arrived, in the name of the whole Council, and which had just been published in the 'Moniteur of Ghent,' contained an eloquent exposition of the liberal policy acknowledged by the monarch. But the party thus rejected were not disposed to yield; they surrounded the King they were unable to control, and found their strongest roots in his own family and bosom friends. The Count d'Artois was their ostensible chief, and M. de Blacas their discreet but steady ally. Through them they hoped to gain a victory as necessary as it was difficult.

I requested the Duke de Duras to demand for me a private audience of the King. The King received me the next day, June 1st, and detained me nearly an hour. I have no turn for the minute and settled parade of such interviews; I shall therefore only relate of this, and of the impressions which it produced on me, what still appears to be worthy of remembrance.

Two points have remained strongly imprinted upon my memory—the impotence and dignity of the King. There was in the aspect and attitude of this old man, seated immovably and as if nailed to his arm-chair, a haughty serenity, and, in the midst of his feebleness, a tranquil confidence in the power of his name and rights, which surprised and touched me. What I had to say could not fail to be displeasing to him; and from respect, not calculation, I began with what was agreeable: I spoke of the royalist feeling which day by day exhibited itself more vehemently in Paris. I then related to him several anecdotes and couplets of songs, in corroboration of this. Such light passages entertained and pleased him, as men are gratified with humorous recitals, who have no sources of gaiety within themselves.

I told him that the hope of his return was general. "But what is grievous, Sire, is that, while believing in the re-establishment of the monarchy, there is no confidence in its duration." "Why is this?" I continued; "when the great artisan of revolution is no longer there, monarchy will become permanent; it is clear that, if Bonaparte returns to Elba, it will only be to break out again; but let him be disposed of, and there will be an end to revolutions also.—People cannot thus flatter themselves, Sire; they fear something beyond Bonaparte, they dread the weakness of the royal government; its wavering between old and new ideas, between past and present interests, and they fear the disunion, or at least the incoherence of its ministers."

The King made no reply. I persisted, and mentioned M. de Blacas. I said that I was expressly charged by men whom the King knew to be old, faithful, and intelligent servants, to represent to him the mistrust which attached itself to that name, and the evil that would result from it to himself. "I will fulfil all that I have promised in the Charter; names are not concerned with that; France has nothing to do with the friends I entertain in my palace, provided no act emanates from them injurious to the country? Speak to me of more serious causes of uneasiness." I entered into some details, and touched on various points of party intrigues and menaces. I also spoke to the King, of the Protestants in the south, of their alarms, of the violence even of which, in some instances, they had already been the objects. "This is very bad," said he: "I will do all I can to stop it; but I cannot prevent everything,—I cannot, at the same time, be a liberal and an absolute king." He questioned me upon several recent occurrences, and respecting some members of the Imperial Administration. "There are two, Sire, who, knowing that I was about to seek an audience of the King, have requested me to mention their names, and to assure him of their devotion." "Who are they?"—"The Arch-chancellor and M. Molé." "For M. Molé, I rely upon him, and am glad of his support; I know his worth. As to M. Cambacérès, he is one of those whom I neither ought nor wish to hear named." I paused there. I was not ignorant that at that time the King was in communication with Fouché, a much more objectionable regicide than Cambacérès; but I was a little surprised that the secret relations caused by pressing emergency did not prevent him from maintaining aloud, and as a general theory, a line of conduct most natural under his circumstances. He was certainly far from foreseeing the disgust that would ensue from his connection with the Duke of Otranto. He dismissed me with some commonplace words of kindness, leaving on me the impression of a sensible and liberal mind, outwardly imposing, shrewd with individuals, careful of appearances, thinking little, and not profoundly informed, and almost as incapable of the errors which destroy, as of the great strokes which establish the future of royal dynasties.

I then visited M. de Blacas. He had evinced some prepossession against me. "What brings this young man here?" said he to Baron d'Eckstein, Commissary-General of Police to the King of the Netherlands, at Ghent. "He comes from I know not who, with some mission that I am ignorant of, to the King." He was fully acquainted both with my mission and my friends. However, he received me with perfect civility, and I must add with honourable frankness, inquiring what they said at Paris, and why they were so incensed against him. He spoke to me even of his differences with the Abbé de Montesquiou, complaining of the sallies and whims which had embroiled them to the detriment of the King's service. I replied with equal candour; and his bearing during the whole of our interview was dignified, with a slight degree of reserve, expressing more surprise than irritation. I find in some notes written after I left him, this sentence:—"I am much mistaken if his mistakes do not chiefly proceed from the mediocrity of his intellect."

The situation of M. de Châteaubriand at Ghent was singular. A member of the King's Council, he brilliantly exposed its policy in official publications, and defended them in the 'Moniteur of Ghent' with the same attractive power; but he was dissatisfied with everybody, and no one placed much confidence in him. I believe that neither then nor later did the King or the different Cabinets understand M. de Châteaubriand, or sufficiently appreciate his concurrence or hostility. He was, I admit, a troublesome ally; for he aspired to all things, and complained of all. On a level with the rarest spirits and most exalted imaginations, it was his chimera to fancy himself equal to the greatest masters in the art of government, and to feel bitterly hurt if he were not looked upon as the rival of Napoleon as well as of Milton. Prudent men did not lend themselves to this complaisant idolatry; but they forgot too much what, either as friend or enemy, he to whom they refused it was worth. They might, by paying homage to his genius and satisfying his vanity, have lulled to rest his ambitious dreams; and if they had not the means of contenting him, they ought in either case, from prudence as well as from gratitude, not only to have humoured, but to have gained him over completely to their side. He was one of those towards whom ingratitude was as dangerous as unjust; for they resent passionately, and know how to revenge without treachery. He lived at Ghent in great intimacy with M. Bertin, and assumed thenceforward that influence over the 'Journal des Débats' which he afterwards so powerfully employed. Notwithstanding the cordiality of our first acquaintance, there had been for some time a considerable coolness between us. In 1814 he was discontented with, and spoke ill of the Abbé de Montesquiou and his friends. I was nevertheless equally surprised at and sorry for the injustice and error committed in thinking so little of one they used so much, and I regretted not meeting him oftener, and on a more amicable footing.

In the midst of these discussions, not only of principles and parties, but of private interests and coteries, we waited, at a distance from France, and scarcely knowing how to occupy our minds or time, the issue of the struggle between Napoleon and Europe;—a most painful situation, which I endured to serve the cause I believed and have never ceased to believe just, though I hourly felt its complicated vexations. I shall not linger here to describe them; nothing is more repugnant to my nature than to volunteer a display of my own feelings, especially when I am well aware that many, who listen, cannot or will not understand or believe me. I care little for mistake or invective; either is the natural condition of public life: but I do not feel called upon to enter into useless controversies in my own defence; I know how to wait for justice without demanding it.

The battle of Waterloo terminated our passive anxiety. The King quitted Ghent on the 22nd of June, urged by his trustiest friends, and by his own judgment, not to lose a moment in placing himself between divided France and foreign invasion. I set out the next day with M. Mounier, and on the same evening we rejoined the King at Mons, where he had paused in his journey.

Then burst forth, through the agency of new actors, and by contrivances still unexplained, the dénoûment that I had been despatched to accomplish—the fall of M. de Blacas. I am not disposed to discuss the various accounts given by several who were witnesses of or interested in the event; I shall simply relate what I myself saw on the spot, as I find it detailed in a letter written at Cambray, six days afterwards, to the person to whom, in the absence of immediate communication, I had the pleasure of relating all that occurred:—

"As we entered Mons (M. Mounier and I), we were told that M. de Blacas had been dismissed, and was going as ambassador to Naples; but our surprise was great when we also learned that M. de Talleyrand, who had lately left Vienna for Brussels, to be within reach of coming events, and had arrived at Mons a few hours after the King, had at the same time tendered his resignation; that the King, while refusing to accept it, had received M. de Talleyrand himself coldly, and that he had set out again for Brussels, while, contrary to his advice, the King repaired to Cateau-Cambresis, at that moment the head-quarters of the English army. We understood nothing whatever of these conflicting incidents, and our uneasiness equalled our surprise. We have since been everywhere, we have seen everybody,—those of our friends who preceded us to Mons, and the foreign ministers who followed the King—MM. de Jaucourt, Louis, Beugnot, de Châteaubriand, Pozzo di Borgo, de Vincent;—and, between half confidences, restrained anger, deceptive smiles, and sincere regrets, we have arrived at last at a tolerably clear understanding of the whole matter. The little court of the Count d'Artois, knowing that M. de Talleyrand advised the King not to hurry, and that the Duke of Wellington, on the contrary, recommended him to advance rapidly into France, thought nothing could be better than to drive away both M. de Blacas and M. de Talleyrand, and to separate the King from his constitutional advisers, as well as from his favourite, by inducing him to set out quickly for the head-quarters of the English army, surrounded only by the partisans of Monsieur, from whom they hoped he would select his ministers.

"Our friends were much excited, and the foreigners greatly displeased. The latter demanded in whom they could have confidence with regard to the French question, and with whom they should treat in such a crisis? M. de Talleyrand had returned from Vienna with a great reputation for ability and success; in the eyes of Europe he represented France and the King. The Austrian Minister had just said to him at Brussels, 'I am ordered to consult you on every occasion, and to be guided entirely by your advice.' He himself haughtily maintained his discontent, and sharply repulsed those who would have persuaded him to rejoin the King. After six hours of rather stormy conversation, it was agreed that Pozzo di Borgo should repair to Cateau, and persuade the Duke of Wellington to take some step which should put an end to this strange misunderstanding; and that MM. de Jaucourt, Louis, and Beugnot should at the same time say to the King, that the men in whom he appeared to confide entertained ideas and projects so diametrically opposed to theirs, that it was impossible they could serve him usefully, and therefore requested permission to retire. It is probable that reflections and measures in conformity with these resolutions had already taken place at Cateau; for on the morning of the 25th, at the same time that we received news of the occurrences at Paris, the abdication of Napoleon, and the embassy of the Commissioners to the Allied Sovereigns, a letter arrived at Mons, from the Duke of Wellington to M. de Talleyrand, couched, as I have been assured, in these exact terms:—

"'I regret much that you have not accompanied the King to this place; it is I who have earnestly requested him to enter France at the same time with ourselves. If I could have told you the motives which sway me in this matter, I have no doubt that you would have given the King the same advice. I trust that you will come to hear them.' M. de Talleyrand decided upon setting out instantly; and we determined to accompany him. We rejoined the King here on the 26th. It was high time; for already a proclamation, dated from Cateau, drawn up, it is said, by M. Dambray, gave a false colouring to the re-entrance of his Majesty. We have hastened to substitute another, of which M. Beugnot is the principal author, and which prognosticates a wholesome policy. The King signed it without hesitation. It appeared yesterday, to the great satisfaction of the public of Cambray. I hope it may produce a similar effect in all other quarters."

We indeed hoped and believed that the end of the great crisis which had overthrown France, as well as the smaller one which had agitated the immediate circle of royalty, was at hand. On all sides affairs appeared to tend towards the same issue. The King was in France; a moderate and national line of policy prevailed in his councils, and animated his words. A feeling of loyalty displayed itself everywhere during his progress, not only with his old party, but amongst the masses; every hand was raised towards him, as to a plank of safety in a shipwreck. The people care little for consistency. At this time I saw, in the northern departments, the same popularity surround the exiled King and the vanquished army. Napoleon had abdicated in Paris, and, notwithstanding a few unworthy alternations of dejection and feverish excitement, of resignation and momentary energy, he was evidently incapable of renewing the struggle. The Chamber of Representatives, which, from its first institution, had shown itself unfavourable to the Imperial system, and opposed to revolutionary excesses, appeared to be earnestly occupied in threading a perilous defile, by avoiding all violence and every irrevocable engagement. Popular passion sometimes murmured, but suffered itself to be easily restrained, and even stopped voluntarily, as if unaccustomed to action or dominion. The army, the scattered corps of which had successively re-united round Paris, had given itself up to patriotic fervour, and, together with France, had plunged into an abyss to prove its devotion and avenge its injuries: but amongst its oldest and most illustrious chiefs, some—such as Gouvion St. Cyr, Macdonald, and Oudinot—had refused to join Napoleon, and openly espoused the Royal cause; others—like Ney, Davoust, Soult, and Masséna—protested with stern candour against fatal delusions, considering that their well-tried courage entitled them to utter melancholy truths, to offer sage advice, and to repress, even by the sacrifice of party credit, military excitement or popular disorder; others, in fine, like Drouot, with an influence conferred by true courage and virtue, maintained discipline in the army in the midst of the mortifications of the retreat behind the Loire, and secured its obedience to the authority of a detested civil power. After so many mistakes and misfortunes, and in the midst of all differences of opinion and situation, there existed still a spontaneous desire and a general effort to preserve France from irreparable errors and total ruin.

But tardy wisdom does not avail, and, even when they wish to become prudent, political genius is wanting to those nations who are not accustomed to decide their own affairs or their own destiny. In the deplorable state into which the enterprise of an heroic and chimerical egotism had thrown France, there was evidently only one line of conduct to pursue,—to recognize Louis XVIII., to accept his liberal concessions, and to act in concert with him while treating with the foreign Powers. This was absolutely necessary; for the most limited mind could foresee that the return of the House of Bourbon was an inevitable, and all but an accomplished fact. Such a course became also a duty, to promote peace and to afford the best means of counteracting the evils of invasion; for Louis XVIII. could alone repel them with any show of authority. An auspicious future was thus opened to liberty; for reason whispered, and experience demonstrated, that, after what had passed in France since 1789, despotism could never more be attempted by the princes of the House of Bourbon—an insurmountable necessity compelled them to adopt defined and constitutional government,—if they resorted to extremes, their strength would prove unequal to success. To accept without hesitation or delay the second restoration, and to place the King, of his own accord, between France and the rest of Europe, became the self-evident dictate of patriotism and sound policy.

Not only was this left undone, but every endeavour was used to make it appear that the Restoration was exclusively the work of foreign interference, and to bring upon France, in addition to her military defeat, a political and diplomatic overthrow. It was not independence of the Empire, or good intentions towards the country, that were wanting in the Chamber of the Hundred Days, but intelligence and resolution. It neither lent itself to imperial despotism nor revolutionary violence; it was not the instrument of either of the extreme parties,—it applied itself honestly to preserve France, on the brink of that abyss towards which they had driven her; but it could only pursue a line of negative policy, it tacked timidly about before the harbour, instead of boldly entering,—closing its eyes when it approached the narrow channel, submitting, not from confidence, but from imbecility, to the blindness or infatuation of the old or new enemies by whom the King was surrounded, and appearing sometimes, from weakness itself, to consent to combinations which in reality it tried to elude;—at one moment proclaiming Napoleon II., and at another any monarch whom the sovereign people might please to select.

To this fruitless vacillation of the only existing public authority, one of the most fatally celebrated actors of the worst times of the Revolution, Fouché, owed his importance and ephemeral success.

When honest men fail to understand or execute the designs of Providence, dishonesty undertakes the task. Under the pressure of circumstances, and in the midst of general weakness, corrupt, sagacious, and daring spirits are ever at hand, who perceive at once what may happen, or what may be attempted, and make themselves the instruments of a triumph to which they have no natural claim, but of which they assume the credit, to appropriate the fruits. Such a man was the Duke of Otranto during the Hundred Days,—a revolutionist transformed into a grandee; and desirous of being consecrated in this double character by the ancient royalty of France, he employed, to accomplish his end, all the cleverness and audacity of a reckless intriguer more clear-sighted and sensible than his associates. Perhaps also—for justice ought to retain its scruples even towards those who have none themselves—perhaps a desire to save his country from violence and useless suffering may have had some share in the series of treasons and imperturbable changes of side, by means of which, while deceiving and playing alternately with Napoleon, La Fayette, and Carnot, the Empire, the Republic, and the regicidal Convention, Fouché gained the time that he required to open for himself the doors of the King's cabinet, while he opened the gates of Paris to the King.

Louis XVIII. offered some resistance, but, notwithstanding what he had said to me at Ghent respecting Cambacérès, I doubt whether he objected strongly. He was one of those who are dignified from habit and decorum rather than from a real and powerful emotion of the soul; and propriety disappeared before emergency. He had, as vouchers for the necessities of the case, two authorities who were the best calculated to influence his decision and uphold his honour; the Duke of Wellington and the Count d'Artois both urged him to accept Fouché as a minister:— Wellington, to secure an easy return for the King, and also that he himself, and England with him, might remain the principal author of the Restoration by promptly terminating the war before

Paris, where he feared to be compromised through the violent hatred of the Prussians; the Count d'Artois, with impatient levity, always ready to promise and agree, and already entangled through his most active confidant, M. de Vitrolles, in the snare which Fouché had spread for the Royalists on every side.

I do not believe in the necessity which they urged upon the King. Fouché had no control over Paris; the army had retired; the Federates were more noisy than powerful; the Chamber of Representatives consoled themselves, by discussing a constitution, for not having dared or known how to form a government; no party was either able or disposed to arrest effectually the tide which carried the King along. A little less eagerness, and a little more determination, would have spared him a sad dishonour. By waiting a few days he would have incurred the risk, not of fatal resolutions or violence, but merely of the temporary continuance of disorder and alarm. Necessity presses upon people as well as on kings: that with which Fouché armed himself to become minister to Louis XVIII. was factitious and ephemeral; that which brought Louis XVIII. back to the Tuileries was real, and became hourly more urgent. There was no occasion for him to receive the Duke of Otranto into his cabinet at Arnouville; he might have remained there patiently, for they would soon have sought him. I thought thus at the time, after having passed two days in Paris, where I arrived on the 3rd of July, when the manœuvres of Fouché were following their course. All that I subsequently saw and heard tended to confirm me in this opinion.

CHAPTER IV.: THE CHAMBER OF 1815.: 1815-1816.

FALL OF M. DE TALLEYRAND AND FOUCHÉ.—FORMATION OF THE DUKE DE RICHELIEU'S CABINET.—MY CONNECTION AS SECRETARY-GENERAL OF THE ADMINISTRATION OF JUSTICE WITH M. DE MARBOIS, KEEPER OF THE GREAT SEAL.—MEETING AND ASPECT OF THE CHAMBER OF DEPUTIES.—INTENTIONS AND ATTITUDE OF THE OLD ROYALIST FACTION.—FORMATION AND COMPOSITION OF A NEW ROYALIST PARTY.—STRUGGLE OF CLASSES UNDER THE CLOAK OF PARTIES.—PROVISIONAL LAWS.—BILL OF AMNESTY.—THE CENTRE BECOMES THE GOVERNMENT PARTY, AND THE RIGHT THE OPPOSITION.— QUESTIONS UPON THE CONNECTION BETWEEN THE STATE AND THE CHURCH.—STATE OF THE GOVERNMENT BEYOND THE CHAMBERS.— INSUFFICIENCY OF ITS RESISTANCE TO THE SPIRIT OF REACTION.—THE DUKE OF FELTRI AND GENERAL BERNARD.—TRIAL OF MARSHAL NEY.—CONTROVERSY BETWEEN M. DE VITROLLES AND ME.—CLOSING OF THE SESSION.— MORTIFICATIONS IN THE CABINET.—M. LAINÉ MINISTER OF THE INTERIOR.—I LEAVE THE MINISTRY OF JUSTICE AND ENTER THE STATE COUNCIL AS MASTER OF REQUESTS.—THE CABINET ENTERS INTO CONTESTS WITH THE RIGHT-HAND PARTY.—M. DECAZES.—POSITION OF MESSRS. ROYER-COLLARD AND DE SERRE.—OPPOSITION OF M. DE CHÂTEAUBRIAND.—THE COUNTRY RISES AGAINST THE CHAMBER OF DEPUTIES.—EFFORTS OF M. DECAZES TO BRING ABOUT A DISSOLUTION.—THE KING DETERMINES ON IT.—DECREE OF THE 5TH OF SEPTEMBER, 1816.

Three months had scarcely elapsed and neither Fouché nor M. de Talleyrand were any longer in the Ministry. They had fallen, not under the pressure of any new or unforeseen event, but by the evils connected with their personal situation, and their inaptitude for the parts they had undertaken to play. M. de Talleyrand had effected a miracle at Vienna; by the treaty of alliance concluded on the 3rd January, 1815, between France, England, and Austria, he had put an end to the coalition formed against us in 1813, and separated Europe into two parties, to the advantage of France. But the event of the 20th of March had destroyed his work; the European coalition was again formed against the Emperor and against France, who had made herself, or had permitted herself to be made, the instrument of Napoleon. There was no longer a chance of breaking up this formidable alliance. The same feeling of uneasiness and mistrust of our faith, the same desire for a firm and lasting union, animated the sovereigns and the nations. They had speedily arranged at Vienna the questions which had threatened to divide them. In this fortified hostility against France the Emperor Alexander participated, with extreme irritation towards the House of Bourbon and M. de Talleyrand, who had sought to deprive him of his allies. The second Restoration was no longer like the first, the personal glory and work of M. de Talleyrand; the honour was chiefly due to England and the Duke of Wellington. Instigated by self-love and policy, the Emperor Alexander arrived at Paris on the 10th of July, 1815, stern and angrily disposed towards the King and his advisers.

France and the King stood, nevertheless, in serious need of the goodwill of the Russian Emperor, encompassed as they were by the rancorous and eager ambition of Germany. Her diplomatists drew up the geographical chart of our territory, leaving out the provinces of which they desired to deprive us. Her generals undermined, to blow into the air, the monuments which recalled their defeats in the midst of their victories. Louis XVIII. resisted with much dignity these acts of foreign barbarism; he threatened to place his chair of state upon the bridge of Jena, and said publicly to the Duke of Wellington, "Do you think, my Lord, that your Government would consent to receive me if I were again to solicit a refuge?" Wellington restrained to the utmost of his power the violence of Blücher, and remonstrated with him by arguments equally urgent and politic; but neither the dignity of the King, nor the amicable intervention of England were sufficient to curb the overweening pretensions of Germany. The Emperor Alexander alone could keep them within bounds. M. de Talleyrand sought to conciliate him by personal concessions. In forming his cabinet, he named the Duke de Richelieu, who was still absent, Minister of the Royal Household, while the Ministry of the Interior was held in reserve for Pozzo di Borgo, who would willingly have left the official service of Russia to take part in the Government of France. M. de Talleyrand placed much faith in the power of temptations; but, in this instance, they were of no avail. The Duke de Richelieu, probably in concert with the King himself, refused; Pozzo di Borgo did not obtain, or dared not to solicit, the permission of his master to become, once more, a Frenchman. I saw him frequently, and that mind, at once quick and decisive, bold and restless, felt keenly its doubtful situation, and with difficulty concealed its perplexities. The Emperor Alexander maintained his cold reserve, leaving M. de Talleyrand powerless and embarrassed in this arena of negotiation, ordinarily the theatre of his success.

The weakness of Fouché was different, and sprang from other causes. It was not that the foreign sovereigns and their ministers regarded him more favourably than they did M. de Talleyrand, for his admission into the King's cabinet had greatly scandalized monarchical Europe; the Duke of Wellington alone persisted in still upholding him; but none amongst the foreigners either attacked him or appeared anxious for his downfall. It was from within that the storm was raised against him. With a strangely frivolous presumption, he had determined to deliver up the Revolution to the King, and the King to the Revolution, relying upon his dexterity and boldness to assist him in passing and repassing from camp to camp, and in governing one by the other, while alternately betraying both. The elections which took place at this period throughout France, signally falsified his hopes. In vain did he profusely employ agents, and circular addresses; neither obtained for him the slightest influence; the decided Royalists prevailed in nearly every quarter, almost without a struggle. It is our misfortune and our weakness, that in every great crisis the vanquished become as the dead. The Chamber of 1815 as yet appeared only in the distance, and already the Duke of Otranto trembled as though thunderstruck by the side of the tottering M. de Talleyrand. In this opposite and unequal peril, but critical for both, the conduct of these two men was very different. M. de Talleyrand proclaimed himself the patron of constitutional monarchy, boldly and greatly organized as in

England. Modifications conformable to the views of the Liberal party were in some instances immediately acceded to, and in others promised by the Charter. Young men were permitted to enter the Chamber of Deputies. Fourteen Articles relative to the constitution of this Chamber were submitted for the inspection of the next Legislative Assembly. The Peerage was made hereditary. The censorship, to which works under twenty printed sheets had been subjected, was abolished. A grand Privy Council, on important occasions, united the principal men of every party. It was neither the urgent necessity of the moment, nor prevailing public opinion, that imposed on restored royalty these important reforms: they were enacted by the Cabinet from a desire of encouraging free institutions, and of giving satisfaction to the party,—I ought rather to say to the small section of enlightened and impatient spirits.

The real intentions and measures of Fouché were of a more personal nature. Violently menaced by the reaction in favour of royalty, he at first endeavoured to appease by feeding it. He consented to make himself the instrument of proscription against the very men who, but a short time before, were his agents, his confederates, his accomplices, his colleagues, and his friends. At the same time that he published memorials and circulars showing the necessity of clemency and forgetfulness of the past, he placed before the Royal Council a list of one hundred and ten names, to be excluded from all amnesty; and when strict inquiry had reduced this number to eighteen, subject to courts-martial, and to thirty-eight provisionally banished, he countersigned without hesitation the decree which condemned them. A few days afterwards, and upon his request, another edict revoked all the privileges hitherto accorded to the daily papers, imposed upon them the necessity of a new license, and subjected them to the censorship of a commission, in which several of the principal royalist writers, amongst others Messieurs Auger and Fiévée, refused to sit under his patronage. As little did the justice or national utility of his acts affect the Duke of Otranto in 1815, as in 1793; he was always ready to become, no matter at what cost, the agent of expediency. But when he saw that his severe measures did not protect himself, and perceived the rapidly approaching danger, he changed his tactics; the minister of the monarchical reaction became again the factious revolutionist. He caused to be secretly published and circulated, "Reports to the King," and the "Notes to the Foreign Ministers," less calculated to enlighten the authorities he addressed, than to prepare for himself arms and allies against the Government and the party, from which he saw that he was about to be excluded. He was of the number of those who try to make themselves feared, by striving to injure when they are no longer permitted to serve.

Neither the liberal reforms of M. de Talleyrand, nor the revolutionary menaces of the Duke of Otranto, warded off the danger which pressed on them. Notwithstanding their extraordinary abilities and long experience, both mistook the new aspect of the times, either not seeing, or not wishing to see, how little they were in unison with the contests which the Hundred Days had revived. The election of a Chamber decidedly Royalist, surprised them as an unexpected phenomenon; they both fell at its approach, and within a few days of each other; left, nevertheless, after their common downfall, in opposite positions. M. de Talleyrand retained credit; the King and his new Cabinet loaded him with gifts and royal favours; his colleagues during his short administration, Messieurs de Jaucourt, Pasquier, Louis and Gouvion St. Cyr, received signal marks of royal esteem, and retired from the scene of action as if destined to return. Having accepted the trifling and distant embassy to Dresden, Fouché hastened to depart, and left Paris under a disguise which he only changed when he reached the frontier, fearful of being seen in his native land, which he was fated never again to behold.

The Cabinet of the Duke de Richelieu entered upon office warmly welcomed by the King, and even by the party which had gained the ascendency through the present elections. It was indeed a new and thoroughly royalist Ministry. Its head, recently arrived in France, honoured by all Europe, and beloved by the Emperor Alexander, was to King Louis XVIII. what the king himself was to France, the pledge of a more advantageous peace. Two of his colleagues, Messieurs Decazes and Dubouchage, had taken no part in public affairs previous to the Restoration. The four others, Messieurs Barbé-Marbois, de Vaublanc, Coretto, and the Duke of Feltri, had recently given proofs of strong attachment to the regal cause. Their union inspired hope without suspicion, in the public mind, as well as in that of the triumphant party. I was intimately acquainted with M. de Marbois; I had frequently met him at the houses of Madame de Rumford and Madame Suard. He belonged to that old France which, in a spirit of generous liberality, had adopted and upheld, with enlightened moderation, the principles most cherished by the France of the day. I held under him, in the capacity of a confidential friend, the post of Secretary-General to the Ministry of Justice, to which M. Pasquier, then keeper of the great seal, had nominated me under the Cabinet of M. de Talleyrand. Hardly was the new minister installed in office, when the Chamber of Deputies assembled, and in its turn established itself. It was almost exclusively Royalist. With considerable difficulty, a few men, members of other parties, had obtained entrance into its ranks. They found themselves in a state of perpetual discomfort, isolated and ill at ease, as though they were strangers of suspicious character; and when they endeavoured to declare themselves and explain their sentiments, they were roughly driven back into impotent silence. On the 23rd of October, 1815, in the debate on the Bill presented by M. Decazes for the temporary suspension of personal liberty, M. d'Argenson spoke of the reports which had been spread abroad respecting the massacre of Protestants in the south. A violent tumult arose in contradiction of his statements; he explained himself with great reserve. "I name no facts," replied he, "I bring forward no charges; I merely say that vague and contradictory rumours have reached me; ... the very vagueness of these rumours calls for a report from the minister, on the state of the kingdom." M. d'Argenson was not only defeated in his object, and interrupted in his speech, but was expressly called to order for having alluded to facts unfortunately too certain, but which the Government wished to smother up by silencing all debate on the question.

For the first time in five-and-twenty years, the Royalists saw themselves in the ascendant. Thoroughly believing that they had obtained a legitimate triumph, they indulged unreservedly in the enjoyment of power, with a mixture of aristocratic arrogance and new-born zeal, as men do when little accustomed to victory, and doubtful of the strength they are so eager to display.

Very opposite causes plunged the Chamber of 1815 into the extreme reaction which has stamped its historical character. In the first place, and above all others, may be named, the good and evil passions of the Royalists, their moral convictions and personal resentments, their love of order and thirst for vengeance, their pride in the past and their apprehensions for the future, their determination to re-establish honour and respect for holy observances, their old attachments, their sworn pledges, and the gratification of lording it over their conquerors. To the violence of passion was joined a prudent calculation of advantage. To strengthen their party, and to advance individual fortunes, it was essential for the new rulers of France to possess themselves everywhere of place and power; therein lay the field to be worked, and the territory to be occupied, in order to reap the entire fruits of victory. Finally must be added, the empire of ideas, more influential than is commonly supposed, and often exercising more power over men, without their being conscious of it, than prejudice or interest. After so many years of extraordinary events and disputes, the Royalists had, on all political and social questions, systematic views to realize, historical reminiscences to act upon, requirements of the mind to satisfy. They hastened to apply their hands to the work, believing the day at last arrived when they could, once more, assume in their own land, morally as well as physically, in thought and deed, the superiority which had so long been wrested from them.

As it happens in every great crisis of human associations, these opposing principles in the reaction of 1815, had each its special and exclusively effective representative in the ranks of the Royalists. The party had their fighting champion, their political advocate, and their philosopher. M. de la Bourdonnaye led their passions, M. de Villèle their interests, and M. de Bonald their ideas; three men well suited to their parts, for they excelled respectively, the first in fiery attack, the second in prudent and patient manœuvring, and the third in specious, subtle, and elevated exposition; and all three, although unconnected by any previous intimacy, applied their varied talents with unflinching perseverance to the common cause.

And what, after all, was the cause? What was, in reality, the end which the leaders of the party, apparently on the very verge of success, proposed to themselves? Had they been inclined to speak sincerely, they would have found it very difficult to answer the question. It has been said and believed by many, and probably a great portion of the Royalists imagined, in 1815, that their object was to abolish the Charter, and restore the old system: a commonplace supposition of puerile credulity; the battle-cry of the enemies, whether able or blind, of the Restoration. In the height of its most sanguine hopes, the Chamber of 1815 had formed no idea so extreme or audacious. Replaced as conquerors upon the field, not by themselves, but by the errors of their adversaries and the course of European events, the old Royalist party expected that the reverses of the Revolution and the Empire would bring them enormous advantages, and restitution; but they were yet undecided as to the use they should make of victory in the government of France, when they found themselves in the undisturbed possession of power. Their views were as unsettled and confused as their passions were violent; above all things, they coveted victory, for the haughty pleasure of triumph itself, for the definitive establishment of the Restoration, and for their own predominance, by holding power at the centre of government, and throughout the departments by administration.

But in those social shocks there are deeper questions involved than the actors are aware of. The

Hundred Days inflicted on France a much heavier evil than the waste of blood and treasure it had cost her; they lit up again the old quarrel which the Empire had stifled and the Charter was intended to extinguish,—the quarrel between old and new France, between the emigrants and the revolutionists. It was not alone between two political parties, but between two rival classes, that the struggle recommenced in 1815, as it originally exploded in 1789.

An unfavourable position for founding a Government, and, above all, a free Government. A certain degree of excitement and emulation invariably exists between the people and the political parties, which constitutes the very life of the social body, and encourages its energetic and wholesome development. But if this agitation is not confined to questions of legislature and the conduct of public affairs,—if it attacks society in its very basis,—if, instead of emulation between parties, there arises hostility amongst classes, the movement ceases to be healthy, and changes to a destroying malady, which leads on to the most lamentable disorders, and may end in the dissolution of the State. The undue ascendency of one class over another, whether of the aristocracy or the people, becomes tyranny. The bitter and continued struggle of either to obtain the upper hand, is in fact revolution, imminently impending or absolutely declared. The world has witnessed, in two great examples, the diametrically opposite results to which this formidable fact may lead. The contest between the Patricians and Plebeians held Rome for ages between the cruel alternations of despotism and anarchy, which had no variety but war. As long as either party retained public virtue, the republic found grandeur, if not social peace, in their quarrel; but when Patricians and Plebeians became corrupted by dissension, without agreeing on any fixed principle of liberty, Rome could only escape from ruin by falling under the despotism and lingering decline of the Empire. England presents to modern Europe a different spectacle. In England also, the opposing parties of nobles and democrats long contended for the supremacy; but, by a happy combination of fortune and wisdom, they came to a mutual compromise, and united in the common exercise of power: and England has found, in this amicable understanding between the different classes, in this communion of their rights and mutual influence, internal peace with greatness, and stability with freedom.

I looked forward to an analogous result for my own country, from the form of government established by the Charter. I have been accused of desiring to model France upon the example of England. In 1815, my thoughts were not turned towards England; at that time I had not seriously studied her institutions or her history. I was entirely occupied with France, her destinies, her civilization, her laws, her literature, and her great men. I lived in the heart of a society exclusively French, more deeply impregnated with French tastes and sentiments than any other. I was immediately associated with that reconciliation, blending, and intercourse of different classes, and even of parties, which seemed to me the natural condition of our new and liberal system. People of every origin, rank, and calling, I may almost say of every variety of opinion,— great noblemen, magistrates, advocates, ecclesiastics, men of letters, fashion, or business, members of the old aristocracy, of the Constituent Assembly, of the Convention, of the Empire,—lived in easy and hospitable intercourse, adopting without hesitation their altered positions and views, and all apparently disposed to act together in goodwill for the advantage of their country. A strange contradiction in our habits and manners! When social relations, applicable to mental or worldly pleasures, are alone involved, there are no longer distinctions of classes, or contests; differences of situation and opinion cease to exist; we have no thought but to enjoy and contribute in common our mutual possessions, pretensions, and recommendations. But let political questions and the positive interests of life once more spring up,—let us be called upon, not merely to assemble for enjoyment or recreation, but to assume each his part in the rights, the affairs, the honours, the advantages, and the burdens of the social system,—on the instant, all dissensions re-appear; all pretences, prejudices, susceptibilities, and oppositions revive; and that society which had seemed so single and united, resumes all its former divisions and differences.

This melancholy incoherence between the apparent and actual state of French society revealed itself suddenly in 1815. The reaction provoked by the Hundred Days destroyed in the twinkling of an eye the work of social reconciliation carried on in France for sixteen years, and caused the abrupt explosion of all the passions, good or evil, of the social system, against all the works, beneficial or mischievous, of the Revolution.

Attacked also by another difficulty, the party which prevailed at the opening of the session, in the Chamber of 1815, fell into another mistake. The aristocratic classes in France, although generously devoted, in public dangers, to the king and the country, knew not how to make common cause either with the crown or the people; they have alternately blamed and opposed, royal power and public liberty. Isolating themselves in the privileges which satisfied their vanity without giving them real influence in the State, they had not assumed, for three centuries, either with the monarch, or at the head of the nation, the position which seemed naturally to belong to them. After all they had lost, and in spite of all they ought to have learned at the Revolution, they found themselves in 1815, when power reverted to their hands, in the same undefined and shifting position. In its relations with the great powers of the State, in public discussion, in the exercise of its peculiar rights, the Chamber of 1815 had the merit of carrying into vigorous practice the constitutional system, which, in 1814, had scarcely emerged from its torpor under the Empire; but in its new work it lost sight of equity, moderation, and the favourable moment. It wished at the same time to control France and the King. It was independent and haughty, often revolutionary in its conduct towards the monarch, and equally violent and contra-revolutionary as regarded the people. This was to attempt too much; it ought to have chosen between the two, and to have declared itself either monarchical or popular. The Chamber of 1815 was neither the one nor the other. It appeared to be deeply imbued with the spirit of the old system, envenomed by the ideas or examples of the spirit of the revolution; but the spirit of government, even more essential under constitutional than under absolute power, was wanting altogether.

Thus, an opposition was seen to spring up quickly within its own bosom,—an opposition which became at once popular and monarchical, for it equally defended against the ruling party, the crown they had so rashly insulted, and the country they had profoundly disturbed. After some sharp contests, sustained with acrimonious determination on both sides, this opposition, strong in the royal support as in public sympathy, frequently obtained a majority, and became the party of the Government.

I had no seat at that time in the Chamber of Deputies. It has often been said that I took a more important share in the Government of the day than could be attributed to me with truth. I have never complained of this, nor shall I complain now. I accept the responsibility, not only of my own actions, but of those of the friends I selected and supported. The monarchical and constitutional party formed in 1815, became on the instant my own. I shall acknowledge frankly what experience has taught me of their mistakes, while I feel proud of having been enrolled in their ranks.

This party was formed abruptly and spontaneously, without premeditated object, without previous or personal concert, under the simple necessity of the moment, to meet a pressing evil, and not to establish any particular system, or any specific combination of ideas, resolutions, or designs. Its sole policy was at first confined to the support of the Restoration against the reaction: a thankless undertaking, even when most salutary; for it is useless to contend with a headlong counter-current. While you are supporting the power whose flag serves as a cloak to reaction, it is impossible to arrest the entire mischief you desire to check; and you seem to adopt that which you have been unable to subdue. This is one of the inevitable misconstructions which honest men, who act conscientiously, in stormy days, must be prepared to encounter.

Neither in its composition nor plans had the new Royalist party any special or decided character. Amongst its rising leaders, as in its more undistinguished ranks, there were men of every origin and position, collected from all points of the social and political horizon. M. de Serre was an emigrant, and had been a lieutenant in the army of Condé; MM. Pasquier, Beugnot, Siméon, Barante and St. Aulaire, had possessed influence under Napoleon; MM. Royer-Collard and Camille Jordan were opposed to the Imperial system. The same judgment, the same opinion upon the events of the day and the chances of the morrow, upon the rights and legitimate interests of the throne and country, suddenly united these men, hitherto unknown to each other. They combined, as the inhabitants of the same quarter run from all sides and, without acquaintance and never having met before, work in concert to extinguish a great fire.

A fact, however, disclosed itself, which characterized already the new royalist party in the impending struggle. Equally disturbed by the pretensions of the old aristocrats, the monarchy and the citizens formed a close league for mutual support. Louis XVIII. and young France resumed together the policy of their fathers. It is fruitless for a people to deny or forget the past; they cannot either annihilate or abstract themselves from it; situations and emergencies will soon arise to force them back into the road on which they have travelled for ages.

Selected as President by the Chamber itself, and also by the King, M. Lainé, while preserving, with a dignity at the same time natural and slightly studied, the impartiality which his situation required, inclined nevertheless towards the opinions of the moderate minority, and supported them by his moral influence, sometimes even by his words. The ascendency of his character, the gravity of his manners, and, at certain moments, the passionate overflowing of his soul, invested him with an authority which his abilities and knowledge would scarcely have sufficed to command.

The Session had not been many days open, and already, from conversation, from the selection of the officials, from the projects of interior movement which were announced, the Deputies began to know and arrange themselves, but still with doubt and confusion; as, in a battalion unexpectedly called together, the soldiers assemble in disorder, looking for their arms and colours. The Government propositions soon brought the different parties to broad daylight, and placed them in contest. The Session commenced, as might be expected, with measures arising from incidental circumstances. Of the four bills evidently bearing this character, two—the suspension of personal liberty, and the establishment of prevôtal courts—were proposed as exceptional and purely temporary; the others—for the suppression of seditious acts, and for a general amnesty—were intended to be definitive and permanent.

Measures of expediency, and exceptional laws, have been so often and so peremptorily condemned in France, that their very name and aspect suffice to render them suspicious and hateful,—a natural impression, after so much and such bitter experience! They supply notwithstanding, and particularly under a constitutional government, the least dangerous as well as the most efficacious method of meeting temporary and urgent necessities. It is better to suspend openly, and for a given time, a particular privilege, than to pervert, by encroachment and subtlety, the fixed laws, so as to adapt them to the emergency of the hour. The experience of history, in such cases, confirms the suggestions of reason. In countries where political liberty is finally established, as in England, it is precisely after it has obtained a signal triumph, that the temporary suspension of one or more of its special securities has, under pressing circumstances, been adopted as a Government measure. In ruder and less intelligent times, under the dominion of momentary danger, and as an immediate defence, those rigorous and artful statutes were enacted in perpetuity, in which all tyrannies have found arms ready made, without the odium of forging them, and from which a more advanced civilization, at a later period, has found it so difficult to escape.

It is necessary, I admit, to enable these exceptional laws to accomplish their end without too much danger, that, beyond the scope of their operation and during their continuance, the country should retain enough general liberty, and the authorities sufficient real responsibility, to confine these measures within their due limits, and to control their exercise. But, in spite of the blindness and rage of the beaten parties, we have only to read the debates in the Chambers of 1815, and the publications of the time, to be convinced that at that epoch liberty was far from having entirely perished; and the history of the ministers who were then in power unanswerably demonstrates that they sustained the weight of a most effective responsibility.

Of the two temporary bills introduced into the Chamber in 1815, that respecting the prevôtal courts met with the least opposition. Two very superior men, MM. Royer-Collard and Cuvier, had consented to become its official advocates, in the character of Royal Commissioners; and during the discussion, M. Cuvier took the lead. The debate was a very short one; two hundred and ninety members voted for the bill, ten only rejected it. The division may create surprise. The bill, in principle, comprised the heaviest possible infringement on common right, and the most formidable in practical application, by the suppression, in these courts, of the greater part of the privileges accorded in the ordinary modes of jurisdiction. A clause in the bill went almost to deprive the King of his prerogative of pardon, by ordering the immediate execution of the condemned criminals, unless the prevôtal court itself assumed the functions of grace by recommending them to royal clemency. One of the most enthusiastic Royalists of the right-hand party, M. Hyde de Neuville, objected energetically, but without effect, to a clause so harsh and anti-monarchical. The two most intractable of passions, anger and fear, prevailed in the Chamber; it had its own cause, as well as that of the King, to defend and avenge, and persuaded itself that it could neither strike too soon nor too strongly when both were attacked.

On this occasion, as well as on others, the memory of M. Cuvier has been unjustly treated. He has been accused of pusillanimity and servile ambition. The charge indicates little knowledge of human nature, and insults a man of genius on very slight grounds. I lived much with M. Cuvier. Firmness in mind and action was not his most prominent quality; but he was neither servile, nor governed by fear in opposition to his conscience. He loved order, partly for his own personal security, but much more for the cause of justice, civilization, the advantage of society, and the progress of intellect. In his complaisance for power, he was more governed by sincere inclination than egotism. He was one of those who had not learned from experience to place much confidence in liberty, and whom the remembrance of revolutionary anarchy had rendered easily accessible to honest and disinterested apprehensions. In times of social disturbance, men of sense and probity often prefer drifting towards the shore, to running the risk of being crushed, with many dear objects, on the rocks upon which the current may carry them.

In the debate on the bill which suspended for a year the securities for personal liberty, M. Royer-Collard, while supporting the Government, marked the independence of his character, and the mistrustful foresight of the moralist with regard to the power which the politician most desired to establish. He demanded that the arbitrary right of imprisonment should be entrusted only to a small number of functionaries of high rank, and that the most exalted of all, the Ministers, should in every case be considered distinctly responsible. But these amendments, which would have prevented many abuses without interfering with the necessary power, were rejected. Inexperience and precipitation were almost universal at the moment. The Cabinet and its most influential partisans in the Chambers had scarcely any knowledge of each other; neither had yet learned to conceive plans in combination, to settle the limits or bearing of their measures, or to enter on a combat with preconcerted arrangements.

A combined action and continued understanding, however, between the Government and the moderate Royalists, became every day more indispensable; for the divergence of several new parties which began to be formed, and the extent of their disagreements, manifested themselves with increasing strength from hour to hour. In proposing the act intended to repress sedition, M. de Marbois, a gentle and liberal nature, inclined to mild government, and little acquainted with the violent passions that fermented around him, had merely looked upon these acts as ordinary offences, and had sent the criminals before the tribunals of correctional police, to be punished by imprisonment only. Better informed as to the intentions of a portion of the Chamber, the committee appointed to examine the bill, of which M. Pasquier was the chairman, endeavoured to restrain the dissentients, while satisfying them to a certain extent. Amongst seditious acts, the committee drew a line between crimes and offences, assigning crimes to the Court of Assizes, to be punished by transportation, and prescribing for simple offences fine and imprisonment. This was still too little for the ultra-members of the party. They demanded the penalty of death, hard labour, and confiscation of property. These additions were refused, and the Chamber, by a large majority, passed the bill as amended by the committee. Undoubtedly there were members of the right-hand party who would not have dared to contest the propositions of MM. Piet and de Salaberry, but who rejoiced to see them thrown out, and voted for the bill. How many errors would men escape, and how many evils would they avoid, if they had the courage to act as they think right, and to do openly what they desire!

All these debates were but preludes to the great battle ready to commence, on the most important of the incidental questions before the Chamber. It is with regret that I use the word question. The amnesty was no longer one. On returning to France, the King, by his proclamation from Cambray, had promised it; and, with kings, to promise is to perform. What sovereign could refuse the pardon, of which he has given a glimpse to the condemned criminal? The royal word is not less pledged to a nation than to an individual. But in declaring, on the 28th of June, 1815, that he would only except from pardon "the authors and instigators of the plot which had overturned the throne," the King had also announced "that the two Chambers would point them out to the punishment of the laws;" and when, a month later, the Cabinet had, upon the report of the Duke of Otranto, arrested the individuals excepted in the two lists, the decree of the 24th of July again declared that "the Chambers should decide upon those amongst them who should be expatriated or brought to trial." The Chambers were therefore inevitably compromised. The amnesty had been declared, and yet it still remained a question, a bill was still considered necessary.

Four members of the Chamber of Deputies hastened to take the initiative in this debate, three of them with extreme violence, M. de la Bourdonnaye being the most vehement of the three. He had energy, enthusiasm, independence, political tact as a partisan, and a frank and impassioned roughness, which occasionally soared to eloquence. His project, it was said, would have brought eleven hundred persons under trial. Whatever might be the correctness of this calculation, the three propositions were tainted with two capital errors: they assumed, in fact, that the catastrophe of the 20th of March had been the result of a widely-spread conspiracy, the authors of which ought to be punished as they would have been in ordinary times, and by the regular course of law, if they had miscarried; they assigned to the Chambers the right of indicating, by general categories, and without limit as to number, the conspirators to be thus dealt with, although the King, by his decree of the 24th of July preceding, had merely conferred on them the power of deciding, amongst the thirty-eight individuals specially excepted by name, which should be banished and which should be brought to trial. There was thus, in these projects, at the same time, an act of accusation under the name of amnesty, and an invasion of the powers already exercised, as well as of the limits already imposed, by the royal authority.

The King's Government by no means mistook the bearing of such resolutions, and maintained its rights, its acts, and promises with suitable dignity. It hastened to check at once the attempt of the Chamber. The bill introduced by the Duke de Richelieu on the 8th of December, was a real act of amnesty, with no other exceptions than the fifty-six persons named in the two lists of the decree of the 24th of July, and belonging to the family of the Emperor Napoleon. A single additional clause, the fatal consequences of which were assuredly not foreseen, had been introduced into the preamble: the fifth article excepted from the amnesty all persons against whom prosecutions had been ordered or sentences passed before the promulgation of the law,—a lamentable reservation, equally contrary to the principle of the measure and the object of its framers. The character and essential value of an amnesty consist in assigning a term to trials and punishments, in arresting judicial action in the name of political interest, and in re-establishing confidence in the public mind, with security in the existing state of things, at once producing a cessation of sanguinary scenes and dangers. The King's Government had already, by the first list of exceptions in the decree of the 24th of July, imposed on itself a heavy burden. Eighteen generals had been sent before councils of war. Eighteen grand political prosecutions, after the publication of the amnesty, would have been much even for the strongest and best-established government to bear. The Duke de Richelieu's Cabinet, by the fifth article of the bill, imposed on itself, in addition, the prospective charge of an indefinite number of political prosecutions, which might rise up in an indefinite time; and no one could possibly foresee in what part of the kingdom, or under what circumstances. The evil of this short-sightedness continued, with repeated instances rapidly succeeding each other, for more than two years. It was the prolonged application of this article which destroyed the value and almost the credit of the amnesty, and compromised the royal Government in that reaction of 1815 which has left such lamentable reminiscences.

A member of the right-hand party, who was soon destined to become its leader, and who until then had taken no share in the debate, M. de Villèle, alone foresaw the danger of the fifth article, and hesitated not to oppose it. "This article," said he, "seems to me too vague and expansive; exceptions to amnesty, after such a rebellion as that which has taken place in our country, deliver over inevitably to the rigour of the laws all the excepted individuals. Now rigorous justice demands that, in such cases, none should be excepted but the most guilty and the most dangerous. Having no pledge or certain proof that the individuals attainted by the fifth article have deserved this express exception, I vote that the article be struck out." Unfortunately for the Government, this vote of the leader of the opposition passed without effect.

Independently of the question itself, this discussion produced an important result: it settled the division of the Chamber into two great parties, the right-hand side and the centre; the one the opponent, and the other the ally of the Cabinet. The differences of opinion which manifested themselves on this occasion were too keen, and were maintained on both sides with too much animosity, not to become the basis of a permanent classification. The right-hand party persisted in requiring several categories of exceptions to the amnesty, confiscations under the name of indemnity for injuries done to the State, and the banishment of the regicides who had been implicated during the Hundred Days. The centre, and the Cabinet in union, firmly resisted these propositions. M. Royer-Collard and M. de Serre, amongst others, exhibited in the course of this debate as much political intelligence as moral rectitude and impassioned eloquence. "It is not always the number of executions that saves empires," said M. Royer-Collard; "the art of governing men is more difficult, and glory is acquired at a loftier price. If we are prudent and skilful, we shall find that we have punished enough; never, if we are not so." M. de Serre applied himself chiefly to oppose the confiscations demanded under the title of indemnities. "The revolutionists have acted thus," said he; "they would do the same again if they could recover power. It is precisely for this reason that you ought not to imitate their detestable example; and by a distorted interpretation of an expression which is not open and sincere, by an artifice scarcely worthy of the theatre.... Gentlemen, our treasury may be low, but let it be pure." The categories and the indemnities were definitively rejected. At the last moment, and in the midst of almost universal silence, the banishment of the regicides was alone inscribed upon the act. Under the advice of his ministers, the King felt that he could not, in obedience to the will of Louis XVI., refuse his sanction to the amnesty, and leave this formidable question in suspense. There are Divine judgments which human authority ought not to forestall; neither is it called upon to reject them when they are declared by the course of events.

To the differences on the questions of expediency, every day were added the disagreements on the questions of principle. The Government itself excited but few. A bill on elections, introduced by the Minister of the Interior, M. de Vaublanc, was the only one which assumed this character. The debate was long and animated. The leading men on the opposite sides of the Chamber, MM. de Villèle, de la Bourdonnaye, de Bonald, Royer-Collard, Pasquier, de Serre, Beugnot, and Lainé, entered into it anxiously. But the ministerial plan was badly conceived, based upon incompatible foundations, and giving to the elections more of an administrative than of a political character. The principal orators of the Centre rejected it, as well as a counter-project proposed by the committee, in which the right-hand party prevailed, and which the Cabinet also disapproved. The last proposal was ultimately carried, but with important amendments, and vehemently opposed to the last. The Chamber of Deputies passed it by a weak majority, and in the Chamber of Peers it was thrown out. Although the different parties had clearly indicated their impressions and desires on the electoral system, the details were as yet obscure and unsettled. The question remained in abeyance. From the Chamber itself emanated the other propositions which involved matters of principle; they sprang from the right-hand party, and all tended to the same point—the position of the Church in the State. M. de Castelbajac proposed that the bishops and ministers should be authorized to receive and hold in perpetuity, without requiring the sanction of Government, all donations of property, real or personal, for the maintenance of public worship or ecclesiastical establishments. M. de Blangy demanded that the condition of the clergy should be materially improved, and that the married priests should no longer enjoy the pensions which had been given to them in their clerical character. M. de Bonald called for the abolition of the law of divorce. M. Lachèze-Murel insisted that the custody of the civil records should be given back to the ministers of religion. M. Murard de St. Romain attacked the University, and argued that public education should be confided to the clergy. The zeal of the new legislators was, above all other considerations, directed towards the re-establishment of religion and the Church, as the true basis of social power.

At the outset, the uneasiness and opposition excited by these proposals were less animated than we can at present imagine. More immediate dangers occupied the adversaries of Government and the public mind. A general sentiment in favour of religion as a necessary principle of order and morality, prevailed throughout the country; a sentiment revived even by the crisis of the Hundred Days, the moral wounds which that crisis had revealed, and the social dangers it had partially disclosed. The Catholic Church had not yet become the mark of the reaction which a little later was raised against it. The clergy took no direct part in these debates. The University had been, under the Empire, an object of suspicion and hostility on the part of the Liberals. The movement in favour of religious influences scarcely astonished those whom it displeased. But in the very bosom of the Chamber whence this movement emanated, there were enlightened understandings, who at once perceived its full range, and I foresaw the angry dissensions which sooner or later would be stirred up in the new social system by some of these propositions, so utterly opposed to its most fundamental and cherished principles. They applied themselves, with resolute good sense, to extract from the measures introduced, a selection conformable to the true interests of society and the Church. The law of divorce was abolished. The position of the parish priests, of the assistant ministers, and of several ecclesiastical establishments received important amelioration. The scandal of married clergymen still receiving official pensions ceased. But the proposal of assigning to the clergy the care of the civil records, and the control of public instruction, fell to the ground. The University, well defended and directed by M. Royer-Collard, intact. And with regard to the privilege for the clergy, of receiving every kind of donation without the interference of the civil authorities, the Chamber of Peers, on a report, as judicious as it was elegantly composed, by the Abbé de Montesquiou, reduced it to these conditions,—that none but religious establishments recognized by law should exercise this right, and that in every individual instance the authority of the King should be indispensable. The Chamber of Deputies adopted the measure thus amended, and from this movement, which threatened to disturb so completely the relations of the Church and State, nothing eventuated to infringe seriously either on the old maxims or the modern principles of French society.

The Cabinet co-operated loyally in these debates and wise resolutions, but with less decision and ascendency than that evinced by the moderate Royalists in the Chambers. It brought into the question neither the depth of thought, nor the power of eloquence, which give a Government the control over legislative assemblies, and raise it, even in spite of its deficiencies, in public estimation. The Duke de Richelieu was universally respected. Amongst his colleagues, all men of high character and loyalty, there were several who were endowed with rare knowledge, ability, and courage. But the Cabinet wanted unity and brilliant reputation; important conditions under any system, but pre-eminently so under a free government.

Outside the Chambers, the Ministry had to sustain a still more weighty load than the pressure from within, and one which they were not better able to encounter. France had become a prey, not to the most tyrannical or the most sanguinary, but to the most vexatious and irritating of all the passing influences which the vicissitudes of frequent revolutions impose upon a nation. A party long vanquished, trampled on, and finally included in a general amnesty, the party of the old Royalty, suddenly imagined that they had become masters, and gave themselves up passionately to the enjoyment of a new power which they looked upon as an ancient right. God forbid that I should revive the sad remembrances of this reaction! I only desire to explain its true character. It was, in civil society, in internal administration, in local affairs, and nearly throughout the entire land of France, a species of foreign invasion, violent in certain places, offensive everywhere, and which occasioned more evil to be dreaded than it actually inflicted; for these unexpected victors threatened and insulted even where they refrained from striking. They seemed inclined to indemnify themselves by arrogant temerity, for their impotence to recover all that they had lost; and to satisfy their own consciences in the midst of their revenge, they tried to persuade themselves that they were far from inflicting on their enemies the full measure of what they had themselves suffered.

Strangers to the passions of this party, impressed with the mischief they inflicted on the Royal cause, and personally wounded by the embarrassments they occasioned to the Government, the Duke de Richelieu and the majority of his colleagues contended with honest sincerity against them. Even by the side of the most justly condemned proceedings during the reaction of 1815, and which remained entirely unpunished, we find traces of the efforts of the existing authorities either to check them, prevent their return, or at least to repel the sad responsibility of permitting them. When the outrages against the Protestants broke out in the departments of the south, and more than six weeks before M. d'Argenson spoke of them in the Chamber of Deputies, a royal proclamation, countersigned by M. Pasquier, vehemently denounced them, and called upon the magistrates for their suppression. After the scandalous acquittal, by the Court of Assize at Nismes, of the assassin of General Lagarde, who had protected the free worship of the Protestants, M. Pasquier demanded and obtained, from the Court of Appeal, the annulment of this sentence, in the name of the law, and as a last protestation of discarded justice. In spite of every possible intervention of delay and impediment, the proceedings commenced at Toulouse, and ended in a decree of the prevôtal court at Pau, which inflicted five years' imprisonment on two of the murderers of General Ramel. Those of Marshal Brune had never been seriously pursued; but M. de Serre, being appointed Chancellor, compelled justice to resume its course; and the Court of Assize at Riom condemned to death, in default of appearance, the assassins they were unable to apprehend. Tardy and insufficient amends, which reveal the weakness of authority, as well as the resistance with which it was opposed! Even the ministers most subservient to the extreme royalist party endeavoured to check while supporting them, and took care to contribute less assistance than they had promised. At the very time when the Government divided the old army into classes, to get rid of all the suspected officers, the Minister of War, the Duke of Feltri, summoned to the direction of the staff of his department General de Meulan, my brother-in-law, a brave soldier, who had entered the service as a private in 1797, and had won his promotion on the field of battle by dint of wounds. M. de Meulan was a royalist, but extremely attached to the army and his comrades, and deeply grieved by the severities with which they were oppressed. I witnessed his constant efforts to obtain justice for them, and to secure the continuance in the ranks, or re-admission, of all those whom he believed to be disposed to serve the King with honest loyalty. The undertaking was difficult. In 1816, one of our most able and distinguished officers of engineers, General Bernard, had been placed on half-pay, and lived in exile at Dôle. The United States of America offered him the command of that branch of service in the Republic, with considerable advantages. He accepted the proposal, and asked the permission of his minister. The Duke of Feltri summoned him to his presence, and tried to induce him to abandon this design, by offering to appoint him to any situation in France which he considered suitable. "You promise me," said Bernard, "what you are unable to perform; place me as you intend, and in a fortnight I shall be so denounced that you will have no power to support me, and so harassed that I should voluntarily resign. While the Government has no more strength than at present, it can neither employ nor protect me. In my corner, I am at the mercy of a sub-prefect and police magistrate, who can arrest and imprison me; who sends for me every day, and compels me to wait in his ante-chamber to be ill received at last. Suffer me to go to America. The United States are the natural allies of France. I have decided, and, unless imprisoned, I shall certainly take my departure." His passport was then given to him. The Duke de Berry complained to General Haxo of the course adopted by General Bernard. "After the manner in which he has been treated," replied Haxo, "I am only surprised that he has not gone before; it is by no means certain that I shall not some day follow his example."

Nothing can explain, better than this simple fact, the situation of the King's ministers at that time, and the sincerity as well as the timidity of their wishes to be prudent and just.

A great act, resolutely conceived and accomplished, on a great occasion, was necessary to raise the executive authority from the reputation as well as the actual mischief of this weakness, and to emancipate it from the party under which it succumbed while resisting. Today, so long removed as we are from that time, the more I reflect on it in the calm freedom of my judgment, the more I am convinced that the trial of Marshal Ney afforded a most propitious opportunity for such an act as that to which I now allude. There were undoubtedly weighty reasons for leaving justice to its unfettered course. Society and the royal power both required that respect for, and a salutary dread of, the law should repossess men's minds. It was important that generations formed during the vicissitudes of the Revolution and the triumphs of the Empire, should learn, by startling examples, that all does not depend on the strength and success of the moment; that there are certain inviolable duties; that we cannot safely sport with the fate of governments and the peace of nations; and that, in this momentous game, the most powerful and the most eminent risk their honour and their lives. In a political and moral sense these considerations were of the greatest importance. But another prominent truth, equally moral and political, ought to have weighed heavily in the balance against an extreme decision. The Emperor Napoleon had reigned long and brilliantly, acknowledged and admired by France and Europe, and supported by the devotion of millions of men,—by the people as well as by the army. Ideas of right and duty, sentiments of respect and fidelity, were confused and antagonistic in many minds. There were two actual and natural governments in presence of each other; and many, without perversity, might have hesitated which to choose. The King, Louis XVIII. and his advisers might in their turn, without weakness, have taken into consideration this moral confusion, of which Marshal Ney presented the most illustrious example. The greater his offence against the King, with the more safety could they place clemency by the side of justice, and display, over his condemned head, that greatness of mind and heart which has also its full influence in establishing power and commanding fidelity. The very violence of the reaction in favour of royalty, the bitterness of party passions, their thirst for punishment and vengeance, would have imparted to this act a still greater brilliancy of credit and effect; for boldness and liberty would have sprung from it as natural consequences. I heard at that time a lady of fashion, usually rational and amiable, call Mademoiselle de Lavalette "a little wretch," for aiding her mother in the escape of her father. When such extravagancies of feeling and language are indulged in the hearing of kings and their advisers, they should be received as warnings to resist, and not to submit. Marshal Ney, pardoned and banished after condemnation, by royal letters deliberately promulgated, would have given to kingly power the aspect of a rampart raising itself above all, whether friends or enemies, to stay the tide of blood; it would have been, in fact, the reaction of 1815 subdued and extinguished, as well as that of the Hundred Days.

I do not pretend to have thought and said then, all that I say and think at present. I was sorrowful and perplexed. The King's ministers were in a similar predicament. They believed that they neither could nor ought to recommend clemency. In this momentous contingency, power knew not how to be great, sometimes the only method of becoming strong. Controlled but not overthrown, and irritated while defeated, by these alternations of concession and resistance, the Right-hand party, now become decidedly the Opposition, sought, while complaining and hesitating, some channel of escape from their position at once powerful and impotent,—some breach through which they might give the assault to the Government, enter the citadel, and establish themselves firmly there. A man of mind and courage, ambitious, restless, clever, and discontented, as well on his own account as for the sake of his party, ventured an attack extremely daring in reality, but circumspect in form, and purely theoretical in appearance. M. de Vitrolles, in a short pamphlet entitled 'Of the Ministry under a Representative Government,' said:—"France in every quarter expresses the necessity, profoundly acknowledged, of sterner action in the Government. I have examined the causes of this universal feeling, and the reasons which could explain why the different Administrations that have succeeded each other within the last eighteen months have not given the King's Cabinet the character of strength and unity which the Ministers themselves feel to be so essential. I believe that I have found them in the incoherence which existed between the nature of the adopted government and the ministerial organization, which it had not been considered necessary to modify, while at the same time we received a new division of power, and that power assumed an entirely new character of action." Appealing at every sentence to the practice and example of England, M. de Vitrolles argued that the Ministry, which he called an institution, should have perfect unity in itself, a predominant majority in the Chambers, and an actual responsibility in the conduct of affairs, which would ensure for it, with the Crown, the requisite influence and dignity. On these three conditions alone could the Government be effective. A strange reminiscence to refer to at the present day! By the most confidential intimate of the Count d'Artois, and to establish the old royalist party in power, parliamentary legislation was for the first time recommended and demanded for France, as a necessary consequence of representative government.

I undertook to repulse this attack by unmasking it. I explained, in reply, the essential principles of representative government, their true meaning, their real application, and the conditions under which they could be usefully developed, in the state in which France had been plunged by our revolutions and dissensions. Above all, I endeavoured to expose the bitterness of party spirit which lay behind this polished and erudite tilting-match between political rhetoricians, and the underhand blows which, in the insufficiency of their public weapons, they secretly aimed at each other. I believe my ideas were sound enough to satisfy intelligent minds who looked below the surface and onwards to the future; but they had no immediate and practical efficacy. When the great interests of nations and the contending passions of men are at stake, the most ingenious speculative arguments are a mere war of display, which has no influence on the course of events. As soon as the budget was voted, and on the very day of its announcement, the session was closed, and the Chambers of 1815 retired, having strenuously exercised, both in defence and attack, the free privileges conferred on France by the Charter; but divided into two Royalist parties: the one wavering and uneasy, although in the possession of power; the other full of expectation, and looking forward, with the opening of the next session, to a more decisive success, and both in a state of mutual irritation.

Notwithstanding their doubts and weaknesses, the advantage remained with the Cabinet and its adherents. For the first time since France had been a prey to the Revolution, the struggles of liberty assisted the advocates of a moderate policy, and essentially checked, if not completely subdued, their opponents. The waves of reaction murmured, but rose no more. The Cabinet, strongly supported in the Chambers, possessed the confidence of the King, who entertained a high esteem for the Duke de Richelieu, and a friendly disposition, becoming daily more warm, towards his young Minister of Police, M. Decazes. Eight days after the closing of the session, the Cabinet gained an important accession to its internal strength, and an eloquent interpreter of its public policy. M. Lainé replaced M. de Vaublanc as Minister of the Interior. As a slight compensation to the right-hand party, M. de Marbois, who had rendered himself very objectionable to them, was dismissed from the Ministry of Justice, and the Chancellor, M. Dambray, resumed the seals. M. de Marbois was one of those upright and well-informed men, but at the same time neither quick-sighted nor commanding, who assist power by opinion rather than force. He had opposed the reaction with more integrity than energy, and served the King with dignity, without acquiring personal influence. In October 1815, at a moment of the most violent agitation, the King expressed much anxiety for the introduction of the bill respecting the prevôtal courts. It was settled in council that the Chancellor and the Minister of War should prepare it together. A few days after, the King asked for it rather impatiently. "Sire," answered M. de Marbois, "I am ashamed to tell your Majesty that it is ready." He resigned office honourably, although with some regret. At the same time I left the post of Secretary-General to the Ministry of Justice. While there, M. de Marbois had treated me with confidence inspired by sympathy. Finding it disagreeable to remain under M. Dambray, to whom my Protestant extraction and opinions were equally unsuited, I re-assumed the place of Master of Requests in the State Council.

The Chambers had scarcely adjourned, when the conspiracy of Grenoble, planned by Didier, and that called the plot of the patriots, at Paris, in 1816, came, one upon the other, to put the moderation of the Cabinet to the proof. The details forwarded by the magistrates of the department of the Isère were full of exaggeration and declamatory excitement. The mode of repression ordered by the Government was precipitately rigorous. Grenoble had been the cradle of the Hundred Days. It was thought expedient to strike Bonapartism heavily, in the very place where it had first exploded. A natural opportunity presented itself here of dealing firmly with the abettors of treason, while in another quarter strong resistance was opposed to the advocates of reaction. Moderation sometimes becomes impatient of its name, and yields to the temptation of forgetting it for the moment.

The Government nevertheless continued to be moderate, and the public were not deceived as to the course adopted. Although M. Decazes, from the nature of his department, was the minister on whom measures of inquiry and suppression devolved, he was at the same time looked upon, and truly, as the protector of the oppressed, and of all who were suspected without cause. By natural disposition and magisterial habit, he loved justice in his heart. A stranger to all party antipathies, penetrating, fearless, indefatigably active, and as prompt in benevolence as in duty, he exercised the power which the special laws conferred on him with measure and discretion; enforcing them as much against the spirit of reaction and persecution as against detected conspiracy, and continually occupied himself in preventing or repairing the abuses in which the inferior authorities indulged. Thus he advanced equally in the good opinion of the country and the favour of the King. People and parties have an infallible instinct by which they recognize, under the most complicated circumstances, those who attack and those who defend them, their friends and their enemies. The ultra-royalists soon began to look upon M. Decazes as their chief adversary, and the moderates to regard him as their most valuable ally.

At the same time, and during the silence of the tribune, the chief representatives of moderate policy in the Chambers eagerly sought opportunities of bringing their views before the public, of proclaiming their principles, and of rallying, round the King and the constitutional government, the still hesitating support of the nation at large. It affords me much gratification to recall here the words, perhaps forgotten, of three justly celebrated men, all personal friends of my own; they demonstrate (as I think, with some brilliancy) the spirit of the monarchical party attached to the state of society which the times had engendered in France, and the opinions and sentiments they were anxious to disseminate.

On the 6th of July, 1816, M. de Serre, in establishing, as first President, the Royal Court at Colmar, spoke as follows:—"Liberty, that pretext of all seditious ambition,—liberty, which is nothing more than the reign of law, has ever been the first privilege buried with the laws under the ruins of the throne. Religion itself is in danger when the throne and laws are attacked; for everything on earth is derived from heaven, and there is perfect harmony between all divine and human institutions. If the latter are overturned, the former cannot be respected. Let all our efforts, then, be exerted to combine, purify, and strengthen that monarchical and Christian spirit which inspires the sentiment of every sacrifice to duty! Let our first care be to obtain universal respect for the Charter which the King has granted to us. Undoubtedly our laws, our Charter, may be improved; and we neither require to interdict regret for the past nor hope for the future. But let us commence by submitting heartily and without reserve to the laws as they exist; let us place this first check on the impatient restlessness to which we have been surrendered for twenty-five years; let us teach ourselves this primary conviction, that we know how to adopt and to be satisfied with a defined system. The rest may be left to time."

Six weeks later, on the 19th of August, M. Royer-Collard, when presiding over the distribution of prizes at the general meeting of the University, addressed these words to the young students:—"Today, when the reign of falsehood has ceased, and the legitimacy of power, which is truth in government, permits a more unshackled play to all salutary and generous doctrines, public instruction beholds its destinies elevated and expanded. Religion demands from it pure hearts and disciplined minds; the State looks for habits profoundly monarchical; science, philosophy, and literature expect new brilliancy and distinction. These will be the benefits bestowed by a prince to whom his people already owe so much gratitude and love. He, who has made public liberty flourish under the shadow of his hereditary throne, will know well how to base, on the tutelary principles of empires, a system of teaching worthy of the enlightened knowledge of the age, and such as France demands from him, that she may not descend from the glorious rank she occupies amongst nations."

At the expiration of eight days more, in an assembly exclusively literary, a man who had never held public office, but for half or more than half a century a sincere and steady friend to liberty, M. Suard, perpetual secretary of the French Academy, in giving an account to that body of the examination in which he had decreed the prize to M. Villemain for his 'Panegyric on Montesquieu,' expressed himself in these terms:—"The instability of governments generally proceeds from indecision as to the principles which ought to regulate the exercise of power. A prince enlightened by the intelligence of the age, by experience, and a superior understanding, bestows on royal authority a support which no other can replace, in that Charter which protects the rights of the monarch, while it guarantees to the nation all those that constitute true and legitimate liberty. Let us rally under this signal of alliance between the people and their king. Their union is the only certain pledge for the happiness of both. Let the Charter be for us what the holy ark that contained the tables of the law was for the Hebrews of old. If the shade of the great publicist who has shed light on the principles of constitutional monarchies could be present at the triumph which we now award him, he would confirm with his sanction the sentiments I venture to express."

An assembly so unanimous in opinion and intention, composed of such men, representing so many important sections of society, and voluntarily grouped round the King and his ministers, constituted in themselves a great political fact. A certain index was supplied, that, in the opinion of the moderate party, enlightened minds were not wanting to comprehend the conditions of the new system, or serious dispositions for its support. As yet, however, they only formed the scattered elements and seeds of a great conservative party under a free government. Time was necessary for this party to unite, to consolidate its natural strength, and to render itself acceptable to the country. Would time be given for this difficult undertaking? The question was doubtful. A formidable crisis approached; the Chamber of 1815 was on the point of re-opening, and undoubtedly still more ardent and aggressive than during the preceding session. The party which prevailed there had not only to retrieve their checks, and their designs, but they had also recent insults to avenge. During the recess they had been the objects of animated attack. The Government everywhere opposed their influence; the public loudly manifested towards them mistrust and antipathy; they were alternately charged with fanaticism and hypocrisy, with incapacity and vindictive obstinacy. Popular-anger and ridicule assailed them with unrestrained license. From notes collected at the time, I quote literally a few specimens of the sarcastic hostility with which they were pursued:—

"April 10th, 1816.—Before adjourning, the Chamber of Deputies has organized itself into a chapel. Treasurer and secretary, M. Laborie. Contractor for burials, M. de La Bourdonnaye. Grave-digger, M. Duplessis-Grénédan. Superintendent, M. de Bouville, and in his capacity of vice-president—rattlesnake. Dispenser of holy water (promise-maker), M. de Vitrolles. General of the Capuchins, M. de Villèle; and he deserves the post for his voice. Grand almoner, M. de Marcellus, who gives a portion of his own estate to the poor. Bellringers, M. Hyde de Neuville," etc. etc.

"May, 1816.—Here is the Charter which a majority of the Chamber proposes to confer upon us.—Article. The fundamental principles of the constitution may be changed as often as we wish; nevertheless, seeing that stability is desirable, they shall not be changed more than three times a year.—Art. Every law emanates from the King; this is the first evidence of the right of petition accorded to all frenchmen.—Art. The laws shall be executed according to the pleasure of the Deputies, each in their respective departments.—Art. Every representative shall have the nomination to all posts within his district."

"July 1816.—They say the King is slightly indisposed. He will be very ill indeed if he is obliged to keep his Chamber for five years."

Such were the public expressions respecting this assembly, one of the most honourable members of which, M. de Kergorlay, said, a few months before, "The Chamber had not yet whispered when the former Ministry already fell; let it speak, and the present Government will scarcely last eight days."

The Ministry, however, had held its ground, and still continued to do so; but it was evidently impossible that it could stand firm against the Chamber, once more assembled with redoubled animosity. They well knew that the Opposition was determined to renew the most violent attacks upon the existing authorities. M. de Châteaubriand printed his 'Monarchy according to the Charter;' and although this able pamphlet was not yet published, everybody knew the superior skill with which the author could so eloquently blend falsehood with truth, how brilliantly he could compound sentiments and ideas, and with what power he could entangle the blinded and unsettled public in this dazzling chaos. Neither the Ministry nor the Opposition attempted to deceive themselves as to the nature and consequences of the struggle about to commence. The question of persons was merely the symbol and cloak of the great social and political topics in dispute between the two parties. The point to be decided was, whether power should pass over to the Right-hand party, such as it had exhibited itself during the session lately terminated; that is, whether the theories of M. de Bonald and the passions of M. de La Bourdonnaye, feebly qualified by the prudence and influence, as yet unripened, of M. de Villèle, should become the rule of the King's policy.

I am not now, neither was I in 1815, amongst those who considered the Right-hand party unfit to govern France. On the contrary, I had already, although less profoundly and clearly than at present, adopted the opinion, that a concurrence of all the enlightened and independent classes, whether old or new, was absolutely necessary to rescue our country from the impending alternations of anarchy or despotism, and that without their union we could never long preserve order and liberty together. Perhaps too I might include this natural tendency amongst the reasons, not absolutely defined, which led me to desire the Restoration. Hereditary monarchy, become constitutional, presented itself to my mind both as a principle of stability, and as a natural and worthy means of reconciliation and conversion amongst the classes and parties who had been so long and continually at war. But in 1816, so soon after the revolutionary shock of the Hundred Days, and before the counter-revolutionary reaction of 1815 had subsided, the accession of the Right-hand party to power, would have been very different from the victory of men capable of governing without social disturbance, although under an unpopular system. It would have been the Revolution and the Counter-revolution once more in active contest, under an attack of raging fever; and thus the Throne and the Charter, the internal peace and security of France as well as her liberties, would be endangered by this struggle, before the eyes of Europe encamped within our territory and in arms around the combatants.

Under these menacing circumstances, M. Decazes had the rare merit of finding and applying a remedy to the gigantic evil. He was the first, and for some time the only one amongst the Ministers, who looked upon the dissolution of the Chamber of 1815 as equally necessary and possible. Undoubtedly personal interest had a share in his bold perspicuity; but I know him well enough to feel convinced, that his devotion to the country and the King powerfully contributed to his enlightened decision; and his conduct at this crisis displayed at least as much patriotism as ambition.

He had a double labour of persuasion to accomplish; first to win over his two principal colleagues, the Duke de Richelieu and M. Lainé, and afterwards the King himself. Both sincerely attached to a moderate policy, the Duke and M. Lainé were undecided, timid under great responsibility, and more disposed to wait the progress of difficulties and dangers, than to surmount by confronting them. Amongst the Duke's immediate circle were many ultra-royalists, who exercised no influence over him, and whom he even treated rudely when they displayed their violence; but he was unwilling to declare open war against them. M. Lainé, scrupulous in his resolves and fearful for their consequences, was sensitive on the point of vanity, and disinclined to any measure not originating with himself. The King's irresolution was perfectly natural. How could he dissolve the first Chamber, avowedly royalist, which had been assembled for twenty-five years,—a Chamber he had himself declared incomparable, and which contained so many of his oldest and most faithful friends? What dangers to himself and his dynasty might spring up on the day of such a decree! and even now, what discontent and anger already existed in his family and amongst his devoted adherents, and consequently what embarrassment and vexation thereby recoiled upon himself.

But Louis XVIII. had a cold heart and an unfettered mind. The rage and ill-temper of his relatives affected him little, when he had once firmly resolved not to be influenced by them. It was his pride and pleasure to fancy himself a more enlightened politician than all the rest of his race, and to act in perfect independence of thought and will. On more than one occasion, the Chamber, if not in direct words, at least in act and manner, had treated him with disrespect almost amounting to contempt, after the fashion of a revolutionary assembly. It became necessary for him to show to all, that he would not endure the display of such feelings and principles either from his friends or enemies. He regarded the Charter as his own work, and the foundation of his glory. The right-hand party frequently insulted and sometimes threatened a direct attack upon the Charter. The defence lay with the King. This gave him an opportunity of re-establishing it in its original integrity. During the administration of M. de Talleyrand he had, reluctantly and against his own conviction, modified several articles, and submitted fourteen others to the revision of the legislative authorities. To cut short this revision, and to return to the pure Charter, was to restore it a second time to France, and thus to establish, for the country and himself, a new pledge of security and peace.

During more than two months, M. Decazes handled all these points with much ability and address; determined, but not impatient, persevering, yet not obstinate, changing his topic according to the tempers he encountered, and day by day bringing before these wavering minds the facts and arguments best adapted to convince them. Without taking his principal friends unconnected with the Cabinet into the full and daily confidence of his labours, he induced them, under a promise of secrecy, to assist him by reasons and reflections which he might bring under the eyes of the King, while they gave variety to his own views. Several amongst them transmitted notes to him with this object; I contributed one also, particularly bearing on the hopes which those numerous middle classes placed in the King, who desired no more than to enjoy the productive repose they derived from him, and whom he alone could secure from the dangerous uncertainty to which the Chamber had reduced them. Different in origin and style, but all actuated by the same spirit and tending to the same end, these argumentative essays became gradually more and more efficacious. Having at last decided, the Duke de Richelieu and M. Lainé concurred with M. Decazes to bring over the King, who had already formed his resolution, but chose to appear undecided, it being his pleasure to have no real confidant but his favourite. The three ministers who were known to be friends of the right-hand party, M. Dambray, the Duke of Feltri, and M. Dubouchage, were not consulted; and it was said that they remained in total ignorance of the whole affair to the last moment. I have reason to believe that, either from respect to the King, or from reluctance to enter into contest with the favourite, they soon reconciled themselves to a result which they plainly foresaw.

Be this as it may, on Wednesday, the 14th of August, the King held a cabinet council; the sitting was over, and the Duke of Feltri had already risen to take his departure. The King desired him to resume his place again. "Gentlemen," said he, "there is yet a question of immediate urgency,—the course to be taken with respect to the Chamber of Deputies. Three months ago I had determined to re-assemble it. Even a month since, I retained the same intention; but all that I have seen, and all that comes under my daily observation, proves so clearly the spirit of faction by which that Chamber is governed, the dangers which it threatens to France and to myself have become so apparent, that I have entirely changed my opinion. From this moment, then, you may consider the Chamber as dissolved. Start from that point, gentlemen, prepare to execute the measure, and in the meantime preserve the most inviolable secrecy on the subject. My decision is absolute." When Louis XVIII. had formed a serious resolution and intended to be obeyed, he had a tone of dignity and command which cut short all remonstrance. During three weeks, although the question deeply occupied all minds, and in spite of some returns of hesitation on the part of the King himself, the secret of the resolution adopted was so profoundly kept, that the Court believed the Chamber would re-assemble. It was only on the 5th of September, after the King had retired to bed, that Monsieur received information through the Duke de Richelieu, from his Majesty, that the decree for the dissolution was signed, and would be published in the 'Moniteur' on the following morning.

The surprise and anger of Monsieur were unbounded; he would have hastened at once to the King; the Duke de Richelieu withheld him, by saying that the King was already asleep, and had given peremptory orders that he should not be disturbed. The Princes, his sons, accustomed to extreme reserve in the King's presence, appeared to approve rather than condemn. "The King has acted wisely," said the Duke de Berry; "I warned those gentlemen of the Chamber that they had indulged in too much license." The Court was thrown into consternation, on hearing of a stroke so totally unexpected. The party against whom it was aimed, attempted some stir in the first instance. M. de Châteaubriand added an angry Postscript to his 'Monarchy according to the Charter,' and evinced symptoms of resistance, more indignant than rational, to the measures decreed, in consequence of some infraction of the regulations of the press, to retard the publication of his work. But the party, having reflected a little, prudently stifled their anger, and began immediately to contrive means for re-engaging in the contest. The public, or, I ought rather to say, the entire land, loudly proclaimed its satisfaction. For honest, peaceably disposed people, the measure was a signal of deliverance; for political agitators, a proclamation of hope. None were ignorant that M. Decazes had been its first and most effectual advocate. He was surrounded with congratulations, and promises that all men of sense and substance would rally round him; he replied with modest satisfaction, "This country must be very sick indeed for me to be of so much importance."

CHAPTER V.: GOVERNMENT OF THE CENTRE.: 1816-1821.

COMPOSITION OF THE NEW CHAMBER OF DEPUTIES.—THE CABINET IN A
MAJORITY.—ELEMENTS OF THAT MAJORITY, THE CENTRE PROPERLY SO
CALLED, AND THE DOCTRINARIANS.—TRUE CHARACTER OF THE CENTRE.—
TRUE CHARACTER OF THE DOCTRINARIANS, AND REAL CAUSE OF THEIR
INFLUENCE.—M. DE LA BOURDONNAYE AND M. ROYER-COLLARD AT THE
OPENING OF THE SESSION.—ATTITUDE OF THE DOCTRINARIANS IN THE DEBATE
ON THE EXCEPTIONAL LAWS.—ELECTORAL LAW OF FEBRUARY 5TH, 1817.—THE
PART I TOOK ON THAT OCCASION.—OF THE ACTUAL AND POLITICAL POSITION
OF THE MIDDLE CLASSES.—MARSHAL GOUVION ST. CYR, AND HIS BILL FOR
RECRUITING THE ARMY, OF THE 10TH OF MARCH, 1818.—BILL RESPECTING THE
PRESS, OF 1819, AND M. DE SERRE.—PREPARATORY DISCUSSION OF THESE BILLS
IN THE STATE COUNCIL.—GENERAL ADMINISTRATION OF THE COUNTRY.—
MODIFICATION OF THE CABINET FROM 1816 TO 1820.—IMPERFECTIONS OF THE
CONSTITUTIONAL SYSTEM.—ERRORS OF INDIVIDUALS.—DISSENSIONS BETWEEN
THE CABINET AND THE DOCTRINARIANS.—THE DUKE DE RICHELIEU
NEGOCIATES, AT AIX-LA-CHAPELLE, THE ENTIRE RETREAT OF FOREIGN TROOPS
FROM FRANCE.—HIS SITUATION AND CHARACTER.—HE ATTACKS THE BILL ON
ELECTIONS.—HIS FALL.—CABINET OF M. DECAZES.—HIS POLITICAL WEAKNESS,
NOTWITHSTANDING HIS PARLIAMENTARY SUCCESS.—ELECTIONS OF 1819.—
ELECTION AND NON-ADMISSION OF M. GRÉGOIRE.—ASSASSINATION OF THE
DUKE DE BERRY.—FALL OF M. DECAZES.—THE DUKE DE RICHELIEU RESUMES
OFFICE.—HIS ALLIANCE WITH THE RIGHT-HAND PARTY.—CHANGE IN THE LAW
OF ELECTIONS.—DISORGANIZATION OF THE CENTRE, AND PROGRESS OF THE
RIGHT-HAND PARTY.—SECOND FALL OF THE DUKE DE RICHELIEU.—
M. DE VILLÈLE AND THE RIGHT-HAND PARTY OBTAIN POWER.

A violent outcry was raised, as there ever has been and always will be, against ministerial
interference at the elections. This is the sour consolation of the beaten, who feel the necessity of
accounting for their defeat. Elections, taken comprehensively, are almost always more genuine
than interested and narrow-minded suspicion is disposed to allow. The desires and ability of the
powers in office, exercise over them only a secondary authority. The true essence of elections
lies in the way in which the wind blows, and in the impulse of passing events. The decree of the
5th of September, 1816, had given confidence to the moderate party, and a degree of hope to the
persecuted of 1815. They all rallied round the Cabinet, casting aside their quarrels, antipathies,
and private rancours, combining to support the power which promised victory to the one and
safety to the other.

The victory, in fact, remained with the Cabinet, but it was one of those questionable triumphs
which left the conquerors still engaged in a fierce war. The new Chamber comprised, in the
centre a ministerial majority, on the right a strong and active opposition, and on the left a very

small section, in which M. d'Argenson and M. Lafitte were the only names recognized by the public.

The ministerial majority was formed from two different although at that time closely-united elements,—the centre, properly called the grand army of power, and the very limited staff of that army, who soon received the title of doctrinarians.

I shall say of the centre of our assemblies since 1814, what I have just said of M. Cuvier; it has been misunderstood and calumniated, when servility and a rabid desire for place have been named as its leading characteristics. With it, as with others, personal interests have had their weight, and have looked for their gratification; but one general and just idea formed the spirit and bond of union of the party,—the idea that, in the present day, after so many revolutions, society required established government, and that to government all good citizens were bound to render their support. Many excellent and honourable sentiments,—family affection, a desire for regular employment, respect for rank, laws, and traditions, anxieties for the future, religious habits,—all clustered round this conviction, and had often inspired its votaries with rare and trusting courage. I call these persevering supporters of Government, citizen Tories; their defamers are weak politicians and shallow philosophers, who neither understand the moral instincts of the soul, nor the essential interests of society.

The doctrinarians have been heavily attacked. I shall endeavour to explain rather than defend them. When either men or parties have once exercised an influence over events, or obtained a place in history, it becomes important that they should be correctly known; this point accomplished, they may rest in peace and submit to judgment.

It was neither intelligence, nor talent, nor moral dignity—qualities which their acknowledged enemies have scarcely denied them—that established the original character and political importance of the doctrinarians.

Other men of other parties have possessed the same qualities; and between the relative pretensions of these rivals in understanding, eloquence, and sincerity, public opinion will decide. The peculiar characteristic of the doctrinarians, and the real source of their importance in spite of their limited number, was that they maintained, against revolutionary principles and ideas, ideas and principles contrary to those of the old enemies of the Revolution, and with which they opposed it, not to but to reform and purify it in the name of justice and truth. The great feature, dearly purchased, of the French revolution was, that it was a work of the human mind, its conceptions and pretensions, and at the same time a struggle between social interests. Philosophy had boasted that it would regulate political economy, and that institutions, laws, and public authorities should only exist as the creatures and servants of instructed reason,—- an insane pride, but a startling homage to all that is most elevated in man, to his intellectual and moral attributes! Reverses and errors were not slow in impressing on the Revolution their rough lessons; but even up to 1815 it had encountered, as commentators on its ill-fortune, none but implacable enemies or undeceived accomplices,—the first thirsting for vengeance, the last eager for rest, and neither capable of opposing to revolutionary principles anything beyond a retrograde movement on the one side, and the scepticism of weariness on the other. "There was nothing in the Revolution but error and crime," said the first; "the supporters of the old system were in the right."—"The Revolution erred only in excess," exclaimed the second; "its principles were sound, but carried too far; it has abused its rights." The doctrinarians denied both these conclusions; they refused to acknowledge the maxims of the old system, or, even in a mere speculative sense, to adhere to the principles of the Revolution. While frankly adopting the new state of French society, such as our entire history, and not alone the year 1789, had made it, they undertook to establish a government on rational foundations, but totally opposed to the theories in the name of which the old system had been overthrown, or the incoherent principles which some endeavoured to conjure up for its reconstruction. Alternately called on to combat and defend the Revolution, they boldly assumed from the outset, an intellectual position, opposing ideas to ideas, and principles to principles, appealing at the same time to reason and experience, affirming rights instead of maintaining interests, and requiring France, not to confess that she had committed evil alone, or to declare her impotence for good, but to emerge from the chaos into which she had plunged herself, and to raise her head once more towards heaven in search of light.

Let me readily admit that there was also much pride in this attempt; but a pride commencing with an act of humility, which proclaims the mistakes of yesterday with the desire and hope of not repeating them today. It was rendering homage to human intelligence while warning it of the limits of its power, respecting the past, without undervaluing the present or abandoning the future. It was an endeavour to bestow on politics sound philosophy, not as a sovereign mistress, but as an adviser and support.

I shall state without hesitation, according to what experience has taught me, the faults which progressively mingled with this noble design, and impaired or checked its success. What I anxiously desire at present is to indicate its true character. It was to this mixture of philosophical sentiment and political moderation, to this rational respect for opposing rights and facts, to these principles, equally new and conservative, anti-revolutionary without being retrograde, and modest in fact although sometimes haughty in expression, that the doctrinarians owed their importance as well as their name. Notwithstanding the numerous errors of philosophy and human reason, the present age still cherishes reasoning and philosophical tastes; and the most determined practical politicians sometimes assume the air of acting upon general ideas, regarding them as sound methods of obtaining justification or credit. The doctrinarians thus responded to a profound and real necessity, although imperfectly acknowledged, of French minds: they paid equal respect to intellect and social order; their notions appeared well suited to regenerate, while terminating the Revolution. Under this double title they found, with partisans and adversaries, points of contact which drew them together, if not with active sympathy, at least with solid esteem: the right-hand party looked upon them as sincere royalists; and the left, while opposing them with acrimony, could not avoid admitting that they were neither the advocates of the old system, nor the defenders of absolute power.

Such was their position at the opening of the session of 1816: a little obscure still, but recognized by the Cabinet as well as by the different parties. The Duke de Richelieu, M. Lainé, and M. Decazes, whether they liked the doctrinarians or not, felt that they positively required their co-operation, as well in the debates of the Chambers as to act upon public opinion. The left-hand party, powerless in itself, accorded with them from necessity, although their ideas and language sometimes produced surprise rather than sympathy. The right, notwithstanding its losses at the elections, was still very strong, and speedily assumed the offensive. The King's speech on opening the session was mild and somewhat indistinct, as if tending rather to palliate the decree of the 5th of September, than to parade it with an air of triumph: "Rely," said he, in conclusion, "on my fixed determination to repress the outrages of the ill-disposed, and to restrain the exuberance of overheated zeal." "Is that all?" observed M. de Châteaubriand, on leaving the royal presence; "if so, the victory is ours:" and on that same day he dined with the Chancellor. M. de la Bourdonnaye was even more explicit. "The King," said he, with a coarse expression, "once more hands his ministers over to us!" During the session of the next day, meeting M. Royer-Collard, with whom he was in the habit of extremely free conversation, "Well," said he, "there you are, more rogues than last year." "And you not so many," replied M. Royer-Collard. The right-hand party, in their reviving hopes, well knew how to distinguish the adversaries with whom they would have to contend.

As in the preceding session, the first debates arose on questions of expediency. The Cabinet judged it necessary to demand from the Chambers the prolongation, for another year, of the two provisional laws respecting personal liberty and the daily press. M. Decazes presented a detailed account of the manner in which, up to that period, the Government had used the arbitrary power committed to its hands, and also the new propositions which should restrain it within the limits necessary to remove all apprehended danger. The right-hand party vigorously rejected these propositions, upon the very natural ground that they had no confidence in the Ministers, but without any other reasoning than the usual commonplace arguments of liberalism. The doctrinarians supported the bills, but with the addition of commentaries which strongly marked their independence, and the direction they wished to give to the power they defended. "Every day," said M. de Serre, "the nature of our constitution will be better understood, its benefits more appreciated by the nation; the laws with which you co-operate, will place by degrees our institutions and habits in harmony with representative monarchy; the government will approach its natural perfection,—that unity of principle, design, and action which forms the condition of its existence. In permitting and even in protecting legal opposition, it will not allow that opposition to find resting-points within itself. It is because it can be, and ought to be, watched over and contradicted by independent men, that it should be punctually obeyed, faithfully seconded and served by those who have become and wish to remain its direct agents. Government will thus acquire a degree of strength which can dispense with the employment of extraordinary means: legal measures, restored to their proper energy, will be found sufficient." "There is," said M. Royer-Collard, "a strong objection against this bill; the Government may be asked, 'Before you demand excessive powers, have you employed all those which the laws entrust to you? have you exhausted their efficacy?' ... I shall not directly answer this question, but I shall say to those who put it, 'Take care how you expose your Government to too severe a trial, and one under which nearly all Governments have broken down; do not require from it perfection; consider its difficulties as well as its duties.' ... We wish to arrest its steps in the course it pursues at present, and to impose daily changes. We demand from it the complete development of institutions and constitutional enactments; above all, we require that vigorous unity of principles, system, and conduct without which it will never effectually reach the end towards which it advances. But what it has already done, is a pledge for what it will yet accomplish. We feel a just reliance that the extraordinary powers with which we invest it will be exercised, not by or for a party, but for the nation against all parties. Such is our treaty; such are the stipulations which have been spoken of: they are as public as our confidence, and we thank those who have occasioned their repetition, for proving to France that we are faithful to her cause, and neglect neither her interests nor our own duties."

With a more gentle effusion of mind and heart, M. Camille Jordan held the same language; the bills passed; the right-hand party felt as blows directed against itself the advice suggested to the Cabinet, and the Cabinet saw that in that quarter, as necessary supporters, they had also haughty and exacting allies.

Their demands were not fruitless. The Cabinet, uninfluenced either by despotic views or immoderate passions, had no desire to retain unnecessarily the absolute power with which it had been entrusted. No effort was requisite to deprive it of the provisional laws; they fell successively of themselves,—the suspension of the securities for personal liberty in 1817, the prevôtal courts in 1818, the censorship of the daily press in 1819; and four years after the tempest of the Hundred Days, the country was in the full enjoyment of all its constitutional privileges.

During this interval, other questions, more and less important, were brought forward and decided. When the first overflowing of the reaction of 1815 had a little calmed down, when France, less disturbed with the present, began once more to think of the future, she was called upon to enter on the greatest work that can fall to the lot of a nation. There was more than a new government to establish; it was necessary that a free government should be imbued with vigour. It was written, and it must live,—a promise often made, but never accomplished. How often, from 1789 to 1814, had liberties and political rights been inscribed on our institutes and laws, to be buried under them, and held of no account. The first amongst the Governments of our day, the Restoration, took these words at their true meaning; whatever may have been its traditions and propensities, what it said, it did; the liberties and rights it acknowledged, were taken into real co-operation and action. From 1814 to 1830, as from 1830 to 1848, the Charter was a truth. For once forgetting it, Charles X. fell.

When this work of organization, or, to speak more correctly, when this effectual call to political life commenced in 1816, the question of the electoral system, already touched upon, but without result, in the preceding session, was the first that came under notice. It was included in the scope of the fortieth article of the Charter, which ran thus:—"The electors who nominate the Deputies can have no right of voting, unless they pay a direct contribution of 300 francs, and have reached the age of thirty,"—an ambiguous arrangement, which attempted more than it ventured to accomplish. It evidently contained a desire of placing the right of political suffrage above the popular masses, and of confining it within the more elevated classes of society. But the constitutional legislator had neither gone openly to this point, nor attained it with certainty; for if the Charter required from the electors who were actually to name the Deputies, 300 francs of direct contribution, and thirty years of age, it did not forbid that these electors should be themselves chosen by preceding electoral assemblies; or rather it did not exclude indirect election, nor, under that form, what is understood by the term universal suffrage.

I took part in drawing up the bill of the 5th of February, 1817, which comprised, at that time, the solution given to this important question. I was present at the conferences in which it was prepared. When ready, M. Lainé, whose business it was, as Minister of the Interior, to present it to the Chamber of Deputies, wrote to say that he wished to see me: "I have adopted," he said, "all the principles of this bill, the concentration of the right of suffrage, direct election, the equal privilege of voters, their union in a single college for each department; and I really believe these are the best that could be desired: still, upon some of these points, I have mental doubts and little time to solve them. Help me in preparing the exposition of our objects." I responded, as I was bound, to this confiding sincerity, by which I felt equally touched and honoured. The bill was brought in; and while my friends supported it in the Chamber, from whence my age for the present excluded me, I defended it, on behalf of the Government, in several articles inserted in the 'Moniteur.' I was well informed as to its intent and true spirit, and I speak of it without embarrassment in presence of the universal suffrage, as now established. If the electoral system of 1817 disappeared in the tempest of 1848, it conferred on France thirty years of regular and free government, systematically sustained and controlled; and amidst all the varying influences of parties, and the shock of a revolution, this system sufficed to maintain peace, to develop national prosperity, and to preserve respect for all legal rights. In this age of ephemeral and futile experiments, it is the only political enactment which has enjoyed a long and powerful life. At least it was a work which may be acknowledged, and which deserves to be correctly estimated, even after its overthrow.

A ruling idea inspired the bill of the 5th of February, 1817,—to fix a term to the revolutionary system, and to give vigour to the constitutional Government. At that epoch, universal suffrage had ever been, in France, an instrument of destruction or deceit,—of destruction, when it had really placed political power in the hands of the multitude; of deceit, when it had assisted to annul political rights for the advantage of absolute power, by maintaining, through the vain intervention of the multitude, a false appearance of electoral privilege. To escape, in fine, from that routine of alternate violence and falsehood, to place political power in the region within which the conservative interests of social order naturally predominate with enlightened independence, and to secure to those interests, by the direct election of deputies from the country, a free and strong action upon its Government,—such were the objects, without reserve or exaggeration, of the authors of the electoral system of 1817.

In a country devoted for twenty-five years, on the subject of political elections, whether truly or apparently, to the principle of the supremacy of number, so absurdly called the sovereignty of the people, the attempt was new, and might appear rash. At first, it confined political power to the hands of 140,000 electors. From the public, and even from what was already designated the liberal party, it encountered but slight opposition; some objections springing from the past, some apprehensions for the future, but no declared or active hostility. It was from the bosom of the classes specially devoted to conservative interests, and from their intestine discussions, that the attack and the danger emanated.

During the session of 1815, the old royalist faction, in its moderated views, and when it renounced systematic and retrograding aspirations, had persuaded itself that, at least, the King's favour and the influence of the majority would give it power in the departments as at the seat of government. The decree of the 5th of September, 1816, abolished this double expectation. The old Royalists called upon the new electoral system to restore it, but at once perceived that the bill of the 5th of February was not calculated to produce such an effect; and forthwith commenced a violent attack, accusing the new plan of giving over all electoral power, and consequently all political influence, to the middle classes, to the exclusion of the great proprietors and the people.

At a later period, the popular party, who neither thought nor spoke on the subject in 1817, adopted this argument in their turn, and charged, on this same accusation of political monopoly for the benefit of the middle classes, their chief complaint, not only against the electoral law, but against the entire system of government of which that law was the basis and guarantee.

I collect my reminiscences, and call back my impressions. From 1814 to 1848, under the government of the Restoration, and under that of July, I loudly supported and more than once had the honour of carrying this flag of the middle classes, which was naturally my own. What did we understand by it? Have we ever conceived the design, or even admitted the thought, that the citizens should become a newly privileged order, and that the laws intended to regulate the exercise of suffrage should serve to found the predominance of the middle classes by taking, whether in right or fact, all political influence, on one side from the relics of the old French aristocracy, and on the other from the people?

Such an attempt would have been strangely ignorant and insane. It is neither by political theories nor articles in laws, that the privileges and superiority of any particular class are established in a State. These slow and pedantic methods are not available for such a purpose; it requires the force of conquest or the power of faith. Society is exclusively controlled by military or religious ascendency; never by the influence of the citizens. The history of all ages and nations is at hand to prove this to the most superficial observer.

In our day, the impossibility of such a predominance of the middle classes is even more palpable. Two ideas constitute the great features of modern civilization, and stamp it with its formidable activity; I sum them up in these terms:—There are certain universal rights inherent in man's nature, and which no system can legitimately withhold from any one; there are individual rights which spring from personal merit alone, without regard to the external circumstances of birth, fortune, or rank, and which every one who has them in himself should be permitted to exercise. From the two principles of legal respect for the general rights of humanity, and the free development of natural gifts, ill or well understood, have proceeded, for nearly a century, the advantages and evils, the great actions and crimes, the advances and wanderings which revolutions and Governments have alternately excited in the bosom of every European community. Which of these two principles provokes or even permits the exclusive supremacy of the middle classes? Assuredly neither the one nor the other. One opens to individual endowments every gate; the other demands for every human being his place and his portion: no greatness is unattainable; no condition, however insignificant, is counted as nothing. Such principles are irreconcilable with exclusive superiority; that of the middle classes, as of every other, would be in direct contradiction to the ruling tendencies of modern society.

The middle classes have never, amongst us, dreamed of becoming privileged orders; and no rational mind has ever indulged in such dreams for them. This idle accusation is but an engine of war, erected under cover of a confusion of ideas, sometimes by the hypocritical dexterity, and at others by the blind infatuation of party spirit. But this does not prevent its having been, or becoming again, fatal to the peace of our social system; for men are so constructed that chimerical dangers are the most formidable they can encounter: we fight boldly with tangible substances, but we lose our heads, either from fear or anger, when in presence of phantoms.

It was with real dangers that we had to cope in 1817, when we discussed the electoral system of France. We saw the most legitimate principles and the most jealous interests of the new state of society indistinctly menaced by a violent reaction. We felt the spirit of revolution spring up and ferment around us, arming itself, according to old practice, with noble incentives, to cover the march and prepare the triumph of the most injurious passions. By instinct and position, the middle classes were the best suited to struggle with the combined peril. Opposed to the pretensions of the old aristocracy, they had acquired, under the Empire, ideas and habits of government. Although they received the Restoration with some mistrust, they were not hostile to it; for under the rule of the Charter, they had nothing to ask from new revolutions. The Charter was for them the Capitol and the harbour; they found in it the security of their conquests, and the triumph of their hopes. To turn to the advantage of the ancient monarchy, now become constitutional, this anti-revolutionary state of the middle classes, to secure their co-operation with that monarchy by giving them confidence in their own position, was a line of policy clearly indicated by the state of facts and opinions. Such was the bearing of the electoral bill of 1817. In principle this bill cut short the revolutionary theories of the supremacy of numbers, and of a specious and tyrannical equality; in fact, it brought the new society under shelter from the threats of counter-revolution. Assuredly, in proposing it, we had no intention of establishing any antagonism between the great and small proprietors; but when the question was so laid down, we evinced no hesitation; we supported the bill firmly, by maintaining that the influence, not exclusive but preponderating, of the middle classes was confirmed, on one side by the spirit of free institutions, and on the other in conformity with the interests of France as the Revolution had changed her, and with the Restoration itself as the Charter had defined when proclaiming it.

The election bill occupied the session of 1816. The bill for recruiting was the great subject and work of the session of 1817. The right-hand party opposed it with vehement hostility: it disputed their traditions and disturbed their monarchical tendencies. But the party had to contest with a minister as imperturbable in his convictions and will as in his physiognomy. Marshal Gouvion St. Cyr had a powerful, original, and straightforward mind, with no great combination of ideas, but passionately wedded to those which emanated from himself. He had resolved to give back to France what she no longer possessed—an army. And an army in his estimate was a small nation springing from the large one, strongly organized, formed of officers and soldiers closely united, mutually knowing and respecting each other, all having defined rights and duties, and all well trained by solid study or long practice to serve their country effectually when called upon.

Upon this idea of an army, according to the conception of Marshal St. Cyr, the principles of his bill were naturally framed. Every class in the State was required to assist in the formation of this army. Those who entered in the lowest rank were open to the highest, with a certain advantage in the ascending movement of the middle classes. Those who were ambitious of occupying at once a higher step, were compelled in the first instance to pass certain examinations, and then to acquire by close study the particular knowledge necessary to their post. The term of service, active or in reserve, was long, and made military life in reality a career. The obligations imposed, the privileges promised, and the rights recognized for all, were guaranteed by the bill.

Besides these general principles, the bill had an immediate result which St. Cyr ardently desired. It enrolled again in the new army, under the head of veterans and reserve, the remains of the old discharged legions, who had so heroically endured the penalty of the errors committed by their crowned leader. It effaced also, in their minds, that reminiscence of a distasteful past, while by a sort of special Charter it secured their future.

No one can deny that this plan for the military organization of France, embraced grand ideas and noble sentiments. Such a bill accorded with the moral nature and political conduct of Marshal Gouvion St. Cyr, who possessed an upright soul, a proud temperament, monarchical opinions, and republican manners; and who, since 1814, had given equal proofs of loyalty and independence. When he advocated it in the tribune, when, with the manly solemnity and disciplined feeling of an experienced warrior, at once a sincere patriot and a royalist, he recapitulated the services and sufferings of that nation of old soldiers which he was anxious for a few years longer to unite with the new army of France, he deeply moved the public and the Chambers; and his powerful language, no less than the excellent propositions of his bill, consecrated it on the instant in the affectionate esteem of the country.

Violently attacked in 1818, Marshal St. Cyr's recruiting bill has been since that date several times criticised, revised, and modified. Its leading principles have resisted assault, and have survived alteration. It has done more than last, through soundness of principle; it has given, by facts, an astounding denial to its adversaries. It was accused of striking a blow at the monarchy; on the contrary, it has made the army more devotedly monarchical than any that France had ever known,—an army whose fidelity has never been shaken, either in 1830 or 1848, by the influence of popular opinion, or the seduction of a revolutionary crisis. Military sentiment, that spirit of obedience and respect, of discipline and devotion, one of the chief glories of human nature, and the necessary pledge of the honour as of the safety of nations, had been powerfully fomented and developed in France by the great wars of the Revolution and the Empire. It was a precious inheritance of those rough times which have bequeathed to us so many burdens. There was danger of its being lost or enfeebled in the bosom of peaceful inaction, and during endless debates on liberty. It has been firmly maintained in the army which the law of 1818 established and incessantly recruits. This military sentiment is not only preserved; it has become purified and regulated. By the honesty of its promises and the justice of its arrangements in matters of privilege and promotion, the bill of Marshal St. Cyr has imbued the army with a permanent conviction of its rights, of its own legal and individual rights, and, through that feeling, with an instinctive attachment to public order, the common guarantee of all rights. We have witnessed the rare and imposing sight of an army capable of devotion and restraint, ready for sacrifices, and modest in pretension, ambitious of glory, without being athirst for war, proud of its arms, and yet obedient to civil authority. Public habits, the prevailing ideas of the time, and the general character of our civilization have doubtless operated much upon this great result; but the bill of Marshal St. Cyr has had its full part, and I rejoice in recording this honourable distinction, which, amongst so many others, belongs to my old and glorious friend.

The session of 1818, which opened in the midst of a ministerial crisis, had to deal with another question not more important, but even more intricate and dangerous. The Cabinet determined to leave the press no longer under an exceptional and temporary law. M. de Serre, at that time Chancellor, introduced three bills on the same day, which settled definitively the penalty, the method of prosecution, and the qualification for publishing, in respect to the daily papers, while at the same time they liberated them from all censorship.

I am one of those who have been much assisted and fiercely attacked by the press. Throughout my life, I have greatly employed this engine. By placing my ideas publicly before the eyes of my country, I first attracted her attention and esteem. During the progress of my career, I have ever had the press for ally or opponent; and I have never hesitated to employ its weapons, or feared to expose myself to its blows. It is a power which I respect and recognize willingly, rather than compulsorily, but without illusion or idolatry. Whatever may be the form of government, political life is a constant struggle; and it would give me no satisfaction—I will even say more— I should feel ashamed of finding myself opposed to mute and fettered adversaries. The liberty of the press is human nature displaying itself in broad daylight, sometimes under the most attractive, and at others under the most repelling aspect; it is the wholesome air that vivifies, and the tempest that destroys, the expansion and impulsive power of steam in the intellectual system. I have ever advocated a free press; I believe it to be, on the whole, more useful than injurious to public morality; and I look upon it as essential to the proper management of public affairs, and to the security of private interests. But I have witnessed too often and too closely its dangerous aberrations as regards political order, not to feel convinced that this liberty requires the restraint of a strong organization of effective laws and of controlling principles. In 1819, my friends and I clearly foresaw the necessity of these conditions; but we laid little stress upon them, we were unable to bring them all into operation, and we thought, moreover, that the time had arrived when the sincerity as well as the strength of the restored monarchy was to be proved by removing from the press its previous shackles, and in risking the consequences of its enfranchisement.

The greater part of the laws passed with reference to the press, in France or elsewhere, have either been acts of repression, legitimate or illegitimate, against liberty, or triumphs over certain special guarantees of liberty successively won from power, according to the necessity or opportunity of gaining them. The legislative history of the press in England supplies a long series of alternations and arrangements of this class.

The bills of 1819 had a totally different character. They comprised a complete legislation, conceived together and beforehand, conformable with certain general principles, defining in every degree liabilities and penalties, regulating all the conditions as well as the forms of publication, and intended to establish and secure the liberty of the press, while protecting order and power from its licentiousness;—an undertaking very difficult in its nature, as all legislative enactments must be which spring from precaution more than necessity, and in which the legislator is inspired and governed by ideas rather than commanded and directed by facts. Another danger, a moral and concealed danger, also presented itself. Enactments thus prepared and maintained become works of a philosopher and artist, the author of which is tempted to identify himself with them through an impulse of self-love, which sometimes leads him to lose sight of the external circumstances and practical application he ought to have considered. Politics require a certain mixture of indifference and passion, of freedom of thought and restrained will, which is not easily reconciled with a strong adhesion to general ideas, and a sincere intent to hold a just balance between the many principles and interests of society.

I should be unwilling to assert that in the measures proposed and passed in 1819, on the liberty of the press, we had completely avoided these rocks, or that they were in perfect harmony with the state of men's minds, and the exigencies of order at that precise epoch. Nevertheless, after an interval of nearly forty years, and on reconsidering these measures now with my matured judgment, I do not hesitate to look on them as grand and noble efforts of legislation, in which the true points of the subject were skilfully embraced and applied, and which, in spite of the mutilation they were speedily doomed to undergo, established an advance in the liberty of the press, properly understood, which sooner or later cannot fail to extend itself.

The debate on these bills was worthy of their conception. M. de Serre was gifted with eloquence singularly exalted and practical. He supported their general principles in the tone of a magistrate who applies, and not as a philosopher who explains them. His speech was profound without abstraction, highly coloured but not figurative; his reasoning resolved itself into action. He expounded, examined, discussed, attacked, or replied without literary or even oratorical preparation, carrying up the strength of his arguments to the full level of the questions, fertile without exuberance, precise without dryness, impassioned without a shadow of declamation, always ready with a sound answer to his opponents, as powerful on the impulse of the moment as in prepared reflection, and, when once he had surmounted a slight hesitation and slowness at the first onset, pressing on directly to his end with a firm and rapid step, and with the air of a man deeply interested, but careless of personal success, and only anxious to win his cause by communicating to his listeners his own sentiments and convictions.

Different adversaries presented themselves during the debate, from those who had opposed the bills for elections and recruiting the army. The right-hand party attacked the two latter propositions; the left assailed the measures regarding the press. MM. Benjamin Constant, Manuel, Chauvelin, and Bignon, with more parliamentary malice than political judgment, overwhelmed them with objections and amendments slightly mingled with very qualified compliments. Recent elections had lately readmitted into the assembly these leaders of the Liberals in the Chamber of the Hundred Days. They seemed to think of nothing but how to bring once more upon the scene their party, for three years beaten down, and to re-establish their own position as popular orators. Some of the most prominent ideas in the drawing up of these three bills, were but little in conformity with the philosophic and legislative traditions which since 1791 had become current on the subject. They evidently comprised a sincere wish to guarantee liberty, and a strong desire not to disarm power. It was a novel exhibition to see Ministers frankly recognizing the liberty of the press, without offering up incense on its shrine, and assuming that they understood its rights and interests better than its old worshippers. In the opposition of the left-hand party at this period, there was much of routine, a great deal of complaisance for the prejudices and passions of the press attached to their party, and a little angry jealousy of a cabinet which permitted liberal innovation. The public, unacquainted with political factions, were astonished to see bills so vehemently opposed which diminished the penalties in force against the press, referred to a jury all offences of that class, and liberated the journals from the censorship,—measures which in their eyes appeared too confident. The right-hand party held dexterously aloof, rejoicing to see the Ministers at issue with reviving opponents who were likely soon to become their most formidable enemies.

It was during this debate that I ascended the tribune for the first time. M. Cuvier and I had been appointed, as Royal Commissioners, to support the proposed measures,—a false and weak position, which demonstrates the infancy of representative government. We do not argue politics as we plead a cause or maintain a thesis. To act effectively in a deliberative assembly, we must ourselves be deliberators; that is to say, we must be members, and hold our share with others in free thought, power, and responsibility. I believe that I acquitted myself with propriety, but coldly, of the mission I had undertaken. I sustained, against M. Benjamin Constant, the general responsibility for the correctness of the accounts given of the proceedings of the Chambers, and, against M. Daunou, the guarantees required by the bill for the establishment of newspapers. The Chamber appeared to appreciate my arguments, and listened to me with attention. But I kept on the reserve, and seldom joined in the debate; I have no turn for incomplete positions and prescribed parts. When we enter into an arena in which the affairs of a free country are discussed, it is not to make a display of fine thoughts and words; we are bound to engage in the struggle as true and earnest actors.

As the recruiting bill had established a personal and political reputation for Marshal Gouvion St. Cyr, so the bills on the press effected the same for M. de Serre. Thus, at the issue of a violent crisis of revolution and war, in presence of armed Europe, and within the short space of three sessions, the three most important questions of a free system—the construction of elective power, the formation of a national army, and the interference of individual opinions in public affairs through the channel of the press—were freely proposed, argued, and resolved; and their solution, whatever might be the opinion of parties, was certainly in harmony with the habits and wishes of that honest and peaceably disposed majority of France who had sincerely received the King and the Charter, and had adopted their government on mature consideration.

During this time, many other measures of constitutional organization, or general legislation, had been accomplished or proposed. In 1818, an amendment of M. Royer-Collard settled the addition to the budget of an annual law for the supervision of public accounts; and in the course of the following year, two ministers of finance, the Baron Louis and M. Roy, brought into operation that security for the honest appropriation of the revenue. By the institution of smaller "Great-books" of the national debt, the state of public credit became known in the departments. Other bills, although laid before the Chambers, produced no result; three, amongst the rest, may be named: on the responsibility of Ministers, on the organization of the Chamber of Peers into a court of justice, and on the alteration of the financial year to avoid the provisional vote of the duty. Others again, especially applicable to the reform of departmental and parochial administrations, and to public instruction, were left in a state of inquiry and preliminary discussion. Far from eluding or allowing important questions to linger, the Government laboriously investigated them, and forestalled the wishes of the public, determined to submit them to the Chambers as soon as they had collected facts and arranged their own plans.

I still preserve a deep remembrance of the State Council in which these various bills were first discussed. This Council had not then any defined official existence or prescribed action in the constitution of the country; politics nevertheless were more prominently argued there, and with greater freedom and effect, than at any other time; every shade, I ought rather to say every variation, of the royalist party, from the extreme right to the edge of the left, were there represented; the politicians most in repute, the leaders of the majority in the two Assemblies, were brought into contact with the heads of administration, the old senators of the Empire, and with younger men not yet admissible to the Chambers, but introduced by the Charter into public life. MM. Royer-Collard, de Serre, and Camille Jordan sat there by the side of MM. Siméon, Portalis, Molé, Bérenger, Cuvier, and Allent; and MM. de Barante, Mounier, and myself deliberated in common with MM. de Ballainvilliers, Laporte-Lalanne, and de Blaire, unswerving representatives of the old system. When important bills were examined by the Council, the Ministers never failed to attend. The Duke de Richelieu often presided at the general sittings. The discussion was perfectly free, without oratorical display or pretension, but serious, profound, varied, detailed, earnest, erudite, and at the same time practical. I have heard Count Bérenger, a man of disputatious and independent temper, and a quasi-republican under the Empire, maintain there, with ingenious and imposing subtlety, universal suffrage, and distinctions of qualification for voting, against direct election and the concentrated right of suffrage. MM. Cuvier, Siméon, and Allent were the constant defenders of traditional and administrative influence. My friends and I argued strongly for the principles and hopes of liberty strongly based, which appeared to us the natural consequences of the Charter and the necessary conditions for the prosperity of the

Restoration. Reforms in criminal legislation, the application of trial by jury to offences of the press, the introduction of the elective principle into the municipal system, were argued in the Council of State before they were laid before the Chambers. The Government looked to the Council, not only for a study of all questions, but for a preparatory and amicable experience of the ideas, desires, and objections it was destined to encounter at a later period, in a rougher contest, and a more tumultuous theatre.

The Cabinet, composed as it was at the time when the decree of the 5th of September, 1816, appeared, was not equal to that line of policy, continually increasing in moderation, sometimes resolutely, liberal, and, if not always provident, at least perpetually active. But the same progress which accompanied events, affected individuals. During the course of the year 1817, M. Pasquier, Marshal Gouvion St. Cyr, and M. Molé replaced M. Dambray, the Duke of Feltri, and M. Dubouchage in the departments of justice, war, and the marine. From that time the Ministers were not deficient either in internal unity, or in parliamentary and administrative talent. They endeavoured to infuse the same qualities into all the different branches and gradations of government, and succeeded tolerably in the heart of the State. Without reaction or any exclusive spirit, they surrounded themselves with men sincerely attached to a constitutional policy, and who by their character and ability had already won public esteem. They were less firm and effective in local administration; although introducing more changes than are generally believed, they were unable to reconcile them with their general policy. In many places, acts of violence, capricious temper, haughty inexperience, offensive pretension and frivolous alarm, with all the great and little party passions which had possessed the Government of 1815, continued to weigh upon the country. These proceedings kept up amongst the tranquil population a strong sentiment of uneasiness, and sometimes excited active malcontents to attempts at conspiracy and insurrection, amplified at first with interested or absurd credulity, repressed with unmitigated rigour, and subsequently discussed, denied, extenuated, and reduced almost to nothing by never-ending explanations and counter-charges. From thence arose the mistakes, prejudices, and false calculations of the local authorities; while the supreme powers assumed alternately airs of levity or weakness, which made them lose, in the eyes of the multitude, the credit of that sound general policy from which they, the masses, experienced little advantage. The occurrences at Lyons in June 1817, and the long debates of which they became the subject after the mission of redress of the Duke of Ragusa, furnish a lamentable example of the evils which France at this period had still to endure, although at the head of government the original cause had disappeared.

Things are more easily managed than men. These same Ministers, who were not always able to compel the prefects and mayors to adopt their policy, and who hesitated to displace them when they were found to be obstinate or incapable, were ever prompt and effective when general administration was involved, and measures not personal were necessary for the public interest. On this point, reflection tells me that justice has not been rendered to the Government of the day; religious establishments, public instruction, hospital and prison discipline, financial and military administration, the connection of power with industry and commerce, all the great public questions, received from 1816 to 1820 much salutary reform and made important advances. The

Duke de Richelieu advocated an enlightened policy and the public good; he took pride in contributing to both. M. Lainé devoted himself with serious and scrupulous anxiety to the superintendence of the many establishments included in his department, and laboured to rectify existing abuses or to introduce salutary limitations. The Baron Louis was an able and indefatigable minister, who knew to a point how regularity could be established in the finances of the State, and who employed for that object all the resources of his mind and the unfettered energy of his will. Marshal Gouvion St. Cyr had, on every branch of military organization, on the formation and internal system of the different bodies, on the scientific schools as well as on the material supplies, ideas at once systematic and practical, derived either from his general conception of the army or from long experience; and these he carried into effect in a series of regulations remarkable for the unity of their views and the profound knowledge of their details. M. Decazes was endowed with a singularly inquiring and inventive mind in seeking to satisfy doubts, to attempt improvements, to stimulate emulation and concord for the advantage of all social interests, of all classes of citizens, in connection with the Government; and these combined objects he invariably promoted with intelligent, amiable, and eager activity. In a political point of view, the Administration left much to regret and to desire; but in its proper sphere it was liberal, energetic, impartial, economical from probity and regularity, friendly to progress at the same time that it was careful of order, and sincerely impressed with the desire of giving universal prevalence to justice and the public interest.

Here was undoubtedly a sensible and sound Government, in very difficult and lamentable circumstances; and under such rule the country had no occasion to lament the present or despair of the future. Nevertheless this Government gained no strength by permanence; its enemies felt no discouragement, while its friends perceived no addition to their power or security. The Restoration had given peace to France, and laboured honestly and successfully to restore her independence and rank in Europe. Under this flag of stability and order, prosperity and liberty sprang up again together. Still the Restoration was always a disputed question.

If we are to believe its enemies, this evil was inherent and inevitable. According to them the old system, the emigrants, the foreigners, the hatreds and suspicions of the Revolution devoted the House of Bourbon to their obstinately precarious situation. Without disputing the influence of such a fatal past, I cannot admit that it exercised complete empire over events, or that it suffices in itself to explain why the Restoration, even in its best days, always was and appeared to be in a tottering state. The mischief sprang from more immediate and more personal causes. In the Government of that date there were organic and accidental infirmities, vices of the political machine and errors of the actors, which contributed much more than revolutionary remembrances to prevent its firm consolidation.

A natural and important disagreement exists between the representative government instituted by the Charter, and the administrative monarchy founded by Louis XIV. and Napoleon. Where administration and policy are equally free, when local affairs are discussed and decided by local authorities or influences, and neither derive their impulse nor solution from the central power, which never interferes except when the general interest of the State absolutely requires it to do so,—as in England, and in the United States of America, in Holland and Belgium, for instances,—the representative system readily accords with an administrative Government which never appeals to its co-operation except on important and rare occasions. But when the supreme authority undertakes at the same time to govern with freedom, and to administer by centralization,—when it has to contend, at the seat of power, for the great affairs of the State, and to regulate, under its own responsibility, in all the departments, the minor business of every district,—two weighty objections immediately present themselves: either the central power, absorbed by the care of national questions, and occupied with its own defence, neglects local affairs, and suffers them to fall into disorder and inaction; or it connects them closely with general questions, making them subservient to its own interests; and thus the whole system of administration, from the hamlet to the palace, degenerates into an implement of government in the hands of political parties who are mutually contending for power.

I am certainly not called upon today to dwell on this evil; it has become the hackneyed theme of the adversaries of representative government, and of political liberty. It was felt long before it was taken advantage of; but instead of employing it against free institutions, an attempt was made to effect its cure. To achieve this end, a double work was to be accomplished; it was necessary to infuse liberty into the administration of local affairs, and to second the development of the local forces capable of exercising authority within their own circle. An aristocracy cannot be created by laws, either at the extremities or at the fountain-head of the State; but the most democratic society is not stripped of natural powers ready to display themselves when called into action. Not only in the departments, but in the divisions, in the townships and villages, landed property, industry, employments, professions, and traditions have their local influences, which, if adopted and organized with prudence, constitute effectual authority. From 1816 to 1848, under each of the two constitutional monarchies, whether voluntarily or by compulsion, the different cabinets have acted under this conviction; they have studied to relieve the central Government, by remitting a portion of its functions, sometimes to the regular local agents, and at others to more independent auxiliaries. But, as it too often happens, the remedy was not rapid enough in operation; mistrust, timidity, inexperience, and routine slackened its progress; neither the authorities nor the people knew how to employ it with resolution, or to wait the results with patience. Thus compelled to sustain the burden of political liberty with that of administrative centralization, the newly-born constitutional monarchy found itself compromised between difficulties and contradictory responsibilities, exceeding the measure of ability and strength which could be reasonably expected from any Government.

Another evil, the natural but not incurable result of these very institutions, weighed also upon the Restoration. The representative system is at the bottom, and on close analysis, a system of mutual sacrifices and dealings between the various interests which coexist in society. At the same time that it places them in antagonism, it imposes on them the absolute necessity of arriving at an intermediate term, a definite measure of reciprocal understanding and toleration which may become the basis of laws and government. But also, at the same time, by the publicity and heat of the struggle, it throws the opposing parties into an unseemly exaggeration of vehemence and language, and compromises the self-love and personal dignity of human nature. Thus, by an inconsistency teeming with embarrassment, it daily renders more difficult that agreement or submission which, in the end, it has also made indispensable. Herein is comprised an important difficulty for this system of government, which can only be surmounted by a great exercise of tact and conciliation on the part of the political actors themselves, and by a great preponderance of good sense on that of the public, which in the end recalls parliamentary factions and their leaders to that moderation after defeat, from which the inflated passion of the characters they have assumed too often tends to estrange them.

This necessary regulator, always difficult to find or institute, was essentially wanting to us under the Restoration; on entering the course, we were launched, without curb, on this precipice of extreme demonstrations and preconceived ideas, the natural vice of parties in every representative government. How many opportunities presented themselves from 1816 to 1830, when the different elements of the monarchical party could, and in their struggle ought to have paused on this brink, at the point where the danger of revolution commenced for all! But none had the good sense or courage to exercise this provident restraint; and the public, far from imposing it on them, excited them still more urgently to the combat,—as at a play, in which people delight to trace the dramatic reflection of their own passions.

A mischievous, although inevitable, distribution of parts between the opposing parties aggravated still more, from 1816 to 1820, this want of forecast in men, and this extravagance of public passions. Under the representative system, it is usually to one of the parties distinctly defined and firmly resolved in their ideas and desires, that the government belongs: sometimes the systematic defenders of power, at others the friends of liberty, then the conservatives, and lastly the innovators, direct the affairs of the country; and between these organized and ambitious parties are placed the unclassed opinions and undecided wishes, that political chorus which is ever present watching the conduct of the actors, listening to their words, and ready to applaud or condemn them according as they satisfy or offend their unfettered judgment. This is, in fact, the natural bias and true order of things under free institutions. It is well for Government to have a public and recognized standard, regulated on fixed principles, and sustained in action by steady adherents; it derives from that position, not only the strength and consistent coherence that it requires, but the moral dignity which renders power more easy and gentle by placing it higher in the estimation of the people. It is not the chance of events or the personal ambition of men alone, but the interests and inclination of the public, which have produced, in free countries, the great, acknowledged, permanent, and trusty political parties, and have usually confided power to their hands. At the Restoration it was impossible, from 1816 to 1820, to fulfil this condition of a Government at once energetic and restrained. The two great political parties which it found in action, that of the old system and of the revolution, were both at the time incapable of governing by maintaining internal peace with liberty; each had ideas and passions too much opposed to the established and legal order they would have had to defend; they accepted with great reluctance, and in a very undefined sense, the one the Charter, and the other the old Monarchy. Through absolute necessity, power returned to the hands of the political choir; the floating and impartial section of the Chambers, the centre, was called to the helm. Under a free system, the Centre is the habitual moderator and definitive judge of Government, but not the party naturally pretending to govern. It gives or withholds the majority, but its mission is not to conquer it. And it is much more difficult for the centre than for strongly organized parties to win or maintain a majority; for when it assumes government, it finds before it, not undecided spectators who wait its acts to pass judgment on them, but inflamed adversaries resolved to combat them beforehand;—a weak and dangerous position, which greatly aggravates the difficulties of Government, whether engaged in the display of power, or the protection of liberty.

Not only was this the situation of the King's Government from 1816 to 1820, but even this was not regularly and powerfully established. Badly distributed amongst the actors, the characters were doubtfully filled in the interior of this new and uncertain party of the centre, on whom the government, through necessity, devolved. The principal portion of the heads of the majority in the Chambers held no office. From 1816 to 1819, several of those who represented and directed the centre, who addressed and supported it with prevailing influence, who defended it from the attacks of the right and left-hand parties, who established its power in debate and its credit with the public, MM. Royer-Collard, Camille Jordan, Beugnot, and de Serre, were excluded from the Cabinet. Amongst the eminent leaders of the majority, two only, M. Lainé and M. Pasquier were ministers. The Government, therefore, in the Chambers, relied on independent supporters who approved of their policy in general, but neither bore any part in the burden, nor acknowledged any share in the responsibility.

The doctrinarians had acquired their parliamentary influence and moral weight by principles and eloquence rather than by deeds; they maintained their opinions without applying them to practice; the flag of thought and the standard of action were in different hands. In the Chambers, the Ministers often appeared as the clients of the orators; the orators never looked upon their cause as identical with that of the Ministers; they preserved this distinction while supporting them; they had their own demands to make before they assented; they qualified their approval, and even sometimes dissented altogether. As the questions increased in importance and delicacy, so much the more independence and discord manifested themselves in the bosom of the ministerial party, with dangerous notoriety. During the session of 1817, M. Pasquier, then Chancellor, presented a bill to the Chamber of Deputies, which, while temporarily maintaining the censorship of the daily papers, comprised in other respects some modifications favourable to the liberty of the press. M. Camille Jordan and M. Royer-Collard demanded much greater concessions, particularly the application of trial by jury to press offences; and the bill, reluctantly passed by the Chamber of Deputies, was thrown out by the Chamber of Peers, when the Duke de Broglie urged the same amendments on similar principles. In 1817 also, a new Concordat had been negotiated and concluded at Rome by M. de Blacas. It contained the double and contradictory defect of invading by some of its specifications the liberties of the old Gallican Church; while, by the abolition of the Concordat of 1801, it inspired the new French society with lively alarms for its civil liberties. Little versed in such matters, and almost entirely absorbed in the negotiations for relieving France from the presence of foreigners, the Duke de Richelieu had confided this business to M. de Blacas, who was equally ignorant and careless of the importance of the old or new liberties of France, whether civil or religious. When this Concordat, respecting which the Ministers themselves were discontented and doubtful when they had carefully examined it, was presented to the Chamber of Deputies by M. Lainé, with the measures necessary for carrying it into effect, it was received with general disfavour. In committee, in the board appointed to report on it, in the discussions in the hall of conference, all the objections, political and historical, of principle or circumstance, that the bill could possibly excite, were argued and explained beforehand, so as to give warning of the most obstinate and dangerous debate. The doctrinarians openly declared for this premature opposition; and their support produced a strong effect, as they were known to be sincere friends to religion and its influences. It is true, M. Royer-Collard was accused of being a Jansenist; and thus an attempt was made to depreciate him in the eyes of the true believers of the Catholic Church. The reproach was frivolous. M. Royer-Collard had derived, from family traditions and early education, serious habits, studious inclinations, and an affectionate respect for the exalted minds of Port-Royal, for their virtue and genius; but he neither adopted their religious doctrines nor their systematic conclusions on the relative ties between Church and State. On all these questions he exercised a free and rational judgment, as a stranger to all extreme passion or sectarian prejudice, and not in the least disposed, either as Catholic or philosopher, to engage in obscure and endless quarrels with the Church. "I seek not to quibble with religion," he was wont to say; "it has enough to do to defend itself and us from impiety." The opposition of M. Royer-Collard to the Concordat of 1817 was the dissent of a politician and enlightened moralist, who foresaw the mischief which the public discussion, and adoption or rejection of this bill, would inflict on the influence of the Church, the credit of the Restoration, and the peace of the country. The Cabinet had prudence enough not to brave a danger which it had created, or suffered to grow on its steps. The report on the bill was indefinitely adjourned, and a fresh negotiation was opened with Rome by sending Count Portalis on a special mission, which ended in 1819 by the tacit withdrawal of the Concordat of 1817. The Duke de Richelieu, pressed by his colleagues, and his own tardy reflections, coincided in this retrograde movement; but he maintained a feeling of displeasure at the opposition of the doctrinarians and others on this occasion, which he sometimes gratified himself by indulging. In the month of March, 1818, some one, whose name I have forgotten, demanded of him a trifling favour. "It is impossible," replied he sharply; "MM. Royer-Collard, de Serre, Camille Jordan, and Guizot will not suffer it."

I had no reason to complain that my name was included in this ebullition. Although not a member of the Chamber, I openly adopted the opinions and conduct of my friends; I had both the opportunity and the means, in the discussions of the Council of State, in the drawing-room, and through the press,—channels which all parties employed with equal ardour and effect. In spite of the shackles which restrained the papers and periodical publications, they freely exercised the liberty which the Government no longer attempted to dispute, and to which the most influential politicians had recourse, to disseminate far and wide the brilliant flames or smouldering fire of their opposition. M. de Châteaubriand, M. de Bonald, M. de Villèle, in the 'Conservative,' and

M. Benjamin Constant in the 'Minerva,' maintained an incessant assault on the Cabinet. The Cabinet in its defence, multiplied similar publications, such as the 'Moderator,' the 'Publicist,' and the 'Political and Literary Spectator.' But, for my friends and our cause, the defences of the Cabinet were not always desirable or sufficient; we therefore, from 1817 to 1820, had our own journals and periodical miscellanies,—the 'Courier,' the 'Globe,' the 'Philosophical, Political, and Literary Archives,' and the 'French Review;' and in these we discussed, according to our principles and hopes, sometimes general questions, and at others the incidental subjects of current policy, as they alternately presented themselves. I contributed much to these publications. Between our different adversaries and ourselves the contest was extremely unequal: whether they came from the right or the left, they represented old parties; they expressed ideas and sentiments long in circulation; they found a public predisposed to receive them. We were intruders in the political arena, officers seeking to recruit an army, moderate innovators. We attacked, in the name of liberty, theories and passions long popular under the same denomination. We defended the new French society according to its true rights and interests, but not in conformity with its tastes or habits. We had to conquer our public, while we combated our enemies. In this difficult attempt our position was somewhat doubtful: we were at the same time with and against the Government, royalists and liberals, ministerialists and independents; we acted sometimes in concert with the Administration, sometimes with the Opposition, and we were unable to avail ourselves of all the weapons of either power or liberty. But we were full of faith in our opinions, of confidence in ourselves, of hope in the future; and we pressed forward daily in our double contest, with as much devotion as pride, and with more pride than ambition.

All this has been strenuously denied; my friends and I have often been represented as deep plotters, greedy for office, eager and shrewd in pushing our fortunes through every opening, and more intent on our own ascendency than on the fate or wishes of the country,—a vulgar and senseless estimate, both of human nature and of our contemporary history. If ambition had been our ruling principle, we might have escaped many efforts and defeats. In times when the most brilliant fortunes, political or otherwise, were easily within reach of those who thought of nothing else, we only desired to achieve ours on certain moral conditions, and with the object of not caring for ourselves. Ambition we had, but in the service of a public cause; and one which, either in success or adversity, has severely tried the constancy of its defenders.

The most clear-sighted of the cabinet ministers in 1817, M. Decazes and M. Pasquier, whose minds were more free and less suspicious than those of the Duke de Richelieu and M. Lainé, were not deceived on this point: they felt the necessity of our alliance, and cultivated it with anxiety. But when it becomes a question of how to govern in difficult times, allies are not enough; intimate associates are necessary, devoted adherents in labour and peril. In this character, the doctrinarians, and particularly M. Royer-Collard, their leader in the Chambers, were mistrusted. They were looked upon as at once imperious and undecided, and more exacting than effective. Nevertheless, in November, 1819, after the election of M. Grégoire and in the midst of their projected reforms in the electoral law, M. Decazes, at the strong instigation of M. de Serre, proposed to M. Royer-Collard to join the Cabinet with one or two of his friends.

M. Royer-Collard hesitated at first, then acceded for a moment, and finally declined. "You know not what you would do," said he to M. Decazes; "my method of dealing with affairs would differ entirely from yours: you elude questions, you shift and change them, you gain time, you settle things by halves; I, on the contrary, should attack them in front, bring them into open view, and dissect them before all the world. I should compromise instead of assisting you." M. Royer-Collard was in the right, and defined himself admirably, perhaps more correctly than he imagined. He was more calculated to advise and contest than to exercise power. He was rather a great spectator and critic than an eminent political actor. In the ordinary course of affairs he would have been too absolute, too haughty, and too slow. In a crisis, I question whether his mental reservations, his scruples of conscience, his horror of all public excitement, and his prevailing dread of responsibility, would have permitted him to preserve the cool self-possession, with the firm and prompt determination, which circumstances might have required. M. Decazes pressed him no further.

Even at this moment, after all I have seen and experienced, I am not prone to be discouraged, or inclined to believe that difficult achievements are impossible. However defective may be the internal constitution and combinations of the different parties who co-operate in carrying on public affairs, the upright conduct of individuals may remedy them; history furnishes more than one example of vicious institutions and situations, the evil results of which have been counteracted by the ability of political leaders and the sound sense of the public. But when to the evils of position, the errors of men are added,—when, instead of recognizing dangers in their true tendency, and opposing firm resistance, the chiefs and followers of parties either yield to or accelerate them, then the mischievous effects of pernicious courses inevitably and rapidly develop themselves. Errors were not wanting from 1816 to 1820 in every party, whether of Government or Opposition, of the centre, the right, or the left, of the ministers or doctrinarians. I make no parade of impartiality; in spite of their faults and misfortunes, I continue, with a daily increasing conviction, to look upon the Government I served, and the party I supported, to have been the best; but, for our own credit, let leisure and reflection teach us to acknowledge the mistakes we committed, and to prepare for our cause—which assuredly will not die with us—a more auspicious future.

The centre, in its governing mission, had considerable advantages; it suffered neither from moral embarrassments nor external clogs, it was perfectly free and unshackled,—essential qualifications in a great public career, and which at that time belonged neither to the right nor to the left-hand party.

The right had only accepted the Charter on the eve of its promulgation, and after strenuous resistance; a conspicuous and energetic section of the party still persisted in opposing it. That division which had seats in the Chambers, sided from day to day with the constitutional system,—the officers as intelligent and reflecting men, the soldiers as staunch and contented royalists; but neither, in these recognized capacities, inspired confidence in the country, which looked upon their adhesion to the Charter as constrained or conditional, always insincere and covering other views. The right, even while honestly accepting the Charter, had also party interests to satisfy; when it aspired to power, it was not solely to govern according to its principles, and to place the restored monarchy on a solid basis: it had private misfortunes to repair and positions to re-assume. It was not a pure and regular party of Tory royalists. The emigrants, the remains of the old court and clergy, were still influential amongst them, and eagerly bent on carrying out their personal expectations. By its composition and reminiscences, the party was condemned to much reserve and imprudence, to secret aspirations and indiscreet ebullitions, which, even while it professed to walk in constitutional paths, embarrassed and weakened its action at every step.

The situation of the left was no less confused. It represented, at that exact epoch, not the interests and sentiments of France in general, but the interests and sentiments of that portion of France which had ardently, indistinctly, and obstinately promoted and sustained the Revolution, under its republican or imperial form. It cherished against the House of Bourbon and the Restoration an old habit of hostility, which the Hundred Days had revived, which the most rational of the party could scarcely throw off, the most skilful with difficulty concealed, and the gravest considered it a point of honour to display as a protest and corner-stone. In November 1816, a man of probity, as sincere in the renunciation of his opinions of 1789 as he had formerly been in their profession, the Viscount Matthieu de Montmorency, complained, in a drawing-room of the party, that the Liberals had no love for legitimacy. A person present defended himself from this reproach. "Yes," said M. de Montmorency, with thoughtless candour, "you love legitimacy as we do the Charter." A keen satire on the false position of both parties under the government of the Charter and of legitimacy!

But if the right-hand party or the left, if the members of either in the Chambers, had followed only their sincere convictions and desires, the greater portion, I am satisfied, would have frankly accepted and supported the Restoration with the Charter, the Charter with the Restoration. When men are seriously engaged in a work and feel the weight of responsibility, they soon discover the true course, and would willingly follow it. But, both in the right and left, the wisest and best-disposed feared to proclaim the truth which they saw, or to adopt it as their rule of conduct; both were under the yoke of their external party, of its passions as of its interests, of its ignorance as of its passions. It has been one of the sorest wounds of our age, that few men have preserved sufficient firmness of mind and character to think freely, and act as they think. The intellectual and moral independence of individuals disappeared under the pressure of events and before the heat of popular clamours and desires. Under such a general slavery of thought and action, there are no longer just or mistaken minds, cautious or rash spirits, officers or soldiers; all yield to the same controlling passion, and bend before the same wind; common weakness reduces all to one common level; hierarchy and discipline vanish; the last lead the first; for the last press and drive onwards, being themselves impelled by that tyranny from without, of which they have been the most blind and ready instruments.

As a political party, the centre, in the Chambers from 1816 to 1820, was not tainted by this evil. Sincere in its adoption of the Restoration and the Charter, no external pressure could disturb or falsify its position. It remained unfettered in thought and deed. It openly acknowledged its object, and marched directly towards it; selecting, within, the leaders most capable of conducting it there, and having no supporters without who looked for any other issue. It was thus that, in spite of its other deficiencies for powerful government, the centre was at that time the fittest party to rule, the only one capable of maintaining order in the State, while tolerating the liberty of its rivals.

But to reap the full fruits of this advantage, and to diminish at the same time the natural defects of the centre in its mission, it was necessary that it should adopt a fixed idea, a conviction that the different elements of the party were indispensable to each other; and that, to accomplish the object pursued by all with equal sincerity, mutual concessions and sacrifices were called for, to maintain this necessary union. When Divine wisdom intended to secure the power of a human connection, it forbade divorce. Political ties cannot admit this inviolability; but if they are not strongly knit, if the contracting parties are not firmly resolved to break them only in the last extremity and under the most imperious pressure, they soon end, not only in impotence, but in disorder; and by their too easy rupture, policy becomes exposed to new difficulties and disturbances. I have thus pointed out the discrepancies and different opinions which, from the beginning, existed between the two principal elements of the centre: the Ministers, with their pure adherents, on the one side, and the doctrinarians on the other. From the second session after the decree of the 5th of September, 1816, these differences increased until they grew into dissensions.

While acknowledging the influence of the doctrinarians in the Chambers, and the importance of their co-operation, neither the Ministers nor their advocates measured correctly the value of this alliance, or the weight of the foundation from which that value was derived. Philosophers estimate too highly the general ideas with which they are prepossessed; politicians withhold from general ideas the attention and interest they are entitled to demand. Intelligence is proud and sensitive; it looks for consideration and respect, even though its suggestions may be disallowed; and those who treat it lightly or coldly sometimes pay heavily for their mistake. It is, moreover, an evidence of narrow intellect not to appreciate the part which general principles assume in the government of men, or to regard them as useless or hostile because we are not disposed to adopt them as guides. In our days, especially, and notwithstanding the well-merited disrepute into which so many theories have fallen, philosophic deduction, on all the leading questions and facts of policy, is a sustaining power, on which the ablest and most secure ministers would do wisely to rely. The doctrinarians at that period represented this power, and employed it fearlessly against the spirit of revolution, as well as in favour of the constitutional system. The Cabinet of 1816 undervalued the part they played, and paid too little attention to their ideas and desires. The application of trial by jury to offences of the press was not, I admit, unattended by danger; but it was much better to try that experiment, and by so doing to maintain union in the Government party, than to divide it by absolutely disregarding, on this question, M. Camille Jordan, M. Royer-Collard, and their friends.

All power, and, above all, recent power, demands an impression of grandeur in its acts and on its insignia. Order, and the regular protection of private interests, that daily bread of nations, will not long satisfy their wants. To secure these is an inseparable care of Government, but they do not comprise the only need of humanity. Human nature finds the other enjoyments for which it thirsts in opposite distinctions, moral or physical, just or unjust, solid or ephemeral. It has neither enough of virtue nor wisdom to render absolute greatness indispensable; but in every position it requires to see, conspicuously displayed, something exalted, which may attract and occupy the imagination. After the Empire, which had accustomed France to all the delights of national pre-eminence and glory, the spectacle of free and lofty thought displaying itself with moral dignity, and some show of talent, was not deficient in novelty or attraction, while the chance of its success outweighed the value of the cost.

The Ministers were not more skilful in dealing with the personal tempers than with the ideas of the doctrinarians, who were as haughty and independent in character as they were elevated in mind, and ready to take offence when any disposition was evinced to apply their opinions and conduct without their own consent. Nothing is more distasteful to power than to admit, to any great extent, the independence of its supporters; it considers them treated with sufficient respect if taken into confidence, and is readily disposed to view them as servants. M. Lainé, then Minister of the Interior, wrote one morning to M. Cuvier to say that the King had just named him Royal Commissioner, to second a bill which would be presented on the following day to the Chamber of Deputies. He had not only neglected to apprise him before of the duty he was to undertake, but he did not even mention in the note the particular bill he instructed him to support. M. Cuvier, more subservient than susceptible, with power, made no complaint of this treatment, but related it with a smile. A few days before, the Minister of Finance, M. Corvetto, had also appointed M. de Serre Commissioner for the defence of the budget, without asking whether this appointment was agreeable to him, or holding any conference even on the fundamental points of the budget he was expected to carry through. On receiving notice of this nomination, M. de Serre felt deeply offended. "It is either an act of folly or impertinence," said he loudly; "perhaps both." M. de Serre deceived himself; it was neither the one nor the other. M. Corvetto was an extremely polite, careful, and modest person; but he was of the Imperial school, and more accustomed to give orders to agents than to concert measures with members of the Chambers. By habits as well as ideas, the doctrinarians belonged to a liberal system,—troublesome allies of power, on the termination of a military and administrative monarchy.

I know not which is the most difficult undertaking,—to transform the functionaries of absolute power into the supporters of a free Government, or to organize and discipline the friends of liberty into a political party. If the Ministers sometimes disregarded the humour of the doctrinarians, the doctrinarians in their turn too lightly estimated the position and task of the Ministers. They had in reality, whatever has been said of sectarian passions and ideas, neither the ambition nor the vanity of a coterie; they possessed open, generous, and expanded minds, extremely accessible to sympathy; but, too much accustomed to live alone and depend on themselves, they scarcely thought of the effect which their words and actions produced beyond their own circle; and thus social faults were laid to their charge which they had not the least desire to commit. Their political mistakes were more real. In their relations with power, they were sometimes intemperate and offensive in language, unnecessarily impatient, not knowing how to be contented with what was possible, or how to wait for amelioration without too visible an effort. These causes led them to miscalculate the impediments, necessities, and practicable resources of the Government they sincerely wished to establish. In the Chambers, they were too exclusive and pugnacious, more intent on proving their opinions than on gaining converts, despising rather than desiring recruits, and little gifted with the talent of attraction and combination so essential to the leaders of a party. They were not sufficiently acquainted with the difficulties of carrying out a sound scheme of policy, nor with the infinite variety of efforts, sacrifices, and cares which are comprised in the art of governing.

From 1816 to 1818 the vices of their position and the mistakes committed, infused into the Government and its party a continual ferment, and the seeds of internal discord which prevented them from acquiring the necessary strength and consistency. The mischief burst forth towards the end of 1818, when the Duke de Richelieu returned from the conferences of Aix-la-Chapelle, reporting the withdrawal of the foreign armies, the complete evacuation of our territory, and the definitive settlement of the financial burdens which the Hundred Days had imposed on France. On his arrival he saw his Cabinet on the point of dissolution, and vainly attempted to form a new one, but was finally compelled to abandon the power he had never sought or enjoyed, but which, assuredly, he was unwilling to lose by compulsion in the midst of his diplomatic triumph, and to see it pass into hands determined to employ it in a manner totally opposed to his own intentions.

A check like this, at such a moment, and to such a man, was singularly unjust and unseasonable. Since 1815, the Duke de Richelieu had rendered valuable services to France and to the King. He alone had obtained some mitigation to the conditions of a very harsh treaty of peace, which nothing but sincere and sad devotion had induced him to sign, while feeling the full weight of what he sacrificed in attaching to it his illustrious name, and seeking no self-glorification from an act of honest patriotism. No man was ever more free from exaggeration or quackery in the display of his sentiments. Fifteen months after the ratification of peace, he induced the foreign powers to consent to a considerable reduction in the army of occupation. A year later, he limited to a fixed sum the unbounded demands of the foreign creditors of France. Finally, he had just signed the entire emancipation of the national soil four years before the term rigorously prescribed by treaties. The King, on his return, thanked him in noble words: "Duke de Richelieu," he said, "I have lived long enough, since, thanks to you, I have seen the French flag flying over every town in France." The sovereigns of Europe treated him with esteem and confidence. A rare example of a statesman, who, without great actions or superior abilities, had, by the uprightness of his character and the unselfish tenor of his life, achieved such universal and undisputed respect! Although the Duke de Richelieu had only been engaged in foreign affairs, he was better calculated than has been said, not so much to direct effectively as to preside over the internal government of the Restoration. A nobleman of exalted rank, and a tried Royalist, he was neither in mind or feeling a courtier nor an Emigrant; he had no preconceived dislike to the new state of society or the new men; without thoroughly understanding free institutions, he had no prejudice against them, and submitted to their exercise without an effort. Simple in his manners, true and steady in his words, and a friend to the public good, if he failed to exercise a commanding influence in the Chambers, he maintained full authority near the King; and a constitutional Government, resting on the parliamentary centre, could not, at that period, have possessed a more worthy or more valuable president.

But at the close of 1818 the Duke de Richelieu felt himself compelled, and evinced that he was resolved, to engage in a struggle in which the considerations of gratitude and prosperity I have here reverted to proved to be ineffective weapons on his side. In virtue of the Charter, and in conformity with the electoral law of the 5th of February, 1817, two-fifths of the Chamber of Deputies had been renewed since the formation of his Cabinet. The first trial of votes, in 1817, had proved satisfactory to the Restoration and its friends; not more than two or three recognized names were added to the left-hand party, which, even after this reinforcement, only amounted to twenty members. At the second trial in 1818, the party acquired more numerous and much more distinguished recruits; about twenty-five new members, and amongst them MM. de La Fayette, Benjamin Constant, and Manuel, were enrolled in its ranks. The number was still weak, but important as a rallying point, and prognostic. An alarm, at once sincere and interested, exhibited itself at court and in the right-hand party; they found themselves on the eve of a new revolution, but their hopes were also excited: since the enemies of the House of Bourbon were forcing themselves into the Chamber, the King would at length feel the necessity of replacing power in the hands of his friends. The party had not waited the issue of these last elections to attempt a great enterprise. Secret notes, drawn up under the eye of the Count d'Artois, and by his most intimate confidants, had been addressed to the foreign sovereigns, to point out to them this growing mischief, and to convince them that a change in the advisers of the crown was the only safe measure to secure monarchy in France, and to preserve peace in Europe. The Duke de Richelieu, in common with his colleagues, and with a feeling of patriotism far superior to personal interest, felt indignant at these appeals to foreign intervention for the internal government of the country. M. de Vitrolles was struck off from the Privy Council, as author of the principal of the three Secret notes. The European potentates paid little attention to such announcements, having no faith either in the sound judgment or disinterested views of the men from whom they emanated. Nevertheless, after the elections of 1818, they also began to feel uneasy. It was from prudence, and not choice, that they had sanctioned and maintained the constitutional system in France; they looked upon it as necessary to close up the Revolution. If, on the contrary, it once again opened its doors, the peace of Europe would be more compromised than ever; for then the Revolution would assume the semblance of legality. But neither in France nor in Europe did any one at that time, even amongst the greatest alarmists and the most intimidated, dream of interfering with the constitutional system; in universal opinion it had acquired with us the privileges of citizenship. The entire evil was imputed to the law of elections. It was at Aix-la-Chapelle, while surrounded by the sovereigns and their ministers, that the Duke de Richelieu was first apprised of the newly-elected members whom this law had brought upon the scene. The Emperor Alexander expressed to him his amazement; the Duke of Wellington advised Louis XVIII. "to unite himself more closely with the Royalists." The Duke de Richelieu returned to France with a determination to reform the electoral law, or no longer to incur the responsibility of its results.

Institutions attacked have no voice in their own defence, and men gladly charge on them their individual errors. I shall not commit this injustice, or abandon a sound idea because it has been compromised or perverted in application. The principle of the electoral law of the 5th of February, 1817, was good in itself, and still remains good, although it was insufficient to prevent the evil of our own want of foresight and intemperate passions.

When a free government is seriously desired, we must choose between the principle of the law of the 5th of February, 1817, and universal suffrage,—between the right of voting confined to the higher classes of society and that extended to the popular masses. I believe the direct and defined right of suffrage to be alone effectual in securing the action of the country upon the Government. On this common condition, the two systems may constitute a real control over power, and substantial guarantees for liberty. Which is to be preferred?—this is a question of epoch, of situation, of degree of civilization, and of form of government. Universal suffrage is well suited to republican associations, small or federative, newly instituted or mature in wisdom and political virtue. The right of voting confined to a more elevated class, and exercised in a strong assumption of the spirit of order, of independence, and intelligence, is more applicable to great single and monarchical states. This was our reason for making it the basis of the law of 1817. We dreaded republican tendencies, which with us, and in our days, are nearly synonymous with anarchy; we regarded monarchy as natural, and constitutional monarchy as necessary, to France; we wished to organize it sincerely and durably, by securing under this system, to the conservative elements of French society as at present constituted, an influence which appeared to us as much in conformity with the interests of liberty as with those of power.

It was the disunion of the monarchical party that vitiated the electoral system of 1817, and took away its strength with its truth. By placing political power in the hands of property, intelligence, independent position, and great interests naturally conservative, the system rested on the expectation that these interests would be habitually united, and would defend, in common accord, order and right against the spirit of license and revolution, the fatal bias of the age. But, from their very first steps, the different elements of the great royalist party, old or new, aristocratic or plebeian, plunged into discord, equally blind to the weakness with which it infected them all, and thus opening the door to the hopes and efforts of their common enemies, the revolutionists. From thence, and not from the electoral law of 1817, or from its principle, came the mischief which in 1818 it was considered desirable to check by repealing that enactment.

I am ready to admit in express terms, for it may be alleged with justice, that, when in 1816 and 1817 we prepared and defended the law of elections, we might have foreseen the state of general feeling under which it was to be applied. Discord between the components of the monarchical party was neither a strange nor a sudden fact; it existed at that time; the Royalists of old and new France were already widely separated. I incline to think that, even had we attached more importance to their future contests, we should still have pursued the same course. We were in presence of an imperative necessity: new France felt that she was attacked, and required defence; if she had not found supporters amongst the Royalists, she would have sought for them, as she has too often done, in the camp of the Revolution. But what may explain or even excuse a fault cannot effect its suppression. Our policy in 1816 and 1817 regarded too lightly the disagreements of the monarchical party, and the possible return of the Revolutionists; we miscalculated the extent of both dangers. It is the besetting error of men entrammelled in the fetters of party, to forget that there are many opposite facts which skilful policy should turn to profitable account, and to pass over all that are not inscribed with brilliancy on their standard.

On leaving Aix-la-Chapelle, where he had been so fortunate, the Duke de Richelieu, although far from presumptuous, expected, I have no doubt, to be equally successful in his design of repealing the law of elections. Success deceives the most unassuming, and prevents them from foreseeing an approaching reverse. On his arrival, he found the undertaking much more difficult than he had anticipated. In the Cabinet, M. Molé alone fully seconded his intentions. M. Decazes and Marshal Gouvion St. Cyr declared strongly for the law as it stood. M. Lainé, while fully admitting that it ought to be modified, refused to take any part in the matter, having been, as he said, the first to propose and maintain it. M. Roy, who had lately superseded M. Corvetto in the department of finance, cared little for the electoral question, but announced that he would not remain in the Cabinet without M. Decazes, whom he considered indispensable, either in the Chambers or near the King's person. Discord raged within and without the Ministry. In the Chambers, the centre was divided; the left defended the law vehemently; the right declared itself ready to support any minister who proposed its reform, but at the same time repudiated M. Decazes, the author of the decree of the 5th of September, 1816, and of all its consequences. The public began to warm into the question. Excitement and confusion went on increasing. It was evidently not the electoral law alone, but the general policy of the Restoration and the Government of France, that formed the subject of debate.

In a little work which the historians of this period, M. de Lamartine amongst others, have published, the King, Louis XVIII. himself has related the incidents and sudden turns of this ministerial crisis, which ended, as is well known, in the retirement of the Duke de Richelieu, with four of his colleagues, and in the promotion of M. Decazes, who immediately constructed a new Cabinet, of which he was the head, without appearing to preside, while M. de Serre, appointed to the seals, became the powerful organ in the Chambers, and the maintenance of the law of elections was adopted as the symbol. Two sentiments, under simple forms, pervade this kingly recital: first, a certain anxiety, on the part of the author, that no blame should be attached to him in his royal character, or in his conduct towards the Duke de Richelieu, and a desire to exculpate himself from these charges; secondly, a little of that secret pleasure which kings indulge in, even under heavy embarrassments, when they see a minister fall whose importance was not derived from themselves, and who has served them without expecting or receiving favours.

"If I had only consulted my own opinion," says the King, in concluding his statement, "I should have wished M. Decazes, uniting his lot, as he had always intended, with that of the

Duke de Richelieu, to have left the Ministry with him." It would have been happy for
M. Decazes if this desire of the King had prevailed. Not that he erred in any point of duty or
propriety by surviving the Duke de Richelieu in office, and in forming a Cabinet without him; an
important misunderstanding on a pressing question had already separated them. M. Decazes,
after tendering his resignation, had raised no obstacle to the Duke's efforts at finding new
colleagues; it was only on the failure of those attempts, frankly avowed by the Duke himself, and
at the formal request of the King, that he had undertaken to form a ministry. As a friend of M. de
Richelieu, and the day before his colleague, there were certainly unpleasant circumstances and
appearances attached to this position; but M. Decazes was free to act, and could scarcely refuse
to carry out the policy he had recommended in council, when that which he had opposed
acknowledged itself incapable. Yet the new Cabinet was not strong enough for the enterprise it
undertook; with the centre completely shaken and divided, it had to contend against the right-
hand party more irritated than ever, and the left evidently inimical, although through decency it
lent to Government a precarious support. The Cabinet of M. Decazes, as a ministerial party,
retained much inferior forces to those which had surrounded the Duke de Richelieu, and had to
contest with two bitter enemies, the one inaccessible to peace or truce, the other sometimes
appearing friendly, but suddenly turning round and attacking the Ministry with eager
malevolence, when an opportunity offered, and with hesitating hostility when compelled to
dissemble.

The doctrinarians, who, in co-operation with M. Decazes, had defended the law of elections,
energetically supported the new Cabinet, in which they were brilliantly represented by
M. de Serre. Success was not wanting at the commencement. By a mild and active
administration, by studied care of its partisans, by frequent and always favourably received
appeals to the royal clemency in behalf of the exiles still excepted from amnesty, even including
the old regicides, M. Decazes sought and won extensive popularity; Marshal Gouvion St. Cyr
satisfied the remnants of the old army, by restoring to the new the ablest of its former leaders;
M. de Serre triumphantly defended the Ministry in the Chambers; his bills, boldly liberal, and his
frank opposition to revolutionary principles, soon acquired for him, even with his adversaries, a
just reputation for eloquence and sincerity. In the parliamentary arena it was an effective and
upright Ministry; with the country it was felt to be a Government loyally constitutional. But it
had more brilliancy than strength; and neither its care of individual interests, nor its successes in
the tribune, were sufficient to rally round it the great Government party which its formation had
divided. Discord arose between the Chambers themselves. The Chamber of Peers, by adopting
the proposition of the Marquis Barthélemy, renewed the struggle against the electoral law. In
vain did the Chamber of Deputies repel this attack; in vain did the Cabinet, by creating sixty new
Peers, break down the majority in the palace of the Luxembourg; these half triumphs and legal
extremes decided nothing. Liberal governments are condemned to see the great questions
perpetually revived which revolutions bequeath to society, and which even glorious despotism
suspends without solving. The right-hand party was passionately bent on repossessing the power
which had recently escaped them. The left defended, at any cost, the Revolution, more insulted

than in danger. The centre, dislocated and doubtful of the future, wavered between the hostile parties, not feeling itself in a condition to impose peace on all, and on the point of being confounded in the ranks of one side or the other. The Cabinet, ever victorious in daily debate, and supported by the King's favour, felt itself nevertheless feebly surrounded and precariously placed, with the air of expecting a favourable or a hostile incident, to bring the security it wanted, or to overthrow it altogether.

The events which men call accidents are never wanting in such situations. During the space of a few months the Cabinet of 1819 experienced two,—the election of M. Grégoire, and the assassination of the Duke de Berry; and these two decided its fate.

It is difficult to look upon the election of M. Grégoire as an accident; it was proposed and settled beforehand in the central committee established at Paris to superintend elections in general, and which was called the managing committee. This particular election was decided on at Grenoble in the college assembled on the 11th of September, 1819, by a certain number of votes of the right-hand party, which at the second round of balloting were carried to the credit of the left-hand candidate, and gave him a majority which otherwise he could not have obtained. To excuse this scandal, when it became known, some apologists pretended that M. Grégoire was not in fact a regicide, because, even though he had approved of the condemnation of Louis XVI. in his letters to the Convention, his vote at least had not been included in the fatal list. Again, when the admission of the deputy was disputed in the Chamber, the left-hand party, to get rid of him, while eluding the true cause of refusal, eagerly proposed to annul the election on the ground of irregularity. When improvident violence fails, men gladly shelter themselves under pusillanimous subtlety. It was unquestionably in the character of a Conventional regicide, and with premeditated reflection, not by any local or sudden accident, that M. Grégoire had been elected. No act was ever more deliberately arranged and accomplished by party feelings. Sincere in the perverse extravagancies of his mind, and faithful to his avowed principles, although forgetful and weak in their application, openly a Christian, and preaching tolerance under the Convention, while he sanctioned the most unrelenting persecution of the priests who refused to submit to the yoke of its new church; a republican and oppositionist under the Empire, while consenting to be a senator and a Count, this old man, as inconsistent as obstinate, was the instrument of a signal act of hostility against the Restoration, to become immediately the pretext for a corresponding act of weakness. A melancholy end to a sad career!

The assassination of the Duke de Berry might with much more propriety be called an accident. On the trial it was proved by evidence that Louvel had no accomplices, and that he was alone in the conception as in the execution of his crime. But it was also evident that hatred against the Bourbons had possessed the soul and armed the hand of the murderer. Revolutionary passions are a fire which is kindled and nourished afar off; the orators of the right obtained credit with many timid and horror-stricken minds, when they called this an accident;—as it is also an accident if a diseased constitution catches the plague when it infects the air, or if a powder-magazine explodes when you strike fire in its immediate neighbourhood.

M. Decazes endeavoured to defend himself against these two heavy blows. After the election of M. Grégoire, he undertook to accomplish alone what at the close of the preceding year he had refused to attempt in concert with the Duke de Richelieu. He determined to alter the law of elections. It was intended that this change should take place in a great constitutional reform meditated by M. de Serre, liberal on certain points, monarchical on others, and which promised to give more firmness to royalty by developing representative government. M. Decazes made a sincere effort to induce the Duke de Richelieu, who was then travelling in Holland, to return and reassume the presidency of the Council, and to co-operate with him in the Chambers for the furtherance of this bold undertaking. The King himself applied to the Duke de Richelieu, who positively declined, more from disgust with public affairs and through diffidence of his own power, than from any remains of ill-humour or resentment. Three actual members of the Cabinet of 1819, General Dessoles, Marshal Gouvion St. Cyr, and Baron Louis, declared that they would not co-operate in any attack on the existing law of elections. M. Decazes determined to do without them, as he had dispensed with the Duke de Richelieu, and to form a new Cabinet, of which he became the president, and in which M. Pasquier, General Latour-Maubourg, and M. Roy replaced the three retiring ministers. On the 29th of November the King opened the session. Two months passed over, and the new electoral system had not yet been presented to the Chamber. Three days after the assassination of the Duke de Berry, M. Decazes introduced it suddenly, with two bills to suspend personal liberty, and re-establish the censorship of the daily press. Four days later he fell, and the Duke de Richelieu, standing alone before the King and the danger, consented to resume power. M. Decazes would have acted more wisely had he submitted to his first defeat, and induced the King after the election of M. Grégoire, to take back the Duke de Richelieu as minister. He would not then have been compelled to lower with his own hand the flag he had raised, and to endure the burden of a great miscarriage.

The fall of the Cabinet of 1819, brought on a new crisis, and a fresh progress of the evil which disorganized the great Government party formed during the session of 1815, and by the decree of the 5th of September, 1816. To the successive divisions of the centre, were now added the differences between the doctrinarians themselves. M. de Serre, who had joined the Cabinet with M. Decazes to defend the law of elections, now determined, although sick and absent, to remain there with the Duke de Richelieu to overthrow it, without any of the compensations, real or apparent, which his grand schemes of constitutional reform were intended to supply. I tried in vain to dissuade him from his resolution. In the Chamber of Deputies, M. Royer-Collard and M. Camille Jordan vehemently attacked the new electoral plan; the Duke de Broglie and M. de Barante proposed serious amendments to it in the Chamber of Peers. All the political ties which had been cemented during five years appeared to be dissolved; every one followed his own private opinion, or returned to his old bias. In the parliamentary field, all was uncertainty and confused opposition; a phantom appeared at each extremity, revolution and counter-revolution, exchanging mutual menaces, and equally impatient to come to issue.

Those who wish to give themselves a correct idea of parliamentary and popular excitement, pushed to their extreme limit, and yet retained within that boundary by legal authority and the good sense of the public,—sufficient to arrest the country on the brink of an abyss, although too weak to block up the road that leads to it,—should read the debate on the new electoral bill introduced into the Chamber of Deputies on the 17th of April, 1820, by the second Cabinet of the Duke de Richelieu, and discussed for twenty-six days in that Chamber, accompanied with riotous gatherings without, thoughtlessly aggressive and sternly repressed. If we are to believe the orators of the left, France and her liberties, the Revolution and its conquests, the honour of the present, and the security of the future, were all lost if the ministerial bill should pass. The right, on the other hand, looked upon the bill as scarcely strong enough to save the monarchy for the moment, and declared its resolution to reject every amendment which might diminish its powers. On both sides, pretensions and claims were equally ungovernable. Attracted and excited by this legal quarrel, the students, the enthusiastic young Liberals, the old professional disturbers, the idlers and oppositionists of every class, were engaged daily with the soldiers and the agents of police, in conflicts sometimes sanguinary, and the accounts of which redoubled the acrimony of the debate withindoors. In the midst of this general commotion, the Cabinet of 1820 had the merit of maintaining, while repressing all popular movement, the freedom of legislative deliberation, and of acting its part in these stormy discussions with perseverance and moderation. M. Pasquier, their Minister for Foreign Affairs, endowed with rare self-command and presence of mind, was on this occasion the principal parliamentary champion of the Cabinet; and M. Mounier, Director-General of the Police, controlled the street riots with as much prudence as active firmness. The charge so often brought against so many ministers, against M. Casimir Perrier in 1831, as against the Duke de Richelieu in 1820, of exciting popular commotions only to repress them, does not deserve the notice of sensible men. At the end of a month, all these debates and scenes, within and without, ended in the adoption, not of the ministerial bill, but of an amendment which, without destroying in principle the bill of the 5th of February, 1817, so materially vitiated it, to the advantage of the right, that the party felt themselves bound to be satisfied. The greater portion of the centre, and the more moderate members of the left, submitted for the sake of public peace. The extreme left and the extreme right, M. Manuel and M. de la Bourdonnaye entered a protest. The new electoral system was clearly destined to shift the majority, and, with the majority, power, from the left to the right; but the liberties of France, and the advantages gained by the Revolution, were not endangered by the change.

This question once settled, the Cabinet had to pay its debts to the right-hand party,—rewards to those who had supported it, and punishments to its opposers. In spite of old friendships, the doctrinarians figured of necessity in the last category. If I had desired it, I might have escaped. Not being a member of either Chamber, and beyond the circle of constrained action, I could in my capacity of State Councillor have maintained reserve and silence after giving my advice to the Government; but on entering public life, I had resolved on one uniform course,—to express my true thoughts on every occasion, and never to separate myself from my friends. M. de Serre included me, with good reason, in the measure which removed them from the Council; on the 17th of June, 1820, he wrote to MM. Royer-Collard, Camille Jordan, Barante, and myself, to inform us that we were no longer on the list. The best men readily assume the habits and style of absolute power. M. de Serre was certainly not deficient in self-respect or confidence in his own opinions; he felt surprised that in this instance I should have obeyed mine, without any other more coercive necessity, and evinced this feeling by communicating my removal with unqualified harshness. "The evident hostility," he said to me, "which, without the shadow of a pretext, you have lately exhibited towards the King's Government, has rendered this step inevitable." My answer was simply this:—"I expected your letter. I might have foreseen, and I did anticipate it, when I openly evinced my disapprobation of the acts and speeches of the Ministry. I congratulate myself that I have nothing to alter in my conduct. Tomorrow, as yesterday, I shall belong only and entirely to myself."

The decisive step was taken; power had changed its course with its friends. After having turned it to this new direction, the Duke de Richelieu and his colleagues made sincere efforts during two years to arrest its further progress. They tried all methods of conciliation or resistance; sometimes they courted the right, at others the remains of the centre, and occasionally even the left, by concessions of principle, and more frequently of a personal nature. M. de Châteaubriand was sent as Ambassador to Berlin, and General Clauzel was declared entitled to the amnesty. M. de Villèle and M. Corbière obtained seats in the Cabinet, the first as minister without a portfolio, and the other as president of the Royal Council of Public Instruction; they left it, however, at the expiration of six months, under frivolous pretexts, but foreseeing the approaching fall of the Ministry, and not wishing to be there at the last moment. They were not deceived. The elections of 1821 completed the decimation of the weak battalion which still endeavoured to stand firm round tottering power. The Duke de Richelieu, who had only resumed office on a personal promise from the Count d'Artois of permanent support, complained loudly, with the independent spirit of a nobleman of high rank and of a man of honour, that the word of a gentleman, pledged to him, had not been kept. Vain complaints, and futile efforts! The Cabinet obtained time with difficulty; but the right-hand party alone gained ground. At length, on the 19th of December, 1821, the last shadow of the Government of the Centre vanished with the ministry of the Duke de Richelieu. The right and M. de Villèle seized the reins of power. "The counter-revolution is approaching!" exclaimed the left, in a mingled burst of satisfaction and alarm. M. de Villèle thought differently; a little before the decisive crisis, and after having, in his quality of vice-president, directed for some days the deliberations of the Chamber of Deputies, he wrote as follows to one of his friends:—"You will scarcely believe how my four days of presidency have succeeded. I received compliments on every side, but particularly, I own it to my shame, from the left, whom I have never conciliated. They expected, without doubt, to be eaten up alive by an ultra. They are inexhaustible in eulogium. Finally, those to whom I never speak, now address me with a thousand compliments. I think in this there is a little spite against M. Ravez. But, be that as it may, if a president were just now to be elected, I should have almost every vote in the Chamber.... For myself, impartiality costs me nothing. I look only to the success of the affairs I have undertaken, and have not the slightest prejudice against individuals. I am born for the end of revolutions."

CHAPTER VI.: GOVERNMENT OF THE RIGHT-HAND PARTY.: 1822-1827.

POSITION OF M. DE VILLÈLE ON ASSUMING POWER.—HE FINDS HIMSELF ENGAGED WITH THE LEFT AND THE CONSPIRACIES.—CHARACTER OF THE CONSPIRACIES.—ESTIMATE OF THEIR MOTIVES.—THEIR CONNECTION WITH SOME OF THE LEADERS OF THE PARLIAMENTARY OPPOSITION.—M. DE LA FAYETTE.—M. MANUEL.—M. D'ARGENSON.—THEIR ATTITUDE IN THE CHAMBER OF DEPUTIES.—FAILURE OF THE CONSPIRACIES, AND CAUSES THEREOF.— M. DE VILLÈLE ENGAGED WITH HIS RIVALS WITHIN AND BY THE SIDE OF THE CABINET.—THE DUKE DE MONTMORENCY.—M. DE CHÂTEAUBRIAND AMBASSADOR AT LONDON.—CONGRESS OF VERONA.—M. DE CHÂTEAUBRIAND BECOMES MINISTER OF FOREIGN AFFAIRS.—SPANISH WAR.—EXAMINATION OF ITS CAUSES AND RESULTS.—RUPTURE BETWEEN M. DE VILLÈLE AND M. DE CHÂTEAUBRIAND.—FALL OF M. DE CHÂTEAUBRIAND.—M. DE VILLÈLE ENGAGED WITH AN OPPOSITION SPRINGING FROM THE RIGHT-HAND PARTY.— THE "JOURNAL DES DÉBATS" AND THE MESSRS. BERTIN.—M. DE VILLÈLE FALLS UNDER THE YOKE OF THE PARLIAMENTARY MAJORITY.—ATTITUDE AND INFLUENCE OF THE ULTRA-CATHOLIC PARTY.—ESTIMATE OF THEIR CONDUCT.—ATTACKS TO WHICH THEY ARE EXPOSED.—M. DE MONTLOSIER.— M. BÉRANGER.—ACUTENESS OF M. DE VILLÈLE.—HIS DECLINE.—HIS ENEMIES AT THE COURT.—REVIEW AND DISBANDING OF THE NATIONAL GUARD OF PARIS.—ANXIETY OF CHARLES X.—DISSOLUTION OF THE CHAMBER OF DEPUTIES.—THE ELECTIONS ARE HOSTILE TO M. DE VILLÈLE.—HE RETIRES.— SPEECH OF THE DAUPHINISTS TO CHARLES X.

I now change position and point of view. It was no longer as an actor within, but as a spectator without, that I watched the right-hand party, and am enabled to record my impressions,—a spectator in opposition, who has acquired light, and learned to form a correct judgment, from time.

In December 1821, M. de Villèle attained power by the natural highroad. He reached his post through the qualities he had displayed and the importance he had acquired in the Chambers, and at the head of his party, which he brought in with himself. After a struggle of five years, he accomplished the object prematurely conceived by M. de Vitrolles in 1815,—that the leader of the parliamentary majority should become the head of the Government. Events are marked by unforeseen contradictions. The Charter conducted to office the very individual who, before its promulgation, had been its earliest opponent.

Amongst the noted men of our time, it is a distinctive feature in the career of M. de Villèle, that he became minister as a partisan, and retained that character in his official position, while at the same time endeavouring to establish, amongst his supporters, general principles of government in preference to the spirit of party. This moderator of the right was ever strictly faithful to the interests of that side. Very often unacquainted with the ideas, passions, and designs of his party, he opposed them indirectly and without positive disavowal, resolved never to desert his friends, even though he might be unable to control their course. Not from any general and systematic conviction, but from a sound practical instinct, he readily perceived the necessity of a strong attachment from the leader to his army, to secure a reciprocal feeling from the army to its chief. He paid dearly for this pertinacity; for it justly condemned him to bear the weight of errors which, had he been unfettered, he would never in all probability have committed; but through this sacrifice he held power for six years, and saved his party, during that period, from the extreme mistakes which, after his secession, led rapidly to their ruin. As minister of a constitutional monarchy, M. de Villèle has furnished France with one of the first examples of that fixity of political ties which, in spite of many inconveniences and objections, is essential to the great and salutary effects of representative government.

When M. de Villèle was called on to form a Cabinet, he found the country and the Government under the influence of a violent excitement. There were not alone storms in the Chamber and tumults in the streets; secret societies, plots, insurrections, and a strong effort to overthrow established order, fermented and burst forth in every quarter,—in the departments of the east, west, and south, at Béfort, Colmar, Toulon, Saumur, Nantes, La Rochelle, and even at Paris itself, under the very eyes of the Ministers, in the army as well as in the civil professions, in the royal guards as in the regiments of the line. In less than three years, eight serious conspiracies attacked and endangered the Restoration.

Today, after the lapse of more than thirty years, after so many events of greater importance, when an honest and rational man asks himself what motives could have excited such fierce anger and rash enterprises, he can find none either sufficient or legitimate. Neither the acts of power nor the probabilities of the future had so wounded or threatened the rights and interests of the country as to justify these attempts at utter subversion. The electoral system had been artfully changed; power had passed into the hands of an irritating and suspected party; but the great institutions were still intact; public liberty, though disputed, still displayed itself vigorously; legal order had received no serious blow; the country prospered and regularly advanced in strength. The new society was disturbed, but not disarmed; it was in a condition to wait and defend itself. There were just grounds for an animated and public opposition, but none for conspiracy or revolution.

Nations that aspire to be free incur a prominent danger,—the danger of deceiving themselves on the question of tyranny. They readily apply that name to any system of government that displeases or alarms them, or refuses to grant all that they desire. Frivolous caprices, which entail their own punishment! Power must have inflicted on a country many violations of right, with repeated acts of injustice and oppression bitter and prolonged, before revolution can be justified by reason, or crowned with triumph in the face of its inherent faults. When such causes are wanting to revolutionary attempts, they either fail miserably or bring with them the reaction which involves their own punishment.

But from 1820 to 1823 the conspirators never dreamed of asking themselves if their enterprises were legitimate; they entertained no doubt on the subject. Very different although simultaneous passions, past alarms and prospective temptations, influenced their minds and conduct. The hatreds and apprehensions that attached themselves to the words emigration, feudal system, old form of government, aristocracy, and counter-revolution, belonged to bygone times; but these fears and antipathies were in many hearts as intense and vivid as if they were entertained towards existing and powerful enemies. Against these phantoms, which the folly of the extreme right had conjured up, without the power of giving them substantial vitality, war in any shape was considered allowable, urgent, and patriotic. It was believed that liberty could best be served and saved by rekindling against the Restoration all the slumbering revolutionary fires. The conspirators flattered themselves that they could at the same time prepare a fresh revolution, which should put an end, not only to the restored monarchy, but to monarchy altogether, and by the re-establishment of the Republic lead to the absolute triumph of popular rights and interests. To the greater part of these young enthusiasts, descended from families who had been engaged in the old cause of the first Revolution, dreams of the future united with traditions of the domestic hearth; while maintaining the struggles of their fathers, they indulged their own Utopian chimeras.

Those who conspired from revolutionary hatred or republican hope, were joined by others with more clearly defined but not less impassioned views. I have elsewhere said, in speaking of Washington, "It is the privilege, often corruptive, of great men, to inspire attachment and devotion without the power of reciprocating these feelings." No one ever enjoyed this privilege more than the Emperor Napoleon. He was dying at this very moment upon the rock of St. Helena; he could no longer do anything for his partisans; and he found, amongst the people as well as in the army, hearts and arms ready to do all and risk all for his name,—a generous infatuation for which I am at a loss to decide whether human nature should be praised or pitied.

All these passions and combinations would in all probability have remained futile and unnoticed, had they not found exponents and chiefs in the highest political circles and in the bosom of the great bodies of the State. The popular masses are never sufficient for themselves; their desires and designs must be represented by visible and important leaders, who march at their head and accept the responsibility of the means and end. The conspirators of from 1820 to 1823 knew this well; and upon the most widely separated points, at Béfort as at Saumur, and at each fresh enterprise, they declared that they would not act unless well-known political leaders and Deputies of reputation were associated with them. Everybody knows, at the present day, that the co-operation they required was not withheld.

In the Chamber of Deputies, the opposition to the Government of the Right was comprised of three sections united against it, but differing materially in their views and in their means of hostility. I shall only name the principal members of this confederacy, and who have themselves clearly defined their respective positions. M. de La Fayette and M. Manuel acknowledged and directed the conspiracies. Without ignoring them, General Foy, M. Benjamin Constant, and M. Casimir Perrier, disapproved of their proceedings and declined association. M. Royer-Collard and his friends were absolutely unacquainted with them, and stood entirely aloof.

When my thoughts revert to M. de La Fayette, I am saddened by affectionate regret. I never knew a character more uniformly sincere, generous, and kind, or more ready to risk everything for his pledged faith and cause; his benevolence, although rather indiscriminate in particular cases, was not the less true and expanded towards humanity in general. His courage and devotedness were natural and earnest, serious under an exterior sometimes light, and as genuine as they were spontaneous. Throughout his life he maintained consistency in sentiments and ideas; and he had his days of vigorous resolution, which would have reflected honour on the truest friend of order and resistance to anarchy. In 1791, he opened fire, in the Champ de Mars, on the revolt set up in the name of the people; in 1792, he came in person to demand, on behalf of his army, the suppression of the Jacobins; and he held himself apart and independent under the Empire. But, taking all points into account, he failed in political judgment, in discernment, in a just estimate of circumstances and men; and he had a yielding towards his natural bent, a want of foresight as to the probable results of his actions, with a constant but indistinct yearning after popular favour, which led him on much further than he intended, and subjected him to the influence of men of a very inferior order, directly against his moral nature and political situation. At the first moment, in 1814, he seemed to be well disposed towards the Restoration; but the tendencies of power, and the persevering rancour of the Royalists, soon threw him back into the ranks of opposition. At the close of the Hundred Days, his hostility to the House of Bourbon became declared and active; a republican in soul, without being sufficiently strong or daring to proclaim the Republic, he opposed as obstinately as vainly the return of royalty; and before the Chamber of 1815, excited but not dismayed, he pledged himself, while the Restoration lasted, to enter and never to desert the ranks of its most inveterate enemies. From 1820 to 1823 he was, not the ostensible head, but the instrument and ornament, of every secret society, of every plot and project of revolution; even of those the results of which he would inevitably have denounced and resisted, had they been crowned with success.

No two people could less resemble each other than M. Manuel and M. de La Fayette. While one was open, improvident, and rash in his hostility, the other was in an equal degree reserved, calculating, and prudent even in his violence, although in real character bold and determined. M. de La Fayette was not exactly a high and mighty lord,—that expression does not apply to him,—but a noble gentleman, liberal and popular, not naturally a revolutionist, but one who by enthusiasm or example might be led and would himself lead to repeated revolutions. M. Manuel was the obedient child and able defender of the past revolution, capable of joining Government for its interest—a liberal Government, if animated with revolutionary objects, an absolute Government if unlimited power should be necessary to their supremacy,—but determined to uphold revolution in every case and at any price. His mind was limited and uncultivated, and, either in his general life or in parliamentary debate, without any impress of great political views, or of sympathetic or lofty emotions of the soul, beyond the firmness of his attitude and the lucid strength of his language. Although no advocate, and a little provincial in his style, he spoke and acted as a man of party, calmly persevering and resolved, immovable in the old revolutionary arena, and never disposed to leave it either to become a convert to new measures or to adopt new views. The Restoration, in his opinion, was in fact the old system and the counter-revolution.

After having confronted it in the Chambers with all the opposition which that theatre permitted, he encouraged, without, every plot and effort of subversion; less ready than M. de La Fayette to place himself at their head, less confident in their success, but still determined to keep alive by these means hatred and war against the Restoration, watching at the same time for a favourable opportunity of launching a decisive blow.

M. d'Argenson had less weight with the party than either of his colleagues, although perhaps the most impassioned of the three. He was a sincere and melancholy visionary, convinced that all social evils spring from human laws, and bent on promoting every kind of reform, although he had little confidence in the reformers. By his position in society, the generous tone of his sentiments, the seriousness of his convictions, the attraction of an affectionate although reserved disposition, and the charm of a refined and elegant mind, which extracted from his false philosophy bold and original views, he held, in the projects and preliminary deliberations of the conspiring opposition, a tolerably important place; but he was little suited for action, and ready to discourage it, although always prepared for personal engagement. A chimerical but not hopeful fanaticism is not a very promising temperament for a conspirator.

The issue of all these vain but tragical plots is well known. Dogged at every step by authority, sometimes even persecuted by the interested zeal of unworthy agents, they produced, in the space of two years, in various parts of France, nineteen capital condemnations, eleven of which were carried into effect. When we look back on these gloomy scenes, the mind is bewildered, and the heart recoils from the spectacle of the contrast which presents itself between sentiments and actions, efforts and results; we contemplate enterprises at the same time serious and harebrained, patriotic ardour joined to moral levity, enthusiastic devotion combined with indifferent calculation, and the same blindness, the same perseverance, united to similar impotence in old and young, in the generals and the soldiers. On the 1st of January, 1822, M. de La Fayette arrived in the vicinity of Béfort to place himself at the head of the insurrection in Alsace. He found the plot discovered, and several of the leaders already in arrest; but he also met others, MM. Ary Scheffer, Joubert, Carrel, and Guinard, whose principal anxiety was to meet and warn him by the earliest notice, and to save him and his son (who accompanied him) by leading them away through unfrequented roads. Nine months later, on the 21st of September in the same year, four young non-commissioned officers, Bories, Raoulx, Goubin, and Pommier, condemned to death for the conspiracy of Rochelle, were on the point of undergoing their sentence; M. de La Fayette and the head committee of the Carbonari had vainly endeavoured to effect their escape. The poor sergeants knew they were lost, and had reason to think they were abandoned. A humane magistrate urged them to save their lives by giving up the authors of their fatal enterprise. All four answered, "We have nothing to reveal," and then remained obstinately silent. Such devotion merited more thoughtful leaders and more generous enemies.

In presence of such facts, and in the midst of the warm debates they excited in the Chamber, the situation of the conspiring Deputies was awkward; they neither avowed their deeds nor supported their friends. The violence of their attacks against the Ministry and the Restoration in general, supplied but a poor apology for this weakness. Secret associations and plots accord ill with a system of liberty; there is little sense or dignity in conspiring and arguing at the same time. It was in vain that the Deputies who were not implicated endeavoured to shield their committed and embarrassed colleagues; it was in vain that General Foy, M. Casimir Perrier, M. Benjamin Constant, and M. Lafitte, while protesting with vehemence against the accusations charged upon their party, endeavoured to cast the mantle of their personal innocence over the actual conspirators, who sat by their sides. This manœuvre, more blustering than formidable, deceived neither the Government nor the public; and the conspiring Deputies lost more reputation than they gained security, by being thus defended while they were disavowed, in their own ranks. M. de La Fayette became impatient of this doubtful and unworthy position. During the sitting of the 1st of August, 1822, with reference to the debate on the budget, M. Benjamin Constant complained of a phrase in the act of accusation drawn up by the Attorney-General of Poictiers, against the conspiracy of General Berton, and in which the names of five Deputies were included without their being prosecuted. M. Lafitte sharply called upon the Chamber to order an inquiry into transactions "which," said he, "as far as they affect myself are infamous falsehoods." M. Casimir Perrier and General Foy supported the motion for inquiry. The Cabinet and the right-hand party rejected it, while defending the Attorney-General and his statements. The Chamber appeared perplexed. M. de La Fayette demanded to be heard, and, with a rare and happy expression of ironical pride, said, "Whatever may be my habitual indifference to party accusations and enmities, I feel called upon to add a few words to what has been said by my honourable friends. Throughout the course of a career entirely devoted to the cause of liberty, I have constantly desired to be a mark for the malevolence of the adversaries of that cause, under whatever forms, whether despotic, aristocratic, or monarchical, which they may please to select, to contest or pervert it. I therefore make no complaint, although I may claim the right of considering the word proved, which the Attorney-General has thought proper to apply to me, a little free; but I join with my friends by demanding, as far as we can, the utmost publicity, both within the walls of this Chamber and in the face of the entire nation. Thus I and my accusers, in whatever rank they may be placed, can say to each other, without restraint, all that we have had mutually to reproach ourselves with during the last thirty years."

The challenge was as transparent as it was fierce. M. de Villèle felt the full range of it, which extended even to the King himself; and taking up the glove at once, with a moderation which in its turn was not deficient in dignity, "The orator I follow," said he, "placed the question on its true footing when he said, in speaking of the Chamber, 'as far as we can.' Yes, it is of the utmost importance that, on the subject under discussion, the truth or falsehood should be correctly known; but do we adopt the true method of ascertaining either? Such is not my opinion; if it were, I should at once vote for the inquiry. The proper mode of proceeding appears to me to be, to leave justice to its ordinary course, which no one has a right to arrest.... If members of this Chamber have been compromised in the act of accusation, do they not find their acquittal in the very fact that the Chamber has not been called upon to give them up to be added to the list of the accused? For, gentlemen, it is maintaining a contradiction to say, on the one hand, 'You have placed our names in the requisition for indictment,' and on the other, 'The minister in office has not dared to prosecute, since the Chamber has not been required to surrender us.' And the demand has not been made, because the nature of the process neither imposed it as a duty nor a necessity on the part of the minister to adopt that course. I declare openly, before France, we do not accuse you, because there was nothing in the process which rendered it either incumbent or essential that we should do so. And we should the more readily have fulfilled that duty, since you cannot suppose us so little acquainted with the human heart as not to know that there would be less danger in subjecting you to direct prosecution than in following simply and openly the line marked out by the ordinary course of justice."

At the close of this sitting, M. de Villèle assuredly had good reason to be satisfied with his position and himself. He had exhibited, at the same time, firmness and moderation; by confining himself within the ordinary resources of justice, by disclaiming prosecution to extremity, he had exhibited the arm of power restrained, but ready to strike if necessity should require; he had thus, to a certain extent, defied while he tranquillized the patrons of the conspirators, and had satisfied his own party without irritating their passions. On that day he combined the minister with the tactician of the Chamber.

At the time of which we are speaking, M. de Villèle stood in the first and best phase of his power; he defended monarchy and order against conspiracy and insurrection; in the Chamber of Deputies he had to repel the furious attacks of the left-hand party, and in the Chamber of Peers the more temperate but vigilant illwill of the friends of the Duke de Richelieu. The danger and acrimony of the contest united his whole party around him. Before such a situation, the rivalries and intrigues of the Chamber and the Court hesitated to show themselves; unreasonable expectations were held in check; fidelity and discipline were evidently necessary; the associates of the chief could not desert, and dared not to assail him with their importunities.

But during the course of the year 1822 the conspiracies were subdued, the perils of the monarchy dissipated, the parliamentary combats, although always bitter, had ceased to be questions of life and death, and the preponderance of the right-hand party appeared to be firmly established in the country as in the Chambers. Other difficulties and dangers then began to rise up round M. de Villèle. He had no longer menacing enemies to hold his friends in check; disagreements, demands, enmities, and intrigues beset him on every side. The first attacks sprang from questions of internal policy, and originated in the bosom of his own Cabinet.

I have no desire to pronounce severe judgment on the revolutions which agitated Southern Europe from 1820 to 1822. It is hard to say to nations badly governed, that they are neither wise nor strong enough to remedy their own evils. Above all, in our days, when the desire for good government is intense, and none believe themselves too weak to accomplish what they wish, unrestrained truth on this subject offends many sincere friends of justice and humanity. Experience, however, has supplied numerous inferences. Of the three revolutions which occurred in 1820, those of Naples and Turin evaporated in a few months, without any blow being struck, before the sole appearance of the Austrian troops. The Spanish revolution alone survived, neither abandoned nor established, pursuing its course by violent but uncertain steps, incapable of founding a regular government and of suppressing the resistance with which it was opposed, but still strong enough to keep alive anarchy and civil war. Spain, under the influence of such commotions, was a troublesome neighbour to France, and might become dangerous. The conspirators, defeated at home, found shelter there, and began to weave new plots from that place of refuge. In their turn, the Spanish counter-revolutionists found an asylum in France, and prepared arms on both sides of the Pyrenees. A sanatory line of troops, stationed on our frontier to preserve France from the contagion of the yellow-fever which had broken out in Catalonia, soon grew into an army of observation. The hostile feeling of Europe, much more decided and systematic, co-operated with the mistrust of France. Prince Metternich dreaded a new fit of Spanish revolutionary contagion in Italy; the Emperor Alexander imagined himself called upon to maintain the security of all thrones and the peace of the world; England, without caring much for the success of the Spanish revolution, was extremely anxious that Spain should continue entirely independent, and that French influence should not prevail in the Peninsula. The French Government had to deal with a question not only delicate and weighty in itself, but abounding with still more important complications, and which might lead to a rupture with some, if not with the whole of her allies.

M. de Villèle on succeeding to office, had no very defined ideas as to foreign affairs, or any decidedly arranged plans beyond an unbiassed mind and sensible predilections. During his short association with the Cabinet of the Duke de Richelieu, he had closely observed the policy adopted towards Spain and Italy,—a peaceful policy of non-intervention, and of sound advice to kings and liberals, to liberals as to kings, but of little efficacy in act, and tending, above all other considerations, to keep France beyond the vortex of revolutions and counter-revolutions, and to prevent a European conflagration. In the main, M. de Villèle approved of this policy, and would have desired nothing better than to continue it. He was more occupied with internal government than external relations, and more anxious for public prosperity than diplomatic influence; but, in the accomplishment of his views, he had to contend against the prepossessions of his party, and in this struggle his two principal associates, M. de Montmorency, as Minister for Foreign Affairs, and M. de Châteaubriand, as ambassador at London, contributed more embarrassment than assistance.

On the formation of the Cabinet, he proposed to the King to give M. de Montmorency the portfolio of foreign affairs. "Take care," replied Louis XVIII. "He has a very little mind, somewhat prejudiced and obstinate; he will betray you, against his will, through weakness. When present, he will say he agrees with you, and may perhaps think so at the time; when he leaves you, he will suffer himself to be led by his own bias, contrary to your views, and, instead of being aided, you will be thwarted and compromised." M. de Villèle persevered; he believed that, with the right-hand party, the name and influence of M. de Montmorency were of importance. Not long after, he had an opportunity of satisfying himself that the King had judged correctly. M. de Serre having refused to hold office in the new Cabinet, M. de Villèle, to remove him with the semblance of a compliment, requested the King to appoint him ambassador at Naples. M. de Montmorency, who wanted this post for his cousin the Duke de Laval, went so far as to say that he should resign if it were refused to him. The King and M. de Villèle kept their resolution; M. de Serre went to Naples, and M. de Montmorency remained in the Ministry, but not without discontent at the preponderance of a colleague who had treated him with so little complaisance.

M. de Châteaubriand, by accepting the embassy to London, relieved M. de Villèle from many little daily annoyances; but he was not long satisfied with his new post. He wished to reign in a coterie, and to receive adulation without constraint. He produced less effect in English society than he had anticipated; he wanted more success and of a more varied character; he was looked upon as a distinguished writer, rather than as a great politician; they considered him more opinionated than profound, and too much occupied with himself. He excited curiosity, but not the admiration he coveted; he was not always the leading object of attention, and enjoyed less freedom, while he called forth little of the enthusiastic idolatry to which he had been accustomed elsewhere. London, the English court and drawing-rooms, wearied and displeased him; he has perpetuated the impression in his Memoirs:—"Every kind of reputation," he says, "travels rapidly to the banks of the Thames, and leaves them again with the same speed. I should have worried myself to no purpose by endeavouring to acquire any knowledge of the English. What a life is a London season! I should prefer the galleys a hundred times."

An opportunity soon presented itself, which enabled him to seek in another direction more worldly excitement and popularity. Revolution and civil war went on increasing in Spain from day to day; tumults, murders, sanguinary combats between the people and the royal guards, the troops of the line and the militia, multiplied in the streets of Madrid. The life of Ferdinand VII. appeared to be in question, and his liberty was actually invaded.

M. de Metternich, whose importance and influence in Europe had greatly increased ever since he had so correctly foreseen the weakness, and so rapidly stifled the explosion, of the Italian revolutions, applied his entire attention to the affairs of the Spanish Peninsula, and urged the sovereigns and their ministers to deliberate on them in common accord. As soon as it was settled that a Congress should assemble with this object, at Verona, M. de Châteaubriand made powerful applications, directly and indirectly, to M. de Montmorency and M. de Villèle, to be included in the mission. M. de Montmorency had no idea of acceding to this, fearing to be opposed or eclipsed by such a colleague. The King, Louis XVIII., who had no confidence either in the capacity of M. de Montmorency or the judgment of M. de Châteaubriand, was desirous that M. de Villèle himself should repair to Verona, to maintain the prudent policy which circumstances required. M. de Villèle objected. It would be, he said to the King, too decided an affront to his minister of foreign affairs and his ambassador in London, who were naturally called to this duty; it would be better to send them both, that one might control the other, and to give them specific instructions which should regulate their attitude and language. The King adopted this advice. The instructions, drawn up by M. de Villèle's own hand, were discussed and settled in a solemn meeting of the Cabinet; M. de Châteaubriand knew to a certainty that he owed the accomplishment of his desires to M. de Villèle alone; and eight days after the departure of M. de Montmorency, the King, to secure the preponderance of M. de Villèle, by a signal mark of favour, appointed him President of the Council.

The instructions were strictly defined; they prescribed to the French plenipotentiaries to abstain from appearing, when before the Congress, as reporters of the affairs of Spain, to take no initiative and enter into engagement as regarded intervention, and, in every case, to preserve the total independence of France, either as to act or future resolve. But the inclinations of M. de Montmorency accorded ill with his orders; and he had to treat with sovereigns and ministers who wished precisely to repress the Spanish revolution by the hand of France,—in the first place, to accomplish this work without taking it upon themselves, and also to compromise France with England, who was evidently much averse to French interference. The Prince de Metternich, versed in the art of suggesting to others his own views, and of urging with the air of co-operation, easily obtained influence over M. de Montmorency, and induced him to take with the other Powers the precise initiative, and to enter into the very engagements, he had been instructed to avoid. M. de Châteaubriand, who filled only a secondary post in the official negotiation, kept at first a little on the reserve: "I do not much like the general position in which he has placed himself here," wrote M. de Montmorency to Madame Recamier; "he is looked upon as singularly sullen; he assumes a stiff and uncouth manner, which makes others feel ill at ease in his presence. I shall use every effort, before I go, to establish a more congenial intercourse between him and his colleagues." M. de Montmorency had no occasion to trouble himself much to secure this result. As soon as he had taken his departure, M. de Châteaubriand assumed a courteous and active demeanour at the Congress. The Emperor Alexander, alive to the reputation of the author of the 'Genius of Christianity,' and to his homage to the founder of the 'Holy Alliance,' returned him compliment for compliment, flattery for flattery, and confirmed him in his desire of war with the Spanish revolution, by giving him reason to rely, for that course of policy and for himself, upon his unlimited support. Nevertheless, in his correspondence with M. de Villèle, M. de Châteaubriand still expressed himself very guardedly: "We left," said he, "our determination in doubt; we did not wish to appear impracticable; we were apprehensive that, if we discovered ourselves too much, the President of the Council would not listen to us."

I presume that M. de Villèle fell into no mistake as to the pretended doubt in which M. de Châteaubriand endeavoured to envelop himself. I also incline to think that he himself, at that epoch, looked upon a war with Spain as almost inevitable. But he was still anxious to do all in his power to avoid it, if only to preserve with the moderate spirits, and the interests who dreaded that alternative, the attitude and reputation of an advocate for peace. Sensible men are unwilling to answer for the faults they consent to commit. As soon as he ascertained that M. de Montmorency had promised at Verona that his Government would take such steps at Madrid, in concert with the three Northern Powers, as would infallibly lead to war, M. de Villèle submitted to the King in council these premature engagements, declaring at the same time that, for his part, he did not feel that France was bound to adopt the same line of conduct with Austria, Prussia, and Russia, or to recall at once, as they wished to do, her Minister at Madrid, and thus to give up all renewed attempts at conciliation. It was said that, while using this language, he had his resignation already prepared and visible in his portfolio. Powerful supporters were not wanting to this policy. The Duke of Wellington, recently arrived in Paris, had held a conversation with M. de Villèle, and also with the King, on the dangers of an armed intervention in Spain, and proposed a plan of mediation, to be concerted between France and England, to induce the Spaniards to introduce into their constitution the modifications which the French Cabinet itself should indicate as sufficient to maintain peace. Louis XVIII. placed confidence in the judgment and friendly feeling of the Duke of Wellington; he closed the debate in the Council by saying, "Louis XIV. levelled the Pyrenees; I shall not allow them to be raised again. He placed my family on the throne of Spain; I cannot let them fall. The other sovereigns have not the same duties to fulfil. My ambassador ought not to quit Madrid, until the day when a hundred thousand Frenchmen are in march to replace him." The question thus decided against the promises he had made at Verona, M. de Montmorency, on whom a few days before, and at the suggestion of M. de Villèle, the King had conferred the title of Duke, suddenly tendered his resignation. The 'Moniteur,' in announcing it, published a despatch which M. de Villèle, while holding ad interim the portfolio of foreign affairs, addressed to Count de Lagarde, the King's minister at Madrid, prescribing to him an attitude and language which still admitted some chance of conciliation; and three days later M. de Châteaubriand, after some display of appropriate hesitation, replaced M. de Montmorency as Foreign Minister.

Three weeks had scarcely passed over, when the Spanish Government, controlled by a sentiment of national dignity more magnanimous than enlightened, by popular enthusiasm, and by its own passions, refused all constitutional modification whatever. The ambassadors of the three Northern Powers had already quitted Madrid. The Count de Lagarde remained there. On the refusal of the Spaniards, M. de Châteaubriand recalled him, on the 18th of January, 1823, instructing him at the same time, in a confidential despatch, to suggest the possibility of amicable measures; and of this he also apprised the English Cabinet. These last overtures proved as futile as the preceding ones. At Madrid they had no confidence in the French Ministry; and the Government of London placed too little dependence either on the power or discretion of that of Madrid, to commit itself seriously by engaging the latter, through the weight of English influence, to submit to the concessions, otherwise reasonable, which France required. Affairs had reached the point at which the ablest politicians, without faith in the efficacy of their own views, were unwilling to adopt decided measures.

On the 28th of January, 1823, M. de Villèle determined on war, and the King announced this decision in his speech on opening the session of both Chambers. Nevertheless eight days later, M. de Châteaubriand declared to Sir Charles Stuart, the English ambassador at Paris, that, far from dreaming of establishing absolute power in Spain, France was still ready to entertain the constitutional modifications she had proposed to the Spanish Government, "as sufficient to induce her to suspend hostile preparations, and to renew friendly intercourse between the two countries on the old footing." At the very moment of engaging in war, M. de Châteaubriand, who desired, and M. de Villèle, who was averse to, these extreme measures, equally endeavoured to escape from the responsibility attached to them.

I have nothing to say on the war itself and the course of its incidents. In principle it was unjust, for it was unnecessary. The Spanish revolution, in spite of its excesses, portended no danger to

France or the Restoration. The differences to which it gave rise between the two Governments might have been easily arranged without violating peace. The revolution of Paris, in February, 1848, produced much more serious and better-founded alarms to Europe in general, than the Spanish revolution in 1823 could have occasioned to France. Nevertheless Europe, with sound policy, respected towards France the tutelary principle of the internal independence of nations, which can never be justly invaded except under an absolute and most urgent necessity. Neither do I think that in 1823 the throne and life of Ferdinand VII. were actually in danger. All that has since occurred in Spain justifies the conclusion, that regicide has no accomplices there, and revolution very few partisans. The great and legitimate reasons for war were therefore wanting. In fact, and notwithstanding its success, it led to no profitable result either for Spain or France. It surrendered up Spain to the incapable and incurable tyranny of Ferdinand VII., without putting an end to revolutions; and substituted the barbarities of popular absolutism for popular anarchy. Instead of securing the influence of France beyond Pyrenees, it compromised and annulled it to such an extent that, towards the close of 1823, it was found necessary to have recourse to the mediation of Russia, and to send M. Pozzo di Borgo to Madrid to compel Ferdinand VII. to select more moderate advisers. The Northern Powers and England alone retained any credit in Spain,—the first with the King and the Absolutists, the latter with the Liberals; victorious France was there politically vanquished. In the eyes of clear-sighted judges, the advantageous and permanent effects of the war were of no more value than the causes.

As an expedient of restless policy, as a mere coup-de-main of dynasty or party, the Spanish war fully succeeded. The sinister predictions of its opponents were falsified, and the hopes of its advocates surpassed. Brought under proof together, the fidelity of the army and the impotence of the conspiring refugees were clearly manifested. The expedition was easy but not inglorious, and added much to the personal credit of the Duke d'Angoulême. The prosperity and tranquillity of France received no check. The House of Bourbon exhibited a strength and resolution which the Powers who urged it on scarcely expected; and England, who would have restrained the effort, submitted to it patiently, although with some dissatisfaction. Regarding matters in this light only, M. de Châteaubriand was correct in writing to M. de Villèle from Verona, "It is for you, my dear friend, to consider whether you ought not to seize this opportunity, which may never occur again, of replacing France in the rank of military powers, and of re-establishing the white cockade, in a short war almost without danger, and in favour of which the opinion of the Royalists and of the army so strongly impels you at this moment." M. de Villèle was mistaken in his answer: "May God grant," said he, "for my country and for Europe, that we may not persist in an intervention which I declare beforehand, with the fullest conviction, will compromise the safety of France herself."

After such an event, in which they had taken such unequal shares, the relative positions of these two statesmen became sensibly changed; but the alteration did not yet appear for some time. M. de Châteaubriand endeavoured to triumph with modesty, and M. de Villèle, not very sensitive to the wounds of personal vanity, treated the issue of the war as a general success of the Cabinet, and prepared to turn it to his own advantage, without considering to whom the principal honour might be due. Accustomed to power, he exercised it without noise or parade, and was careful not to clash with his adversaries or rivals, who thus felt themselves led to admit his preponderance as a necessity, rather than humiliated to endure it as a defeat. The dissolution of the Chamber of Deputies became his fixed idea and immediate object. The liberal Opposition was too strong there to allow him to hope that he could carry the great measures necessary to satisfy his party. The Spanish war had led to debates, continually increasing in animosity, which in time produced violence in the stronger, and anger in the weaker party, beyond all previous example. After the expulsion of M. Manuel on the 3rd of March, 1823, and the conduct of the principal portion of the left-hand party, who left the hall with him when he was removed by the gendarmes, it was almost impossible to expect that the Chamber could resume its regular place or share in the government. On the 24th of December, 1823, it was in fact dissolved, and M. de Villèle, putting aside the differences of opinion on the Spanish war, applied his whole attention to ensure the success of the elections and the formation of a new Chamber, from which he could demand with confidence what the right-hand party expected from him, and which, according to his expectation, should secure a long duration of his influence both with that party and with the Court.

M. de Châteaubriand had no such objects to contemplate or effect. Unacquainted with the internal government of the country, and the daily management of the Chambers, he enjoyed the success of his Spanish war, as he called it, with tranquil pride,—ready, on provocation, to become active and bitter. He wanted exactly the qualities which distinguished M. de Villèle, and he possessed those, or rather the instinct and inclination of those, in which M. de Villèle was deficient. Entering late on public life, and until then unknown, with a mind but slightly cultivated, and little distracted from business by the force or variety of his imaginative ideas, M. de Villèle had ever one leading object,—to reach power by faithfully serving his party; and, power once obtained, to hold it firmly, while exercising it with discretion.

Launched on the world almost from infancy, M. de Châteaubriand had traversed the whole range of ideas, attempted every career, aspired to every renown, exhausted some, and approached others; nothing satisfied him. "My capital defect," said he himself, "has been ennui, disgust with everything, perpetual doubt." A strange temperament in a man devoted to the restoration of religion and monarchy! Thus the life of M. de Châteaubriand had been a constant and a perpetual combat between his enterprises and his inclinations, his situation and his nature. He was ambitious, as the leader of a party, and independent, as a volunteer of the forlorn hope; captivated by everything great, and sensitive even to suffering in the most trifling matters, careless beyond measure of the common interests of life, but passionately absorbed, on the stage of the world, in his own person and reputation, and more annoyed by the slightest check than gratified by the most brilliant triumph; in public life, more jealous of success than power, capable in a particular emergency, as he had just proved, of conceiving and carrying out a great design, but unable to pursue in government, with energy and patience, a well-cemented and strongly-organized line of policy. He possessed a sympathetic understanding of the moral impressions of his age and country; more able however, and more inclined, to win their favour by compliance than to direct them to important and lasting advantages; a noble and expanded mind, which, whether in literature or politics, touched all the exalted chords of the human soul, but more calculated to strike and charm the imagination than to govern men; greedy, to an excess, of praise and fame, to satisfy his pride, and of emotion and novelty, as resources from constitutional weariness.

At the very moment when he was achieving a triumph in Spain for the House of Bourbon, he received disappointments from the latter quarter, the remembrance of which he has thought proper to perpetuate himself:—"In our ardour," said he, "after the arrival of the telegraphic despatch which announced the deliverance of the King of Spain, we Ministers hastened to the palace. There I received a warning of my fall,—a pailful of cold water which recalled me to my usual humility. The King and Monsieur took no notice of us. The Duchess d'Angoulême, bewildered with the glory of her husband, distinguished no one.... On the Sunday following, before the Council met, I returned to pay my duty to the royal family. The august Princess said something complimentary to each of my colleagues; to me she did not deign to address a single word: undoubtedly I had no claim to such an honour. The silence of the Orphan of the Temple can never be considered ungrateful." A more liberal sovereign undertook to console M. de Châteaubriand for this royal ingratitude; the Emperor Alexander, with whom he had continued in intimate correspondence, being anxious to signalize his satisfaction, conferred on him and M. de Montmorency, and on them alone, the great riband of the Order of St. Andrew.

M. de Villèle was not insensible to this public token of imperial favour bestowed on himself and his policy; and the King, Louis XVIII., showed that he was even more moved by it. "Pozzo and La Ferronays," said he to M. de Villèle, "have made me give you, through the Emperor Alexander, a slap on the cheek; but I shall be even with him, and mean to pay for it in coin of a better stamp. I name you, my dear Villèle, a knight of my Orders; they are worth more than his." And M. de Villèle received from the King the Order of St. Esprit. It was in vain that a little later, and on the mutual request of the two rivals, the Emperor Alexander conferred on M. de Villèle the Grand Cross of St. Andrew, and the King, Louis XVIII., gave the Saint Esprit to M. de Châteaubriand; favours thus extorted cannot efface the original disappointments.

To these courtly slights were soon added causes of rupture more serious. The dissolution of the Chamber had succeeded far beyond the expectations of the Cabinet. The elections had not returned from the left, or the left centre, more than seventeen oppositionists. Much more exclusively than that of 1815, the new Chamber belonged to the right-hand party; the day had now arrived to give them the satisfaction they had long looked for. The Cabinet immediately brought in two bills, which appeared to be evident preparatives and effectual pledges for the measures most ardently desired. By one, the integral remodelling of the Chamber of Deputies every seven years was substituted for the partial and annual reconstruction as at present in force. This was bestowing on the new Chamber a guarantee of power as of durability. The second bill proposed the conversion of the five per cent. annuities into three per cents; that is to say, a reimbursement, to the holders of stock, of their capital at par, or the reduction of interest. To this great financial scheme was joined a political measure of equal importance,—indemnity to the

Emigrants, with preparations for carrying it into effect. The two bills had been discussed and approved in council. On the question of the septennial renewal of the Chamber of Deputies, M. de Châteaubriand proposed the reduction of age necessary for electors; he failed in this object, but still supported the bill. With respect to the conversion of the funds, the friends of M. de Villèle asserted that M. de Châteaubriand warmly expressed his approbation of the measure, and was even anxious that, by a previous arrangement with the bankers, M. de Villèle should secure the means of carrying it, as a preface to that which was intended to heal the most festering wound of the Revolution.

But the debate in the Chambers soon destroyed the precarious harmony of the Cabinet. The conversion of the funds was vigorously opposed, not only by the numerous interests thereby injured, but by the unsatisfied feeling of the public on a new measure extremely complicated and ill understood. In both Chambers, the greater portion of M. de Châteaubriand's friends spoke against the bill; it was said that he was even hostile to it himself. Some observations were attributed to him on the imprudence of a measure which no one desired, no public necessity called for, and was merely an invention of the bankers, adopted by a Minister of Finance, who hoped to extract reputation from what might lead to his ruin. "I have often seen," he was accused of saying, "people break their heads against a wall; but I have never, until now, seen people build a wall for the express purpose of running their heads against it." M. de Villèle listened to these reports, and expressed his surprise at them; his supporters inquired into the cause. Hints were uttered of jealousy, of ambition, of intrigues to depose the President of the Council, and to occupy his place. When the bill had passed the Chamber of Deputies, the debate in the Chamber of Peers, and the part that M. de Châteaubriand would take in it, were looked forward to with considerable misgivings. He maintained profound silence, not affording the slightest support; and when the bill was thrown out, approaching M. de Villèle, he said to him, "If you resign, we are ready to follow you." He adds, while relating this proposal himself, "M. de Villèle, for sole answer, honoured us with a look which we still have before us. This look, however, made no impression."

It is well known how M. de Châteaubriand was dismissed two days after the sitting. From whence proceeded the rudeness of this dismissal? It is difficult to decide. M. de Châteaubriand attributed it to M. de Villèle alone. "On Whit Sunday, the 6th of June, 1824," says he, "at half-past ten in the morning I repaired to the palace. My principal object was to pay my respects to Monsieur. The first saloon of the Pavillon Marsan was nearly empty; a few persons entered in succession, and seemed embarrassed. An aide-de-camp of Monsieur said to me. 'Viscount, I scarcely hoped to see you here; have you received no communication?' I answered, 'No; what am I likely to receive?' He replied, 'I fear you will soon learn.' Upon this, as no one offered to introduce me to Monsieur, I went to hear the music in the chapel. I was quite absorbed in the beautiful anthems of the service, when an usher told me some one wished to speak with me. It was Hyacinth Pilorge, my secretary. He handed to me a letter and a royal ordinance, saying at the same time, 'Sir, you are no longer a minister.' The Duke de Rauzan, Superintendent of Political Affairs, had opened the packet in my absence, and had not ventured to bring it to me. I found within, this note from M. de Villèle; 'Monsieur le Vicomte,—I obey the orders of the King, in transmitting without delay to your Excellency a decree which his Majesty has just placed in my hand:—The Count de Villèle, President of our Ministerial Council, is charged, ad interim, with the portfolio of Foreign Affairs, in place of the Viscount de Châteaubriand.'"

The friends of M. de Villèle assert that it was the King himself, who in his anger dictated the rude form of the communication. "Two days after the vote," say they, "as soon as M. de Villèle entered the royal cabinet, Louis XVIII. said to him: 'Châteaubriand has betrayed us like a——; I do not wish to receive him after Mass; draw up the order for his dismissal, and let it be sent to him in time; I will not see him.' All remonstrances were useless; the King insisted that the decree should be written at his own desk and immediately forwarded. M. de Châteaubriand was not found at home, and his dismissal was only communicated to him at the Tuileries, in the apartments of Monsieur."

Whoever may have been the author of the measure, the blame rests with M. de Villèle. If it was contrary to his desire, assuredly he had credit enough with the King to prevent it. Contrary to his usual habit, he exhibited more temper on this occasion than coolness or foresight. There are allies who are necessary, although extremely troublesome; and M. de Châteaubriand, despite his pretensions and his whims, was less dangerous as a rival than as an enemy.

Although without connection in the Chambers, and with no control as an orator, he immediately became a brilliant and influential leader of the Opposition, for opposition was his natural bent as well as the excitement of the moment. He excelled in unravelling the instincts of national discontent, and of continually exciting them against authority by supplying them with powerful motives, real or specious, and always introduced with effect. He also possessed the art of depreciating and casting odium on his adversaries, by keen and polished insults constantly repeated, and at the same time of bringing over to his side old opponents, destined soon to resume their former character, but for the moment attracted and overpowered by the pleasure and profit of the heavy blows he administered to their common enemy. Through the favour of the MM. Bertin, he found on the instant, in the 'Journal des Débats,' an important avenue for his daily attacks. As enlightened and influential in politics as in literature, these two brothers possessed the rare faculty of collecting round themselves by generous and sympathetic patronage, a chosen cohort of clever writers, and of supporting their opinions and those of their friends with manly intelligence. M. Bertin de Veaux, the more decided politician of the two, held M. de Villèle in high esteem, and lived in familiar intimacy with him. "Villèle," said he to me one day, "is really born for public business; he has all the necessary disinterestedness and capacity; he cares not to shine, he wishes only to govern; he would be a Minister of Finance in the cellar of his hotel, as willingly as in the drawing-rooms of the first story." It was no trifling matter which could induce the eminent journalist to break with the able minister. He sought an interview with M. de Villèle, and requested him, for the preservation of peace, to bestow on M. de Châteaubriand the embassy to Rome. "I shall not risk such a proposition to the King," replied M. de Villèle. "In that case," retorted M. Bertin, "you will remember that the 'Débats' overthrew the ministries of Decazes and Richelieu, and will do the same by the ministry of

Villèle."—"You turned out the two first to establish royalism," said M. de Villèle; "to destroy mine you must have a revolution."

There was nothing in this prospect to inspire M. de Villèle with confidence, as the event proved; but thirteen years later, M. Bertin de Veaux remembered the caution. When, in 1837, under circumstances of which I shall speak in their proper place, I separated from M. Molé, he said to me with frankness, "I have certainly quite as much friendship for you as I ever had for M. de Châteaubriand, but I decline following you into Opposition. I shall not again try to sap the Government I wish to establish. One experiment of that nature is enough."

At Court, as in the Chamber, M. de Villèle was triumphant; he had not only conquered, but he had driven away his rivals, M. de Montmorency and M. de Châteaubriand, as he had got rid of M. de La Fayette and M. Manuel. Amongst the men whose voices, opinions, or even presence might have fettered him, death had already stepped in, and was again coming to his aid. M. Camille Jordan, the Duke de Richelieu, and M. de Serre were dead; General Foy and the Emperor Alexander were not long in following them. There are moments when death seems to delight, like Tarquin, in cutting down the tallest flowers. M. de Villèle remained sole master. At this precise moment commenced the heavy difficulties of his position, the weak points of his conduct, and his first steps towards decline.

In place of having to defend himself against a powerful opposition of the Left, which was equally to be feared and resisted by the Right and the Cabinet, he found himself confronted by an Opposition emanating from the right itself, and headed, in the Chamber of Deputies, by M. de la Bourdonnaye, his companion during the session of 1815; in the Chamber of Peers and without, by M. de Châteaubriand, so recently his colleague in the Council. As long as he had M. de Châteaubriand for an ally, M. de Villèle had only encountered as adversaries, in the interior of his party, the ultra-royalists of the extreme right, M. de la Bourdonnaye, M. Delalot, and a few others, whom the old counter-revolutionary spirit, intractable passions, ambitious discontent, or habits of grumbling independence kept in a perpetual state of irritation against a power, moderate without ascendency, and clever without greatness. But when M. de Châteaubriand and the 'Journal des Débats' threw themselves into the combat, there was then seen to muster round them an army of anti-ministerialists of every origin and character, composed of royalists and liberals, of old and young France, of the popular and the aristocratic throng. The weak remains of the left-hand party, beaten in the recent elections, the seventeen old members of the Opposition, liberals or doctrinarians, drew breath when they looked on such allies; and, without confounding their ranks, while each party retained its own standard and arms, they combined for mutual support, and united their forces against M. de Villèle.

M. de Châteaubriand has gratified himself by inserting in his Memoirs the testimonies of admiration and sympathy proffered to him at that time by M. Benjamin Constant, General Sebastiani, M. Étienne, and other heads of the liberal section. In the Parliamentary struggle, the left-hand party could only add to the opposers of the right a very small number of votes; but they brought eminent talents, the support of their journals, their influence throughout the country; and, in a headlong, confused attack,—some under cover of the mantle of Royalism, others shielded by the popularity of their allies,—they waged fierce war against the common enemy.

In presence of such an Opposition, M. de Villèle fell into a more formidable danger than that of the sharp contests he had to encounter to hold ground against it: he was given over without protection or refuge to the influence and views of his own friends. He could no longer awe them by the power of the left-hand party, nor find occasionally in the unsettled position of the Chamber a bulwark against their demands. There had ceased to be a formidable balance of oppositionists or waverers; the majority, and a great majority, was ministerial and determined to support the Cabinet; but it had no real apprehension of the adversaries by whom it was attacked. It preferred M. de Villèle to M. de la Bourdonnaye and M. de Châteaubriand, believing him more capable of managing with advantage the interests of the party; but if M. de Villèle went counter to the wishes of that majority, if it ceased to hold a perfect understanding with him, it could then fall back on MM. de Châteaubriand and de la Bourdonnaye. M. de Villèle had no resource against the majority; he was a minister at the mercy of his partisans.

Amongst these were some of opposite pretensions, and who lent him their support on very unequal conditions. If he had only had to deal with those I shall designate as the politicals and laymen of the party, he might have been able to satisfy and govern in concert with them. Notwithstanding their prejudices, the greater part of the country-gentlemen and royalist citizens were neither over-zealous nor exacting; they had fallen in with the manners of new France, and had either found or recovered their natural position in present society, reconciling themselves to constitutional government, since they were no longer considered as the vanquished side. The indemnity to the emigrants, some pledges of local influence, and the distribution of public functions, would have long sufficed to secure their support to M. de Villèle; but another portion of his army, numerous, important, and necessary, the religious department, was much more difficult to satisfy and control.

I am not disposed to revive any of the particular expressions which were then used as weapons of war, and have now become almost insulting. I shall neither speak of the priestly, nor of the congregational party, nor even of the Jesuits. I should reproach myself for reviving by such language and reminiscences the evil, heavy in itself, which France and the Restoration were condemned at that time, the one to fear, and the other to endure.

This evil, which glimmered through the first Restoration, through the session of 1815, and still exists, in spite of so many storms and such increasing intelligence, is, in fact a war declared by a considerable portion of the Catholic Church of France, against existing French society, its principles, its organization, political and civil, its origin and its tendencies. It was during the ministry of M. de Villèle, and above all when he found himself alone and confronted with his party, that the mischief displayed its full force.

Never was a similar war more irrational or inopportune. It checked the reaction, which had commenced under the Consulate, in favour of creeds and the sentiment of religion. I have no desire to exaggerate the value of that reaction; I hold faith and true piety in too much respect to confound them with the superficial vicissitudes of human thought and opinion. Nevertheless the movement which led France back towards Christianity was more sincere and serious than it actually appeared to be. It was at once a public necessity and an intellectual taste. Society, worn out with commotion and change, sought for fixed points on which it could rely and repose; men, disgusted with a terrestrial and material atmosphere, aspired to ascend once more towards higher and purer horizons; the inclinations of morality concurred with the instincts of social interest. Left to its natural course, and supported by the purely religious influence of a clergy entirely devoted to the re-establishment of faith and Christian life, this movement was likely to extend and to restore to religion its legitimate empire.

But instead of confining itself to this sphere of action, many members and blind partisans of the Catholic clergy descended to worldly questions, and showed themselves more zealous to recast French society in its old mould, and so to restore their church to its former place there, than to reform and purify the moral condition of souls. Here was a profound mistake. The Christian Church is not like the pagan Antæus, who renews his strength by touching the earth; it is on the contrary, by detaching itself from the world, and re-ascending towards heaven, that the Church in its hours of peril regains its vigour. When we saw it depart from its appropriate and sublime mission, to demand penal laws and to preside over the distribution of offices; when we beheld its desires and efforts prominently directed against the principles and institutions which constitute today the essence of French society; when liberty of conscience, publicity, the legal separation of civil and religious life, the laical character of the State, appeared to be attacked and compromised,—on that instant the rising tide of religious reaction stopped, and yielded way to a contrary current. In place of the movement which thinned the ranks of the unbelievers to the advantage of the faithful, we saw the two parties unite together; the eighteenth century appeared once more in arms; Voltaire, Rousseau, Diderot, and their worst disciples once more spread abroad and recruited innumerable battalions. War was declared against society in the name of the Church, and society returned war for war:—a deplorable chaos, in which good and evil, truth and falsehood, justice and injustice, were confounded together, and blows hurled at random on every side.

I know not whether M. de Villèle thoroughly estimated, in his own thoughts, the full importance of this situation of affairs, and the dangers to which he exposed religion and the Restoration. His was not a mind either accustomed or disposed to ponder long over general facts and moral questions, or to sound them deeply. But he thoroughly comprehended, and felt acutely, the embarrassment which might accrue from these causes to his own power; and he tried to diminish them by yielding to clerical influence in the government, imposing though limited sacrifices, flattering himself that by these means he should acquire allies in the Church itself, who would aid him to restrain the overweening and imprudent pretensions of their own friends. Already, and shortly after his accession to the ministry, he had appointed an ecclesiastic in good estimation, and whom the Pope had named Bishop of Hermopolis, the Abbé Frayssinous, to the head-mastership of the University. Two months after the fall of M. de Châteaubriand, the Abbé Frayssinous entered the Cabinet as Minister of Ecclesiastical Affairs and Public Instruction—a new department created expressly for him. He was a man of sense and moderation, who had acquired, by Christian preaching without violence, and conduct in which prudence was blended with dignity, a reputation and importance somewhat superior to his actual merits, and which he had no desire to compromise. In 1816 he had been a member of the Royal Commission of Public Education, over which M. Royer-Collard at that time presided; but soon retired from it, not wishing either to share the of his superior or to act in opposition to him. He generally approved of the policy of M. de Villèle; but although binding himself to support it, and while lamenting the blind demands of a portion of the clergy, he endeavoured, when opportunity offered, to excuse and conceal rather than reject them altogether. Without betraying M. de Villèle, he afforded him little aid, and committed him repeatedly by his language in public, which invariably tended more to maintain his own position in the Church than to serve the Cabinet.

Three months only had elapsed since M. de Villèle, separated from his most brilliant colleagues and an important portion of his old friends, had sustained the entire weight of government, when the King Louis XVIII. died. The event had long been foreseen, and M. de Villèle had skilfully prepared for it: he was as well established in the esteem and confidence of the new monarch as of the sovereign who had just passed from the Tuileries to St. Denis; Charles X., the Dauphin, and the Dauphiness, all three looked upon him as the ablest and most valuable of their devoted adherents. But M. de Villèle soon discovered that he had changed masters, and that little dependence could be placed on the mind or heart of a king, even though sincere, when the surface and the interior were not in unison. Men belong, much more than is generally supposed, or than they believe themselves, to their real convictions. Many comparisons, for the sake of contrast, have been drawn between Louis XVIII. and Charles X.; the distinction between them was even greater than has been stated. Louis XVIII. was a moderate of the old system, and a liberal-minded inheritor of the eighteenth century; Charles X. was a true emigrant and a submissive bigot. The wisdom of Louis XVIII. was egotistic and sceptical, but serious and sincere; when Charles X. acted like a sensible king, it was through propriety, from timid and short-sighted complaisance, from being carried away, or from the desire of pleasing,— not from conviction or natural choice. Through all the different Cabinets of his reign, whether under the Abbé de Montesquiou, M. de Talleyrand, the Duke de Richelieu, M. Decazes, and M. de Villèle, the government of Louis XVIII. was ever consistent with itself; without false calculation or premeditated deceit, Charles X. wavered from contradiction to contradiction, from inconsistency to inconsistency, until the day when, given up to his own will and belief, he committed the error which cost him his throne.

During three years, from the accession of Charles X. to his own fall, M. de Villèle not only made no stand against the inconsiderate fickleness of the King, but even profited by it to strengthen himself against his various enemies. Too clear-sighted to hope that Charles X. would persevere in the voluntary course of premeditated and steady moderation which Louis XVIII. had followed, he undertook to make him at least pursue, when circumstances allowed, a line of policy sufficiently temperate and popular to save him from the appearance of being exclusively in the hands of the party to whom in fact his heart and faith were devoted. Skilful in varying his advice according to the necessities and chances of the moment, and aptly availing himself of the inclination of Charles X. for sudden measures, whether lenient or severe, M. de Villèle at one time abolished, and at another revived, the censorship of the journals, occasionally softened or aggravated the execution of the laws, always endeavouring, and frequently with success, to place in the mouth or in the name of the King, liberal demonstrations and effusions, by the side of words and tendencies which recalled the old system and the pretensions of absolute power. The same spirit governed him in the Chambers. His bills were so conceived and presented, as we may say, to the address of the different parties, that all influential opinions were conciliated to a certain extent. The indemnity to the emigrants satisfied the wishes and restored the position of the entire lay party of the right. The recognition of the Republic of Hayti pleased the Liberals. Judicious reforms in the national budget and an administration friendly to sound regulations and actual services, obtained for M. de Villèle the esteem of enlightened men and the general approbation of all public functionaries. The bill on the system of inheritance and the right of primogeniture afforded hope to those who were prepossessed with aristocratic regrets. The bill on sacrilege fostered the passions of the fanatics, and the views of their theorists. Parallel with the spirit of reaction which predominated in these legislative deliberations, as in the enactments of power, an intelligent effort was ever visible to contrive something to the advantage of the spirit of progress. While faithfully serving his friends, M. de Villèle sought for and availed himself of every opportunity that offered of making some compensation to his adversaries.

It was not that the state of his mind was changed in principle, or that he had identified himself with the new and liberally-disposed society which he courted with so much solicitude. After all, M. de Villèle continued ever to be a follower of the old system, true to his party from feeling as well as on calculation. But his ideas on the subject of social and political organization were derived from tradition and habit, rather than from personal and well-meditated conviction. He preserved, without making them his sole rule of conduct, and laid them aside occasionally, without renunciation. A strong practical instinct, and the necessity of success, were his leading characteristics; he had the peculiar tact of knowing what would succeed and what would not, and paused in face of obstacles, either judging them to be insurmountable, or to demand too much time for removal. I find, in a letter which he wrote on the 31st of October, 1824, to Prince Julius de Polignac, at that time ambassador in London, on the projected re-establishment of the law of primogeniture, the strong expression of his inward thought, and of his clear-sighted prudence in an important act. "You would be wrong to suppose," said he, "that it is because entailed titles and estates are perpetual, we do not create any. You give us too much credit; the present generation sets no value on considerations so far removed from their own time. The late King named Count K—— a peer, on the proviso of his investing an estate with the title; he gave up the peerage, rather than injure his daughter to the advantage of his son. Out of twenty affluent families, there is scarcely one inclined to place the eldest son so much above the rest. Egotism prevails everywhere. People prefer to live on good terms with all their children, and, when establishing them in the world, to show no preference. The bonds of subordination are so universally relaxed, that parents, I believe, are obliged to humour their own offspring. If the Government were to propose the re-establishment of the law of primogeniture, it would not have a majority on that question; the difficulty is more deeply seated; it lies in our habits, still entirely impressed with the consequences of the Revolution. I do not wish to say that nothing can be done to ameliorate this lamentable position; but I feel that, in a state of society so diseased, we require time and management, not to lose in a day the labour and fruit of many years. To know how to proceed, and never to swerve from that path, to make a step towards the desired end whenever it can be made, and never to incur the necessity of retreat,—this course appears to me to be one of the necessities of the time in which I have arrived at power, and one of the causes which have led me to the post I occupy."

M. de Villèle spoke truly; it was his rational loyalty to the interests of his party, his patient perseverance in marching step by step to his object, his calm and correct distinction between the possible and impossible, which had made and kept him minister. But in the great transformations of human society, when the ideas and passions of nations have been powerfully stirred up, good sense, moderation, and cleverness will not long suffice to control them; and the day will soon return when, either to promote good or restrain evil, defined convictions and intentions, strongly and openly expressed, are indispensable to the heads of government. M. de Villèle was not endowed with these qualities. His mind was accurate, rather than expanded; he had more ingenuity than vigour, and he yielded to his party when he could no longer direct it. "I am born for the end of revolutions," he exclaimed when arriving at power, and he judged himself well; but he estimated less correctly the general state of society: the Revolution was much further from its end than he believed; it was continually reviving round him, excited and strengthened by the alternately proclaimed and concealed attempts of the counter-principle. People had ceased to conspire; but they discussed, criticized, and contended with undiminished ardour in the legitimate field. There were no longer secret associations, but opinions which fermented and exploded on every side. And, in this public movement, impassioned resistance was chiefly directed against the preponderance and pretensions of the fanatically religious party. One of the most extraordinary infatuations of our days has been the blindness of this party to the fact that the conditions under which they acted, and the means they employed, were directly opposed to the end in view, and leading from rather than conducting to it. They desired to restrain liberty, to control reason, to impose faith; they talked, wrote, and argued; they sought and found arms in the system of inquiry and publicity which they denounced. Nothing could be more natural or legitimate on the part of believers who have full confidence in their creed, and consider it equal to the conversion of its adversaries. The latter are justified in recurring to the discussion and publicity which they expect to serve their cause. But those who consider publicity and free discussion as essentially mischievous, by appealing to these resources, foment themselves the movement they dread, and feed the fire they wish to extinguish. To prove themselves not only consistent, but wise and effective, they should obtain by other means the strength on which they rely: they should gain the mastery; and then, when they have silenced all opposition, let them speak alone, if they still feel the necessity of speaking. But until they have arrived at this point, let them not deceive themselves; by adopting the weapons of liberty, they serve liberty much more than they injure it, for they warn and place it on its guard. To secure victory to the system of order and government to which they aspire, there is but one road;—the Inquisition and Philip

II. were alone acquainted with their trade.

As might naturally be expected, the resistance provoked by the attempts of the fanatical party soon transformed itself into an attack. One royalist gentleman raised the flag of opposition against the policy of M. de Villèle; another assailed the religious controllers of his Cabinet, and not only dragged them before public opinion, but before the justice of the country, which disarmed and condemned them, without inflicting any other sentence than that of its disapprobation in the name of the law.

No one was less a philosopher of the eighteenth century, or a liberal of the nineteenth, than the Count de Montlosier. In the Constituent Assembly he had vehemently defended the Church and resisted the Revolution; he was sincerely a royalist, an aristocrat, and a Catholic. People called him, not without reason, the feudal publicist. But, neither the ancient nobility nor the modern citizens were disposed to submit to ecclesiastical dominion. M. de Montlosier repulsed it, equally in the name of old and new France, as he would formerly have denied its supremacy from the battlements of his castle, or in the court of Philip the Handsome. The early French spirit re-appeared in him, free, while respectful towards the Church, and as jealous of the laical independence of the State and crown, as it was possible for a member of the Imperial State Council to show himself.

At the same moment, a man of the people, born a poet and rendered still more poetical by art, celebrated, excited, and expanded, through his songs, popular instincts and passions in opposition to everything that recalled the old system, and above all against the pretensions and supremacy of the Church. M. Béranger, in his heart, was neither a revolutionist nor an unbeliever; he was morally more honest, and politically more rational, than his songs; but, a democrat by conviction as well as inclination, and carried away into license and want of forethought by the spirit of democracy, he attacked indiscriminately everything that was ungracious to the people, troubling himself little as to the range of his blows, looking upon the success of his songs as a victory achieved by liberty, and forgetting that religious faith and respect for things holy are nowhere more necessary than in the bosom of democratic and liberal associations. I believe he discovered this a little too late, when he found himself individually confronted by the passions which his ballads had fomented, and the dreams he had transformed to realities. He then hastened, with sound sense and dignity, to escape from the political arena, and almost from the world, unchanged in his sentiments, but somewhat regretful and uneasy for the consequences of the war in which he had taken such a prominent part. Under the Restoration, he was full of confidence and zeal, enjoying his popularity with modesty, and more seriously hostile and influential than any had ever been before him.

Thus, after six years of government by the right-hand party, and three of the reign of Charles X., matters had arrived at this point—that two of the chief royalist leaders marched at the head of an opposition, one against the Cabinet, and the other against the Clergy, both becoming from day to day more vigorous and extended, and that the Restoration enumerated a ballad-maker in the first rank of its most dangerous enemies.

This entire mischief and danger was universally attributed to M. de Villèle; on the right or on the left, in the saloons and the journals, amongst the Moderates and the extreme Radicals, he became more and more an object of attack and reproach. As the judicial bodies had acted in affairs which regarded religion, so the literary institutions, on questions which concerned their competence, eagerly seized the opportunity of manifesting their opposition. The University, compressed and mutilated, was in a state of utter discontent. The French Academy made it a duty of honour to protest, in an address which the King refused to receive, but which was nevertheless voted, against the new bill on the subject of the press, introduced to the Chamber in 1826, and withdrawn by the Cabinet three months afterwards. In his own Chamber of Peers, M. de Villèle found neither general goodwill nor a certain majority. Even at the Palais Bourbon and the Tuileries, his two strongholds, he visibly lost ground; in the Chamber of Deputies, the ministerial majority declined, and became sad even in triumph; at the court, several of the King's most trusty adherents, the Dukes de Rivière, de Fitz-James, and de Maillé, the Count de Glandères, and many others,—some through party spirit, and some from monarchical uneasiness,—desired the fall of M. de Villèle, and were already preparing his successors. Even the King himself, when any fresh manifestation of public feeling reached him, exclaimed pettishly, on entering his closet, "Always Villèle! always against Villèle!"

In truth, the injustice was shameful. If the right-hand party had held office for six years, and had used power so as to maintain it, if Charles X. had not only peaceably succeeded Louis XVIII., but had ruled without trouble, and even with some increase of popularity, it was to M. de Villèle, above all others, that they were indebted for these advantages. He had accomplished two difficult achievements, which might have been called great had they been more durable: he had disciplined the old royalist party, and from a section of the court, and a class which had never been really active except in revolutionary contests, he had established during six years a steady ministerial support; he had restrained his party and his power within the general limits of the Charter, and had exercised constitutional government for six years under a prince and with friends who were generally considered to understand it little, and to adopt it with reluctance. If the King and the right-hand party felt themselves in danger, it was themselves, and not M. de Villèle, whom they ought to have accused.

Nevertheless M. de Villèle, on his part, had no right to complain of the injustice to which he was exposed. For six years he had been the head of the Government; by yielding to the King and his partisans when he disapproved their intentions, and by continuing their minister when he could no longer prevent what he condemned, he had admitted the responsibility of the faults committed under his name and with his sanction, although in spite of himself. He endured the penalty of his weakness in the exercise of power, and of his obstinacy in retaining it under whatever sacrifices it might cost him. We cannot govern under a free system, to enjoy the merit and reap the fruit of success, while we repudiate the errors which lead to reverse.

Justice to M. de Villèle requires the acknowledgment that he never attempted to withdraw himself from the responsibility of his government, whether as regarded his own acts or his concessions to his friends. He was never seen to reproach the King or his party with the errors to which he became accessory. He knew how to preserve silence and endure the blame, even while he had the power of justification. In 1825, after the Spanish war, and during the financial debates to which it had given rise, M. de la Bourdonnaye accused him of having been the author of the contracts entered into in 1823, with M. Ouvrard, at Bayonne, for supplying the army, and which had been made the subject of violent attacks. M. de Villèle might have closed his adversary's mouth; for on the 7th of April, 1823, he had written to the Duke d'Angoulême expressly to caution him against M. Ouvrard and his propositions. He took no advantage of this, but contented himself with explaining to the King in a Council, when the Dauphin was present, the situation in which he was placed.

The Dauphin at once authorized him to make use of his letter. "No, Monseigneur," replied M. de Villèle; "let anything happen to me that Heaven pleases, it will be of little consequence to the country; but I should be guilty towards the King and to France, if, to exculpate myself from an accusation, however serious it may be, I should give utterance, beyond the walls of this cabinet, to a single word which could compromise the name of your Royal Highness."

When, notwithstanding his obstinate and confiding disposition, he saw himself seriously menaced, when the cries of "Down with the Ministers! Down with Villèle!" uttered by several battalions of the National Guard, both before and after the review by the King in the Champ-de-Mars on the 29th of April, 1827, had led to their disbanding, and had equally excited the public and disturbed the King himself,—when M. de Villèle felt distinctly that, both in the Chambers and at the , he was too much attacked and shaken to govern with efficiency, he resolutely adopted the course prescribed by the Charter and called for by his position; he demanded of the King the dissolution of the Chamber of Deputies, and a new general election, which should either re-establish or finally overthrow the Cabinet.

Charles X. hesitated; he dreaded the elections, and, although not disposed to support his Minister with more firmness, the chance of his fall, and doubt in the selection of his successors, disturbed him, as much as it was possible for his unreflecting nature to be disturbed. M. de Villèle persisted, the King yielded, and, in defiance of the electoral law which, in 1820, M. de Villèle and the right-hand party had enacted, in spite of their six years of power, in spite of all the efforts of Government to influence the elections, they produced a result in conformity with the state of general feeling,—a majority composed of different elements, but decidedly hostile to the Cabinet. After having carefully examined this new ground, and after having received from various quarters propositions of accommodation and alliance, M. de Villèle, having clearly estimated his chances of strength and durability, retired from office, and recommended the King to return towards the centre, and to call together a moderate Ministry, which he assisted him to construct. Charles X. received his new councillors as he quitted his old ones, with sadness and apprehension, not acting as he wished, and scarcely knowing whether what he did would tend to his advantage. More decided, not through superiority of mind, but by natural courage, the Dauphiness said to him, when she ascertained his resolution, "In abandoning M. de Villèle, you have descended the first step of your throne."

The political party of which M. de Villèle was the head, and which had its own peculiar destinies, with which those of royalty had never been closely allied, might indulge in more gloomy anticipations on their own account; they had employed and lost the only man, belonging to their own ranks, who was capable of showing them legitimately how to acquire and how to exercise power.

CHAPTER VII.: MY OPPOSITION.: 1820-1829.

MY RETIREMENT AT THE MAISONNETTE.—I PUBLISH FOUR INCIDENTAL
ESSAYS ON POLITICAL AFFAIRS: 1. OF THE GOVERNMENT OF FRANCE SINCE THE
RESTORATION, AND OF THE MINISTRY IN OFFICE (1820); 2. OF CONSPIRACIES AND
POLITICAL JUSTICE (1821); 3. OF THE RESOURCES OF THE GOVERNMENT AND THE
OPPOSITION IN THE ACTUAL STATE OF FRANCE (1821); 4. OF CAPITAL
PUNISHMENT FOR POLITICAL OFFENCES (1822).—CHARACTER AND EFFECT OF
THESE PUBLICATIONS.—LIMITS OF MY OPPOSITION.—THE CARBONARI.—VISIT
OF M. MANUEL.—I COMMENCE MY COURSE OF LECTURES ON THE HISTORY OF
THE ORIGIN OF REPRESENTATIVE GOVERNMENT.—ITS DOUBLE OBJECT.—THE
ABBÉ FRAYSSINOUS ORDERS ITS SUSPENSION.—MY HISTORICAL LABOURS.—ON
THE HISTORY OF ENGLAND; ON THE HISTORY OF FRANCE; ON THE RELATIONS
AND MUTUAL INFLUENCE OF FRANCE AND ENGLAND; ON THE PHILOSOPHIC
AND LITERARY TENDENCIES OF THAT EPOCH.—THE FRENCH REVIEW.—THE
GLOBE.—THE ELECTIONS OF 1827.—MY CONNECTIONS WITH THE SOCIETY, 'HELP
THYSELF AND HEAVEN WILL HELP THEE.'—MY RELATIONS WITH THE
ADMINISTRATION OF M. DE MARTIGNAC; HE AUTHORIZES THE REOPENING OF
MY COURSE OF LECTURES, AND RESTORES MY TITLE AS A STATE-
COUNCILLOR.—MY LECTURES (1828-1830) ON THE HISTORY OF CIVILIZATION IN
EUROPE AND IN FRANCE.—THEIR EFFECT.—I AM ELECTED DEPUTY FOR LISIEUX
(DECEMBER, 1829).

When I was struck from the list of State-Councillors, with MM. Royer-Collard, Camille
Jordan, and Barante, I received from all quarters testimonies of ardent sympathy. Disgrace
voluntarily encountered, and which imposes some sacrifices, flatters political friends and
interests indifferent spectators. I determined to resume, in the Faculty of Letters, my course of
modern history. We were then at the end of July. Madame de Condorcet offered to lend me for
several months a country-house, ten leagues from Paris, near Meulan. My acquaintance with her
had never been intimate; her political sentiments differed materially from mine; she belonged
thoroughly and enthusiastically to the eighteenth century and the Revolution: but she possessed
an elevated character, a strong mind, and a generous heart, capable of warm affection; a favour
offered by her sincerely, and for the sole pleasure of conferring it, might be received without
embarrassment. I accepted that which she tendered me, and with the beginning of August I
established myself at the Maisonnette, and there recommenced my literary labours.

At that time I was strongly attached, and have ever since remained so, to public life.
Nevertheless I have never quitted it without experiencing a feeling of satisfaction mixed with my
regret, as that of a man who throws off a burden which he willingly sustained, or who passes
from a warm and exciting atmosphere into a light and refreshing temperature. From the first
moment, my residence at the Maisonnette pleased me. Situated halfway up a hill, immediately
before it was the little town of Meulan, with its two churches, one lately restored for worship, the

other partly in ruins and converted into a magazine; on the right of the town the eye fell upon L'Ile Belle, entirely parcelled out into green meadows and surrounded by tall poplar-trees; in front was the old bridge of Meulan, and beyond it the extensive and fertile valley of the Seine. The house, not too small, was commodious and neatly arranged; on either side, as you left the dining-hall, were large trees and groves of shrubs; behind and above the mansion was a garden of moderate extent, but intersected by walks winding up the side of the hill and bordered by flowers. At the top of the garden was a small pavilion well suited for reading alone, or for conversation with a single companion. Beyond the enclosure, and still ascending, were woods, fields, other country-houses and gardens scattered on different elevations. I lived there with my wife and my son Francis, who had just reached his fifth year. My friends often came to visit me. In all that surrounded me, there was nothing either rare or beautiful. It was nature with her simplest ornaments, and family life in the most unpretending tranquillity. But nothing was wanting. I had space, verdure, affection, conversation, liberty, and employment,—the necessity of occupation, that spur and bridle which human indolence and mutability so often require. I was perfectly content. When the soul is calm, the heart full, and the mind active, situations the most opposite to those we have been accustomed to possess their charms, which speedily become happiness.

I sometimes went to Paris on affairs of business. I find, in a letter which I wrote to Madame Guizot during one of these journeys, the impressions I experienced. "At the first moment I feel pleasure at mixing again and conversing with the world, but soon grow weary of unprofitable words. There is no repetition more tiresome than that which bears upon popular matters. We are eternally listening to what we know already; we are perpetually telling others what they are as well acquainted with as we are: this is, at the same time, insipid and agitating. In my inaction, I prefer talking to the trees, the flowers, the sun, and the wind. Man is infinitely superior to nature; but nature is always equal, and inexhaustible in her monotony; we know that she remains and must remain what she is; we never feel in her presence that necessity of moving in advance, which makes us impatient or weary of the society of men when they fail to satisfy this imperative demand. Who has ever fancied that the trees ought to be red instead of green, or found fault with the sun of today for resembling the sun of yesterday? We demand of nature neither progress nor novelty; and this is why nature draws us from the weariness of the world, while she brings repose from its excitement. It is her attribute to please for ever without changing; but immovable man becomes tiresome, and he is not strong enough to be perpetually in motion."

In the bosom of this calm and satisfying life, public affairs, the part I had begun to take in them, the ties of mutual opinion and friendship I had formed, the hopes I had entertained for my country and myself, continued nevertheless to occupy much of my attention. I became anxious to declare aloud my thoughts on the new system under which France was governed; on what that system had become since 1814, and what it ought to be to keep its word and accomplish its object. Still a stranger to the Chambers, it was there alone that I could enter personally into the field of politics, and assume my fitting place. I was perfectly unfettered, and at an age when disinterested confidence in the empire of truth blends with the honest aspirations of ambition; I pursued the success of my cause, while I hoped for personal distinction. After residing for two months at the Maisonnette, I published, under this title, 'On the Government of France since the Restoration, and the Ministry now in Office,' my first oppositional treatise against the policy which had been followed since the Duke de Richelieu, by allying himself with the right-hand party to change the electoral law, had also changed the seat and tendency of power.

I took up the question, or, to speak more truly, I entered into the contest, on the ground on which the Hundred Days and the Chamber of 1815 had unfortunately placed it:—Who are to exercise, in the government of France, the preponderating influence? the victors or the vanquished of 1789? the middle classes, elevated to their rights, or the privileged orders of earlier times? Is the Charter the conquest of the newly constituted society, or the triumph of the old system, the legitimate and rational accomplishment, or the merited penalty of the revolution?

I borrow from a preface which I added last year to a new edition of my 'Course of Lectures on the History of Civilization in France,' some lines which today, after more than forty years of experience and reflection, convey the faithful impress of my thoughts.

"It is the blind rivalry of the high social classes, which has occasioned the miscarriage of our efforts to establish a free government. Instead of uniting either in defence against despotism, or to establish practical liberty, the nobility and the citizens have remained separate, intent on mutually excluding or supplanting each other, and both refusing to admit equality or superiority. Pretensions unjust in principal, and vain in fact! The somewhat frivolous pride of the nobility has not prevented the citizens of France from rising, and taking their place on a level with the highest in the State. Neither have the rather puerile jealousies of the citizens hindered the nobility from preserving the advantages of family celebrity and the long tenure of situation. In every arranged society which lives and increases there is an internal movement of ascent and acquisition. In all systems that are destined to endure, a certain hierarchy of conditions and ranks establishes and perpetuates itself. Justice, common sense, public advantage, and private interest, when properly understood, all require a reciprocal acknowledgment of these natural facts of social order. The different classes in France have not known how to adopt this skilful equity. Thus they have endured, and have also inflicted on their country, the penalty of their irrational egotism. For the vulgar gratification of remaining, on the one side insolent, on the other envious, nobles and citizens have continued much less free, less important, less secure in their social privileges, than they might have been with a little more justice, foresight, and submission to the divine laws of human associations. They have been unable to act in concert, so as to become free and powerful together; and consequently they have given up France and themselves to successive revolutions."

In 1820, we were far from this free and impartial appreciation of our political history and the causes of our disasters. Re-engaged for five years in the track of the old rivalries of classes and the recent struggles of revolution, we were entirely occupied with the troubles and dangers of the moment, and anxious to conquer, without bestowing much thought on the price or future embarrassments of victory. I upheld with enthusiasm the cause of the new society, such as the Revolution had made it, holding equality in the eye of the law as the first principle, and the middle classes as the fundamental element. I elevated this cause, already so great, by carrying it back to the past, and by discovering its interests and vicissitudes in the entire series of our history. I have no desire to palliate my thoughts or words. "For more than thirteen centuries," I said, "France has comprised two races, the victors and the vanquished. For more than thirteen centuries, the beaten race has struggled to throw off the yoke of its conquerors. Our history is the history of this contest. In our own days, a decisive battle has been fought. That battle is called the Revolution.... The result was not doubtful. Victory declared for those who had been so long subdued. In turn they conquered France, and in 1814 were in possession beyond dispute. The Charter acknowledged this fact, proclaimed that it was founded on right, and guaranteed that right by the pledge of representative government. The King, by this single act, established himself as the chief of the new conquerors. He placed himself in their ranks and at their head, engaging himself to defend with them, and for them, the conquests of the Revolution, which were theirs. The Charter implied such an engagement, beyond all question; for war was on the point of recommencing. It was easy to foresee that the vanquished party would not tamely submit to their defeat. Not that it reduced them to the condition to which they had formerly humiliated their adversaries; they found rights, if they lost privileges, and, while falling from high supremacy, might repose on equality; but great masses of men will not thus abdicate human weakness, and their reason ever remains far in the rear of their necessity. All that preserved or restored to the ancient possessors of privilege a gleam of hope, urged and tempted them to grasp it. The Restoration could not fail to produce this effect. The fall of privilege had entrained the subversion of the throne; it might be hoped that the throne would restore privilege with its own re-establishment. How was it possible not to cherish this hope? Revolutionary France held it in dread. But even if the events of 1814 had not effected the Restoration, if the Charter had been given to us from another source and by a different dynasty, the mere establishment of the representative system, the simple return to liberty, would have sufficed to inflame and rouse up once more to combat the old race, the privileged orders. They exist amongst us; they live, speak, circulate, act, and influence from one end of France to the other. Decimated and scattered by the Convention, seduced and kept under by Napoleon, as soon as terror and despotism cease (and neither are durable) they re-appear, resume position, and labour to recover all that they have lost.... We have conquered the old system, we shall always conquer it; but for a long time still we shall have to combat with it. Whoever wishes to see constitutional order established in France, free elections, independent Chambers, a tribune, liberty of the press, and all other public liberties, must abandon the idea that, in this perpetual and animated manifestation of all society, the counter-revolution can remain mute and inactive."

At the very moment when I recapitulated, in terms so positive and forcible, the situation in which the Revolution, the Restoration, and the Charter had placed France, I foresaw that my words and ideas might be perverted to the advantage of revolutionary passions; and to confine them within their just interpretation, I hastened to add, "In saying that, since the origin of our monarchy, the struggle between two races has agitated France, and that the Revolution has been merely the triumph of new conquerors over the ancient possessors of power and territory, I have not sought to establish any historical filiation, or to maintain that the double fact of conquest and servitude was perpetual, constant, and identical through all ages. Such an assertion would be evidently falsified by realities. During this long progression of time, the victors and the vanquished, the possessors and the possessions—the two races, in fact—have become connected, displaced, and confounded; in their existence and relations they have undergone innumerable vicissitudes. Justice, the total absence of which would speedily annihilate all society, has introduced itself into the effects of power. It has protected the weak, restrained the strong, regulated their intercourse, and has progressively substituted order for violence, and equality for oppression. It has rendered France, in fact, such as the world has seen her, with her immeasurable glory and her intervals of repose. But it is not the less true that throughout thirteen centuries, by the result of conquest and feudalism, France has always retained two positions, two social classes, profoundly distinct and unequal, which have never become amalgamated or placed in a condition of mutual understanding and harmony; which have never ceased to combat, the one to conquer right, the other to retain privilege. In this our history is comprised; and in this sense I have spoken of two races, victors and vanquished, friends and enemies; and of the war, sometimes open and sanguinary, at others internal and purely political, which these two conflicting interests have mutually waged against each other."

On reading over these pages at the present day, and my entire work of 1820, I retain the impression, which I still desire to establish. On examining things closely and by themselves, as an historian and philosopher, I scarcely find any passage to alter. I continue to think that the general ideas therein expressed are just, the great social facts properly estimated, the political personages well understood and drawn with fidelity. As an incidental polemic, the work is too positive and harsh; I do not sufficiently consider difficulties and clouds; I condemn situations and parties too strongly; I require too much from men; I have too little temperance, foresight, and patience. At that time I was too exclusively possessed by the spirit of opposition.

Even then I suspected this myself; and perhaps the success I obtained inspired the doubt. I am not naturally disposed to opposition; and the more I have advanced in life, the more I have become convinced that it is a part too easy and too dangerous. Success demands but little merit, while considerable virtue is requisite to resist the external and innate attractions. In 1820, I had as yet only filled an indirect and secondary position under the Government; nevertheless I fully understood the difficulty of governing, and felt a degree of repugnance in adding to it by attacking those to whom power was delegated. Another conviction began also from that time to impress itself upon me. In modern society, when liberty is displayed, the strife becomes too unequal between the party that governs and those who criticize Government. With the one rests all the burden and unlimited responsibility; nothing is looked over or forgiven: with the others there is perfect liberty and no responsibility; everything that they say or do is accepted and tolerated. Such is the public disposition, at least in France as soon as we become free. At a later period, and when in office, I endured the weight of this myself; but I may acknowledge without any personal reluctance, that while in Opposition I first perceived the unjust and injurious tendency of this feeling.

By instinct, rather than from any reflective or calculated intention, I conceived the desire, as soon as I had committed an act of declared hostility, of demonstrating what spirit of government was not foreign to my own views. Many sensible men inclined to think that from the representative system, in France at least, and in the state in which the Revolution had left us, no sound plan could emanate, and that our ardent longings for free institutions were only calculated to enervate power and promote anarchy. The Revolutionary and Imperial eras had naturally bequeathed this idea; France had only become acquainted with political liberty by revolutions, and with order by despotism; harmony between them appeared to be a chimera. I undertook to prove, not only that this chimera of great minds might become a reality, but that the realization depended upon ourselves; for the system founded by the Charter alone contained, for us, the essential means of regular government and of effective opposition, which the sincere friends of power and liberty could desire. My work, entitled, 'On the Means of Government and Opposition in the Actual State of France,' was entirely dedicated to this object.

In that treatise I entered into no general or theoretic exposition of policy, the idea of which I expressly repudiated. "Perhaps," I said, in my preface, "I may on some future occasion discuss more general questions of predominant interest in regard to the nature and principles of constitutional government, although their solution has nothing to do with existing politics, with the events and actors of the moment. I wish now to speak only of power as it is, and of the best method of governing our great and beautiful country." Entirely a novice and doctrinarian as I then was, I forgot that the same maxims and arts of government must be equally good everywhere, and that all nations and ages are, at the same moment, cast in a similar mould. I confined myself sedulously to my own time and country, endeavouring to show what effective means of government were included in the true principles and regular exercise of the institutions which France held from the Charter, and how they might be successfully put in practice for the legitimate advantage and strengthening of power. With respect to the means of opposition, I followed the same line of argument, convinced myself, and anxious to persuade the adversaries of the then dominant policy, that authority might be controlled without destroying it, and that the rights of liberty might be exercised without shaking the foundations of established order. It was my strong desire and prepossession to elevate the political arena above the revolutionary track, and to imbue the heart of the constitutional system with ideas of strong and legal conservatism.

Thirty-six years have since rolled on. During this long interval I participated, for eighteen of those years, in the efforts of my generation for the establishment of a free government. For some time I sustained the weight of this labour. That government has been overthrown. Thus I have myself experienced the immense difficulty, and endured the painful failure, of this great enterprise. Nevertheless, and I say it without sceptical hesitation or affected modesty, I read over again today what I wrote in 1821, upon the means of government and opposition in the actual state of France, with almost unmingled satisfaction. I required much from power, but nothing, I believe, that was not both capable and necessary of accomplishment. And notwithstanding my young confidence, I remembered, even then, that other conditions were essential to success. "I have no intention," I wrote, "to impute everything to, and demand everything from, power itself. I shall not say to it, as has often been said, 'Be just, wise, firm, and fear nothing;' power is not free to exercise this inherent and individual excellence. It does not make society, it finds it; and if society is impotent to second power, if the spirit of anarchy prevails, if the causes of dissolution exist in its own bosom, power will operate in vain; it is not given to human wisdom to rescue a people who refuse to co-operate in their own safety."

When I published these two attacks upon the attitude and tendencies of the Cabinet, conspiracies and political prosecutions burst forth from day to day, and entailed their tragical consequences. I have already said what I thought on the plots of that epoch, and why I considered them as ill based, as badly conducted, without legitimate motives or effectual means. But while I condemned them, I respected the sincere and courageous devotion of so many men, the greater part of whom were very young, and who, though mistaken, lavished the treasures of their minds and lives upon a cause which they believed to be just. Amongst the trials of our time, I scarcely recognize any more painful than that of these conflicting feelings, these perplexities between esteem and censure, condemnation and sympathy, which I have so often been compelled to bestow on the acts of so many of my contemporaries. I love harmony and light in the human soul as well as in human associations; and we live in an epoch of confusion and obscurity, moral as well as social.

How many men have I known, who, gifted with noble qualities, would in other times have led just and simple lives, but who, in our days, confounded in the problems and shadows of their own thoughts, have become ambitious, turbulent, and fanatical, not knowing either how to attain their object or how to continue in repose!

In 1820, although still young myself, I lamented this agitation of minds and destinies, almost as sad to contemplate as fatal to be engaged in; but while deploring it, I was divided between severe judgment and lenient emotion, and, without seeking to disarm power in its legitimate defence, I felt a deep anxiety to inspire it with generous and prudent equity towards such adversaries.

A true sentiment does not readily believe itself impotent. The two works which I published in 1821 and 1822, entitled, the first, 'On Conspiracies and Political Justice,' and the second, 'On Capital Punishment for Political Offences,' were not, on my part, acts of opposition; I endeavoured to divest them of this character. To mark distinctly their meaning and object, it will suffice for me to repeat their respective epigraphs. On the title-page of the first I inscribed this passage from the prophet Isaiah: "Say ye not, a confederacy, to all them to whom this people shall say, a confederacy;" and on that of the second, the words of St. Paul: "O death, where is thy sting? O grave, where is thy victory?" What I chiefly desired was to convince power itself that sound policy and true justice called for very rare examples of trial and execution in political cases; and that in exercising against all offenders the utmost severity of the laws, it created more perils than it subdued. Public opinion was in accordance with mine; sensible and independent men, taking no part in the passions of the parties engaged in this struggle, found, as I did, that there was excess in the action of the police with reference to these plots, excess in the number and severity of the prosecutions, excess in the application of legal penalties. I carefully endeavoured to restrain these complaints within their just limits, to avoid all injurious comparisons, all attempts at sudden reforms, and to concede to power its necessary weapons.

While discussing these questions, which had sprung up in the bosom of the most violent storms, I sought to transfer them to an elevated and temperate region, convinced that by that course alone my ideas and words would acquire any permanent efficacy. They obtained the sanction of a much more potent ally than myself. The Court of Peers, which at that time had assumed the place assigned to it by the Charter, in judgment on political prosecutions, immediately began to exercise sound policy and true discrimination. It was a rare and imposing sight, to behold a great assembly, essentially political in origin and composition,—a faithful supporter of authority; and at the same time sedulously watchful, not only to elevate justice above the passions of the moment, and to administer it with perfect independence, but also to apply, in the appreciation and punishment of political offences, that intelligent equity which alone could satisfy the reason of the philosopher and the charity of the Christian. A part of the honour due to this grand exhibition belongs to the authorities the time, who not only made no attempt to interfere with the unshackled impartiality of the Court of Peers, but refrained even from objection or complaint. Next to the merit of being themselves, and through their own convictions, just and wise, it is a real act of wisdom on the part of the great ones of the earth, when they adopt without murmur or hesitation the good which has not originated with themselves.

I have lived in an age of political plots and outrages, directed alternately against the authorities to whom I was in opposition and those I supported with ardour. I have seen conspiracies occasionally unpunished, and at other times visited by the utmost rigour of the law. I feel thoroughly convinced that in the existing state of feelings, minds, and manners, the punishment of death in such cases is an injurious weapon which heavily wounds the power that uses it for safety. It is not that this penalty is without denunciatory and preventive efficacy; it terrifies and holds back from conspiracies many who would otherwise be tempted to engage in them. But by the side of this salutary consequence, it engenders others which are most injurious. Drawing no line of distinction between the motives and dispositions which have incited men to the acts it punishes, it stifles in the same manner the reprobate and the dreamer, the criminal and the enthusiast, the wildly ambitious and the devotedly fanatical. By this gross indifference, it offends more than it satisfies moral feeling, irritates more than it restrains, moves indifferent spectators to pity, and appears to those who are interested an act of war falsely invested with the forms of a decree of justice. The intimidation which it conveys at first, diminishes from day to day; while the hatred and thirst of vengeance it inspires become hourly more intense and expansive; and at last the time arrives when the power which fancies itself saved is exposed to the attacks of enemies infinitely more numerous and formidable than those who have been previously disposed of.

A day will also come, I confidently feel, when, for offences exclusively political, the penalties of banishment and transportation, carefully graduated and applied, will be substituted in justice as well as in fact for the punishment of death. Meanwhile I reckon, amongst the most agreeable reminiscences of my life, the fact of my having strenuously directed true justice and good policy to this subject, at a moment when both were seriously compromised by party passions and the dangers to which power was exposed.

These four works, published successively within the space of two years, attracted a considerable share of public attention. The leading members of Opposition in the two Chambers thanked me as for a service rendered to the cause of France and free institutions. "You win battles for us without our help," said General Foy to me. M. Royer-Collard, in pointing out some objections to the first of these Essays ('On the Government of France since the Restoration'), added, "Your book is full of truths; we collect them with a shovel." I repeat without hesitation these testimonies of real approbation. When we seriously undertake to advocate political measures, either in speeches or publications, it becomes most essential to attain our object. Praise is doubly valuable when it conveys the certainty of success. This certainty once established, I care little for mere compliments, from which a certain degree of puerility and ridicule is inseparable; sympathy without affected words has alone a true and desirable charm. I had a right to set some value on that which the Opposition evinced towards me; for I had done nothing to gratify the passions or conciliate the prejudices and after-thoughts which fermented in the extreme ranks of the party.

I had as frankly supported royalty, as I had opposed the Cabinet; and it was evident that I had no desire to consign either the House of Bourbon or the Charter to their respective enemies.

Two opportunities soon presented themselves of explaining myself on this point in a more personal and precise manner. In 1821, a short time after the publication of my 'Essay on Conspiracies and Political Justice,' one of the leaders of the conspiring faction, a man of talent and honour, but deeply implicated in secret societies, that inheritance of tyrannical times which becomes the poison of freedom, came to see me, and expressed with much warmth his grateful acknowledgments. The boldest conspirators feel gratified, when danger threatens, by shielding themselves under the principles of justice and moderation professed by men who take no part in their plots. We conversed freely on all topics. As he was about to leave me, my visitor, grasping me by the arm, exclaimed, "Become one of ours!"—"Who do you call yours?"—"Enter with us into the Charbonnerie; it is the only association capable of overthrowing the Government by which we are humiliated and oppressed."—I replied, "You deceive yourself, as far as I am concerned; I do not feel humiliation or oppression either for myself or my country."—"What can you hope from the people now in power?"—"It is not a question of hope; I wish to preserve what we possess; we have all we require to establish a free government for ourselves. Actual power constantly calls for resistance. In my opinion it does so at this moment, but not to the extent of being subverted. It is very far from having done anything to give us either the right or the means of proceeding to that extremity. We have legal and public arms in abundance to produce reform by opposition. I neither desire your object nor your method of attaining it; you will bring much mischief on all, yourselves included, without success; and if you should succeed, matters would be still worse."

He went away without anger, for he felt a friendship for me; but I had not in the slightest degree shaken his passion for plots and secret societies. It is a fever which admits of no cure, when the soul is once given up to it, and a yoke not to be thrown off when it has been long endured.

A little later, in 1822, when the publications I have spoken of had produced their effect, I received one day a visit from M. Manuel. We had occasionally met at the houses of mutual friends, and lived on terms of good understanding without positive intimacy. He evidently came to propose closer acquaintanceship, with an openness in which perhaps the somewhat restricted character of his mind was as much displayed as the firmness of his temperament; he passed at once from compliments to confidence, and, after congratulating me on my opposition, opened to me the full bearing of his own. He neither believed in the Restoration nor the Charter, held the House of Bourbon to be incompatible with the France of the Revolution, and looked upon a change of dynasty as a necessary consequence of the total alteration in the social system. He introduced, in the course of our interview, the recent death of the Emperor Napoleon, the security which thence resulted to the peace of Europe, and the name of Napoleon II. as a possible and perhaps the best solution of the problems involved in our future. All this was expressed in guarded but sufficiently definite terms, equally without passion or circumlocution, and with a marked intention of ascertaining to what extent I should admit or reject the prospects on which he enlarged. I was unprepared, both for the visit and the conversation; but I stood on no reserve, not expecting to convert M. Manuel to my own views, and with no desire to conceal mine from him. "Far from thinking," I said in reply, "that a change of dynasty is necessary for France, I should look upon it as a great misfortune and a formidable peril. I consider the Revolution of 1789 to be satisfied as well as finished. In the Charter it possesses all the guarantees that its interests and legitimate objects require. I have no fear of a counter-revolution. We hold against it the power of right as well as of fact; and if people were ever mad enough to attempt it, we should always find sufficient strength to arrest their progress. What France requires at present is to expel the revolutionary spirit which still torments her, and to exercise the free system of which she is in full possession. The House of Bourbon is extremely well suited to this double exigence of the country. Its government is anti-revolutionary by nature, and liberal through necessity. I should much dread a power which, while maintaining order, would either in fact or appearance be sufficiently revolutionary to dispense with being liberal. I should be apprehensive that the country would too easily lend itself to such a rule. We require to be a little uneasy as regards our interests, that we may learn how to maintain our rights. The Restoration satisfies while it keeps us on our guard. It acts at the same time as a spur and a bridle. Both are good for us. I know not what would happen if we were without either." M. Manuel pressed me no longer; he had too much sense to waste time in useless words. We continued to discourse without further argument, and parted thinking well, I believe, of each other, but both thoroughly satisfied that we should never act in concert.

While engaged in the publication of these different treatises, I was also preparing my course of lectures on Modern History, which I commenced on the 7th of December, 1820. Determined to make use of the two influential organs with which public instruction and the press supplied me, I used them nevertheless in a very different manner. In my lectures, I excluded all reference to the circumstances, system, or acts of the Government; I checked every inclination to attack or even to criticize, and banished all remembrance of the affairs or contests of the moment. I scrupulously restrained myself within the sphere of general ideas and by-gone facts. Intellectual independence is the natural privilege of science, which would be lost if converted into an instrument of political opposition. For the effective display of different liberties, it is necessary that each should be confined within its own domain; their strength and security depend on this prudent restraint.

While imposing on myself this line of conduct, I did not evade the difficulty. I selected for the subject of my course the history of the old political institutions of Christian Europe, and of the origin of representative government, in the different forms in which it had been formerly attempted, with or without success. I touched very closely, in such a subject, on the flagrant embarrassments of that contemporaneous policy to which I was determined to make no allusion. But I also found an obvious opportunity of carrying out, through scientific paths alone, the double object I had in view. I was anxious to combat revolutionary theories, and to attach interest and respect to the past history of France. We had scarcely emerged from the most furious struggle against that old French society, our secular cradle; our hearts, if not still overflowing with anger, were indifferent towards it, and our minds were confusedly imbued with the ideas, true or false, under which it had fallen. The time had come for clearing out that arena covered with ruins, and for substituting, in thought as in fact, equity for hostility, and the principles of liberty for the arms of the Revolution. An edifice is not built with machines of war; neither can a free system be founded on ignorant prejudices and inveterate antipathies. I encountered, at every step throughout my course, the great problems of social organization, under the name of which parties and classes exchanged such heavy blows,—the sovereignty of the people and the right divine of kings, monarchy and republicanism, aristocracy and democracy, the unity or division of power, the various systems of election, constitution, and action of the assemblies called to co-operate in government. I entered upon all these questions with a firm determination to sift thoroughly the ideas of our own time, and to separate revolutionary excitement and fantasies from the advances of justice and liberty, reconcilable with the eternal laws of social order. By the side of this philosophic undertaking, I pursued another, exclusively historical; I endeavoured to demonstrate the intermitting but always recurring efforts of French society to emerge from the violent chaos in which it had been originally formed, sometimes produced by the conflict, and at others by the accordance of its different elements—royalty, nobility, clergy, citizens, and people,—throughout the different phases of that harsh destiny, and the glorious although incomplete development of French civilization, such as the Revolution had compiled it after so many combats and vicissitudes. I particularly wished to associate old France with the remembrance and intelligence of new generations; for there was as little sense as justice in decrying or despising our fathers, at the very moment when, equally misled in our time, we were taking an immense step in the same path which they had followed for so many ages.

I expounded these ideas before an audience little disposed to adopt or even to take any interest in them. The public who at that time attended my lectures were much less numerous and varied than they became some years later. They consisted chiefly of young men, pupils of the different scientific schools, and of a few curious amateurs of great historical disquisitions. The one class were not prepared for the questions I proposed, and wanted the preparatory knowledge which would have rendered them acceptable. With many of the rest, preconceived ideas of the eighteenth century and the Revolution, in matters of historical and political philosophy, had already acquired that strength, derived from inveterate habit, which rejects discussion, and listens coldly and distrustfully to all that differs from their own opinions. Others again, and amongst these were the most active and accessible dispositions, were more or less engaged in the secret societies, hostile intrigues and plots. With these, my opposition was considered extremely supine. I had thus many obstacles to surmount, and many conversions to effect, before I could bring over to my own views the small circle that listened to my arguments.

But there is always, in a French audience, whatever may be their prejudices, an intellectual elasticity, a relish for efforts of the mind and new ideas boldly set forward, and a certain liberal equity, which disposes them to sympathize, even though they may hesitate to admit conviction. I was at the same time liberal and anti-revolutionary, devoted to the fundamental principles of the new French social system, and animated by an affectionate respect for our ancient reminiscences. I was opposed to the ideas which constituted the political faith of the greater portion of my auditors. I propounded others which appeared suspicious to them, even while they seemed just; they considered me as made up of obscurities, contradictions, and prospective views, which astonished and made them hesitate to follow me. At the same time they felt that I was serious and sincere; they became gradually convinced that my historic impartiality was not indifference, nor my political creed a leaning towards the old system, nor my opposition to every kind of subversive plot a truckling complaisance for power. I gained ground in the estimation of my listeners: some amongst the most distinguished came decidedly over to my views; others began to entertain doubts on the soundness of their theories and the utility of their conspiring practices; nearly all agreed with my just appreciation of the past, and my recommendation of patient and legal opposition to the mistakes of the present. The revolutionary spirit in this young and ardent section of the public was visibly on the decline, not from scepticism and apathy, but because other ideas and sentiments occupied its place in their hearts, and drove it out to make room for their own admission.

The Cabinet of 1822 thought differently. It looked upon my lectures as dangerous; and on the 12th of October in that year, the Abbé Frayssinous, who a few months before had been appointed by M. de Villèle Head Master of the University, commanded me to suspend them. I made no complaint at the time, and I am not now astonished at the measure. My opposition to the Ministry was unconcealed, and although not in the slightest degree mixed up with my course of public instruction, many persons were unable to separate as distinctly as I did, in their impressions, my lectures on the history of past ages from my writings against the policy of the day. I am equally convinced that the Government, by sanctioning this proceeding, deceived itself to its own detriment. In the struggle which it maintained with the spirit of revolution, the ideas I propagated in my teaching were more salutary than the opposition I carried on through the press was injurious; they added more strength to the monarchy, than my criticisms on incidental questions and situations could abstract from the Cabinet. But my free language disturbed the blind partisans of absolute power in the Church and State, and the Abbé Frayssinous, short-witted and weak though honest, obeyed with inquietude rather than reluctance the influences whose extreme violence he dreaded without condemning their exercise.

In the division of the monarchical parties, that which I had opposed plunged more and more into exclusive and extreme measures. My lectures being interdicted, all immediate political influence became impossible to me. To struggle, beyond the circle of the Chambers, against the existing system, it was necessary either to conspire, or to descend to a blind, perverse, and futile opposition. Neither of these courses were agreeable; I therefore completely renounced all party contentions, even philosophical and abstracted, to seek elsewhere the means of still mentally serving my cause with reference to the future.

There is nothing more difficult and at the same time more important in public life, than to know how at certain moments to resign ourselves to inaction without renouncing final success, and to wait patiently without yielding to despair.

It was at this epoch that I applied myself seriously to the study of England, her institutions, and the long contests on which they were founded. Enthusiastically devoted to the political future of my own country, I wished to learn accurately through what realities and mistakes, by what persevering efforts and prudent acts, a great nation had succeeded in establishing and preserving a free government. When we compare attentively the history and social development of France and England, we find it difficult to decide by which we ought to be most impressed,—the differences or the resemblances. Never have two countries, with origin and position so totally distinct, been more deeply associated in their respective destinies, or exercised upon each other, by the alternate relations of peace and war, such continued influence. A province of France conquered England; England for a long time held possession of several provinces of France; and on the conclusion of this national strife, already the institutions and political wisdom of the English were, with the most political spirits of the French, with Louis XI. and Philip de Comines, for example, subjects of admiration. In the bosom of Christianity the two nations have served under different religious standards; but this very distinction has become between them a new cause of contact and intermixture. In England the French Protestants, and in France the persecuted English Catholics, have sought and found an asylum. And when kings have been proscribed in their turn, in France the monarch of England, and in England the sovereign of France, was received and protected. From these respective havens of safety, Charles II., in the seventeenth century, and Louis XVIII. in the nineteenth, departed to resume their dominions. The two nations, or, to speak more correctly, the high classes of the two nations, have mutually adopted ideas, manners, and fashions from each other. In the seventeenth century, the court of Louis XIV. gave the tone to the English aristocracy. In the eighteenth, Paris went to London in search of models. And when we ascend above these historical incidents to consider the great phases of civilization in the two countries, we find that, after considerable intervals in the course of ages, they have followed nearly the same career; and that similar attempts and alternations of order and revolution, of absolute power and liberty, have occurred in both, with singular coincidences and equally remarkable distinctions.

It is, therefore, on a very superficial and erroneous survey that some persons look upon French and English society as so essentially different, that the one could not draw political examples from the other except by factitious and barren imitations. Nothing is more completely falsified by true history, and more opposed to the natural bias of the two countries. Their very rivalries have never broken the ties, apparent or concealed, that exist between them; and, whether they know or are ignorant of it, whether they acknowledge or deny the fact, they cannot avoid being powerfully acted upon, by each other; their ideas, their manners, and their institutions intermingle and modify mutually, as if by an amicable necessity.

Let me at the same time admit, without hesitation, that we have sometimes borrowed from England too completely and precipitately. We have not sufficiently calculated the true character and social condition of French society. France has increased and prospered under the influence of royalty seconding the ascending movement of the middle classes; England, by the action of the landed aristocracy, taking under its charge the liberties of the people. These distinctions are too marked to disappear, even under the controlling uniformity of modern civilization. We have too thoroughly forgotten them. It is the rock and impediment in the way of innovations accomplished under the name of general ideas and great examples, that they do not assume their legitimate part in real and national facts. But how could we have escaped this rock? In the course of her long existence, ancient France has made, at several regular intervals, great efforts to obtain free government. The most powerful influences have either resisted, or failed in the attempt; her best institutions have not co-operated with the necessary changes, or have remained politically ineffective; nevertheless, by a just sentiment of her honour as of her interest, France has never ceased to aspire to a true and permanent system of political guarantees and liberties. She demanded and desired this system in 1789. Through what channels was it sought? From what institution was it expected? So often deceived in her hopes and attempts within, she looked beyond home for lessons and models,—a great additional obstacle to a work already so difficult, but an inevitable one imposed by necessity.

In 1823, I was far from estimating the obstacles which beset us in our labour of constitutional organization as correctly as I do now. I was impressed with the idea that our predecessors of 1789 had held old France, her social traditions and her habits, in too much contempt; and that to bring back harmony with liberty into our country, we ought to lay more stress on our glorious past. At the same moment, therefore, when I placed before the eyes of the French public the history and original monuments of the institutions and revolutions of England, I entered with ardour into the study and exposition of the early state of French society, its origin, laws, and different gradations of development. I was equally desirous to give to my readers information on a great foreign history, and to revive amongst them a taste and inclination for the study of our own.

My labours were certainly in accord with the instincts and requirements of the time; for they were received and seconded by the general movement which then manifested itself in the public mind, and with reference to the Government so much a subject of dispute. It is the happy tendency of the French temperament to change the direction of its course without slackening speed. It is singularly flexible, elastic, and prolific. An obstacle impedes it, it opens another path; if burdened by fetters, it still walks on while bearing them; if restrained on a given point, it leaves it, and rebounds elsewhere. The Government of the right-hand party restrained political life and action within a narrow circle, and rendered them more difficult; the generation which was then beginning to stir in the world, sought, not entirely independent of, but side by side with politics, the employment of its strength and the gratification of its desires: literature, philosophy, history, policy, and criticism assumed a new and powerful flight. While a natural and unfortunate reaction brought back into the field of combat the eighteenth century with its old weapons, the nineteenth displayed itself with its original ideas, tendencies, and features.

I do not quote particular names; those which deserve to be remembered require no repetition; it is the general character of the intellectual movement of the period that I wish to bring into light. This movement was neither exclusively nor directly applied to politics, yet it was from politics that it emanated; it was both literary and philosophic: the human mind, disengaging itself from the interests and disputes of the day, pressed forward through every path that presented itself, in the search and enjoyment of the true and beautiful; but the first impulse came from political liberty, and the hope of contributing to the establishment of a free system was plainly perceptible in the most abstract labours as in the most poetic flights. My friends and I, while originating in 1827 one of the leading periodicals of the age, the 'Revue Française,' selected for its motto this verse of Ovid,—

"Et quod nunc ratio est, impetus ante fuit:"—

"What is now reason, was at first an impulse of passion."

We thus truly conveyed the prevailing spirit around us, and our own personal conviction. The 'Revue Française' was devoted to philosophy, history, literary criticism, and moral and scientific lucubrations; at the same time it was impregnated with the grand political inspirations which for forty years had agitated France. We declared ourselves distinct from our precursors of 1789, strangers to their passions, and not enslaved to their ideas, but inheritors and continuators of their work. We undertook to bring back the new French society to purer principles, to more elevated and equitable sentiments, and to firmer foundations; to that great subject of interest, to the accomplishment of its legitimate hopes and the assurance of its liberties, our efforts and desires were incessantly directed.

Another miscellany, commenced in 1824, and more popular than the 'Revue'—the 'Globe'— bore the same features in a polemic of greater animation and variety. Some young doctrinarians, associated with other writers of the same class, and animated by the same spirit, although with primary ideas and ultimate tendencies of a very different character, were the ordinary editors. Their distinguishing symbols were, in philosophy, spiritualism; in history, intelligent inquiry, impartial and even sympathetic as regarded ancient times and the progressive conditions of human society; in literature, a taste for novelty, variety, liberty, and truth, even under the strangest forms and the most incongruous associations. They defended, or rather advanced their banner with the ardour and pride of youth; enjoying, in their attempts at philosophical, historical, poetical, and critical reform, the satisfaction, at once personal and disinterested, which forms the sweetest reward of intellectual activity; and promising themselves, as always happens, a too extensive and too easy success. Two faults were mingled with these generous aspirations: the ideas developed in the 'Globe' were deficient in a fixed basis and a defined limit; their form was more decided than their foundation; they exhibited minds animated by a noble impulse, but not directed to any single or certain end; and open to an easy, unrestricted course, which excited apprehension that they might themselves drift towards the rocks they cautioned others to avoid. At the same time the spirit of partisanship, inclining men to be wrapped up and isolated in the narrow circle of their immediate associates, without remembering the general public for whom they labour and to whom they speak, exercised too much influence in the pages of the 'Globe.' Turgot intended to write several articles for the 'Encyclopædia.' D'Alembert came one day to ask him for them. Turgot declined: "You incessantly say we," he replied; "the public will soon say you; I do not wish to be so enrolled and classed." But these faults of the 'Globe,' apparent today, were concealed, thirty years ago, by the merit of its opposition; for political opposition was at the bottom of this miscellany, and obtained favour for it with many in the party opposed to the Restoration, to whom its philosophical and literary opinions were far from acceptable. In February, 1830, under the ministry of M. de Polignac, the 'Globe,' yielding to its inclination, became decidedly a great political journal; and from his retirement at Carquerannes, near Hyères, where he had gone to reconcile his labour with his health, M. Augustine Thierry wrote to me as follows:—"What think you of the 'Globe' since it has changed its character? I know not why I am vexed to find in it all those trifling points of news and daily discussion. Formerly we concentrated our thoughts to read it, but now that is no longer possible; the attention is distracted and divided. There are still the same spirit and the same articles, but it is disagreeable to encounter by their side these commonplace and every-day matters." M. Augustine Thierry was right. The 'Globe' sank materially by becoming a political journal, like so many others; but it had not been the less essentially political from its commencement, in tendency and inspiration. Such was the general spirit of the time; and, far from avoiding this, the 'Globe' was deeply impregnated with it.

Even under the controlling influence of the right-hand party, the Restoration made no attempt to stifle this actual but indirect opposition, which they felt to be troublesome though not openly hostile: justice requires that we should remember this to the credit of that epoch. In the midst of the constant alarms excited by political liberty and the efforts of power to restrain it, intellectual freedom maintained itself and commanded respect. This freedom does not supply all the rest; but it prepares them, and, while their accomplishment is suspended, preserves the honour of nations who have not yet learned to conquer or preserve their rights.

While this movement of the mind developed itself and gained strength from day to day, the Government of M. de Villèle pursued its course, more and more perplexed by the pretensions and quarrels of the party which its leader vainly to restrain. One of my friends, endowed with penetrating and impartial judgment, thus wrote to me in December, 1826, from the interior of his department:—"Men who are at the head of a faction are really destined to tremble before their own shadow. I cannot recollect any time when this nullity of the ruling party was more complete.

They do not propound a single doctrine or conviction, or a hope for the future. Even declamation itself seems to be exhausted and futile. Surely M. de Villèle must be allowed the merit of being well acquainted with their helplessness; his success springs from that cause; but this I look upon as an instinctive knowledge: he represents without correctly estimating these people. Otherwise he would discover that he might refuse them everything except places and appointments; provided also that he lends himself to no connection with opposite opinions." When the party, proceeding from exigence to exigence, and the Cabinet from weakness to weakness, found themselves unable to act longer together,—when M. de Villèle, in November 1827, appealed to an election for defence against his rivals in the Chamber and at Court,—we resolutely encountered our share in the contest. Every opposition combined. Under the motto, Aide-toi, le Ciel t'aidera, "Help thyself, and Heaven will help thee," a public association was formed, in which was comprised men of very different general ideas and definitive intentions, who acted in concert with the sole design of bringing about, by legal measures, a change of the majority in the Chamber of Deputies, and the fall of the Cabinet. I as readily joined them, with my friends, as in 1815 I had repaired alone to Ghent to convey to the King, Louis XVIII., the wishes of the constitutional Royalists. Long revolutions engender two opposite vices, rashness and pusillanimity; men learn from them either to plunge blindly into mad enterprises, or to abstain timidly from the most legitimate and necessary actions. We had openly opposed the policy of the Cabinet; it now challenged us to the electoral field to decide the quarrel: we entered it with the same frankness, resolved to look for nothing beyond fair elections, and to accept the difficulties and chances, at first of the combat, and afterwards of the success, if success should attend our efforts.

In the 'Biography' which Béranger has written of himself, I find this paragraph:—"At all times I have relied too much on the people, to approve of secret associations, in reality permanent conspiracies, which uselessly compromise many persons, create a host of inferior rival ambitions, and render questions of principle subordinate to private passions. They rapidly produce suspicion, an infallible cause of defection and even of treachery, and end, when the labouring classes are called in to co-operate, by corrupting instead of enlightening them.... The society, Aide-toi, le Ciel t'aidera, which acted openly, has alone rendered true service to our cause." The cause of M. Béranger and ours were totally distinct. Which of the two would profit most by the electoral services derived from the society of Aide-toi, le Ciel t'aidera? The question was to be speedily solved by the King, Charles X.

The results of the election of 1827 were enormous; they greatly exceeded the fears of the Cabinet and the hopes of the Opposition. I was still in the country when these events became known. One of my friends wrote to me from Paris, "The consternation of the Ministers, the nervous attack of M. de Villèle, who sent for his physician at three o'clock in the morning, the agony of M. de Corbières, the retreat of M. de Polignac to the country, from whence he has no intention to return, although he may be vehemently requested to do so, the terror at the palace, the ever brilliant shooting-parties of the King, the elections so completely unexpected, surprising, and astounding,—here are more than subjects enough to call for prophecies, and to give rise to false predictions on every consequence that may be anticipated." The Duke de Broglie, absent, like myself, from Paris, looked towards the future with more confident moderation. "It will be difficult," he wrote to me, "for the general sound sense which has presided at these elections not to react, to a certain extent, on the parties elected. The Ministry which will be formed during the first conflict, will be poor enough; but we must support it, and endeavour to suppress all alarm. It has already reached me here, that the elections have produced great apprehensions; if I am not deceived, this terror is nothing more than a danger of the moment. If, after the fall of the present Ministry, we are able to get through the year quietly, we shall have won the victory."

When the Ministry of M. de Villèle fell, and the Cabinet of M. de Martignac was installed, a new attempt at a Government of the Centre commenced, but with much less force, and inferior chances of success, than that which in 1816 and 1821, under the combined and separate directions of the Duke de Richelieu and M. Decazes, had defended France and the crown against the supremacy of the right and left-hand parties. The party of the centre, formed at that time under a pressing danger of the country, had drawn much strength from that very circumstance, and either from the right or the left had encountered nothing but animated opposition, but still raw and badly organized, and such as in public estimation was incapable of government. In 1828, on the contrary, the right hand-party, only just ejected from power, after having held it for six years, believed that they were as near recovering as they were capable of exercising office, and attacked with exuberant hope the suddenly created successors who had stepped into their places. In other quarters, the left and the left centre, brought into contact and almost confounded by six years of common opposition, reciprocated mutual understanding in their relations with a Cabinet which they were called on to support, although not emanating from their ranks. As it happens in similar cases, the violent and extravagant members of the party, paralyzed or committed the more moderate and rational to a much greater extent than the latter were able to restrain and guide their troublesome associates. Thus assailed in the Chambers by ambitious and influential rivals, the rising power found there only lukewarm or restrained allies. While from 1816 to 1821 the King, Louis XVIII., gave his sincere and active co-operation to the Government of the Centre, in 1828 the King, Charles X., looked upon the Cabinet which replaced immediately round him the leaders of the right-hand party as an unpleasant trial he was doomed to undergo; but to which he submitted with uneasy reluctance, not believing in its success, and fully determined to endure it no longer than strict necessity compelled.

In this weak position, two individuals, M. de Martignac, as actual head of the Cabinet, without being president, and M. Royer-Collard, as president of the Chamber of Deputies, alone contributed a small degree of strength and reputation to the new Ministry; but they were far from being equal to its difficulties or dangers.

M. de Martignac has left on the minds of all who were acquainted with him, either in public or private life, whether friends or adversaries, a strong impression of esteem and goodwill. His disposition was easy, amiable, and generous; his mind just, quick, and refined, at once calm and liberal; he was endowed with natural, persuasive, clear, and graceful eloquence; he pleased even those from whom he differed. I have heard M. Dupont de l'Eure whisper gently from his place, while listening to him, "Be silent, Siren!" In ordinary times, and under a well-settled constitutional system, he would have been an effective and popular minister; but either in word or act he had more seduction than authority, more charm than power. Faithful to his cause and his friends, he was unable to carry either into government or political debate that simple, fervent, and persevering energy, that insatiable desire and determination to succeed, which rises before obstacles and under defeats, and often wills without absolutely converting opinions. On his own account, more honest and epicurean than ambitious, he held more to duty and pleasure than to power. Thus, although well received by the King and the Chambers, he neither exercised at the Tuileries nor at the Palais Bourbon the authority, nor even the influence, which his sound mind and extraordinary talent ought to have given to him.

M. Royer-Collard, on the contrary, had reached and occupied the chair of the Chamber of Deputies through the importance derived from twelve years of parliamentary contest, recently confirmed by seven simultaneous elections, and by the distinguished mark of esteem which the Chamber and the King had conferred on him. But this importance, real in moral consideration, was politically of little weight. Since the failure of the system of government he had supported, and his own dismissal from the State Council by M. de Serre in 1820, M. Royer-Collard had, I will not say fallen, but entered into a state of profound despondency. Some sentences in letters written to me from his estate at Château-vieux, where he had passed the summer, will more readily explain the condition of his mind at that time. I select the shortest:—

"Aug. 1, 1823.—There is no trace of man here, and I am ignorant of what can be found in the papers; but I do not believe there is anything more to hear. At all events, I am careless on the subject. I have no longer any curiosity, and I well know the reason. I have lost my cause, and I much fear you will lose yours also; for you assuredly will as soon as it becomes a bad one. In these sad reflections the heart closes itself up, but without resignation."

"Aug. 27, 1826.—There cannot be a more perfect or innocent solitude than that in which I have lived until this last week, which has brought M. de Talleyrand to Valençay. It is only through your letter and his conversation, that I am again connected with the world. I have never before so thoroughly enjoyed this kind of life,—some hours devoted to study, the meditations they occasion, a family walk, and the care of a small, domestic administration. Nevertheless, in the midst of this profound tranquillity, on observing what passes, and what we have to expect, the fatigue of a long life entirely wasted in wishes unaccomplished and hopes deceived, makes itself sensibly felt. I hope I shall not give way under it; in the place of illusions, there are still duties which assert their claims."

"Oct. 22, 1826.—After having thoroughly enjoyed this year of the country and of solitude, I shall return with pleasure to the society of living minds. At this moment that society is extremely calm; but without firing cannon, it gains ground, and insensibly establishes its power. I have formed no idea of the coming session. I believe it to be merely through habit and remembrance, that any attention is yet paid to the Chamber of Deputies. It belongs to another world; our time is still distant, fortune has thrown you into the only course of life which has now either dignity or utility. It has done well for you and for us."

M. Royer-Collard was too ambitious and too speedily cast down. Human affairs do not permit so many expectations, and supply greater resources. We should expect less, and not so soon give way to despair. The elections of 1827, the advent of the Martignac Ministry, and his own situation in the chair of the Chamber of Deputies, drew M. Royer-Collard a little from his despondency, but without much restoring his confidence. Satisfied with his personal position, he supported and seconded the Cabinet in the Chamber, but without warmly adopting its policy; preserving carefully the attitude of a gracious ally who wishes to avoid responsibility. In his intercourse with the King he held the same reserve, speaking the truth, and offering sage advice, but without in the slightest degree conveying the idea that he was ready to put in practice the energetic and consistent policy he recommended. Charles X. listened to him with courtesy and surprise, confiding in his loyalty, but scarcely understanding his words, and regarding him as an honest man tainted with inapplicable or even dangerous ideas. Sincerely devoted to the King, and friendly to the Cabinet, M. Royer-Collard served them advantageously in their daily affairs and perils, but held himself always apart from their destiny as from their acts, and without bringing to them, through his co-operation, the strength which ought to have attached to the superiority of his mind and the influence of his name.

I did not at that time return to public office. The Cabinet made no such proposition to me, and I refrained from suggesting it; on either side we were right. M. de Martignac came from the ranks of M. de Villèle's party, and was obliged to keep measures with them; it would not have been consistent in him to hold intimate relations with their adversaries. For my own part, even though I should consider it necessary, I am badly adapted to serve a floating system of policy, which resorts to uncertain measures and expedients instead of acting on fixed and declared ideas. At a distance, I was both able and willing to support the new Ministry. In a close position I should have compromised them. I had, however, my share in the triumph. Without calling me back to exercise the functions of State-Councillor, the title was restored to me; and the Minister of Public Instruction, M. de Vatimesnil, authorized the reopening of my course.

I retain a deep impression of the Sorbonne which I then entered, and of the lectures I delivered there during two years. This was an important epoch in my life, and perhaps I may be permitted to add, a moment of influence on my country. With more care even than in 1821, I kept my lectures free of politics. Not only did I abstain from opposition to the Martignac Ministry, but I scrupulously avoided embarrassing them in the slightest degree. In other respects, I proposed an object to myself sufficiently important, as I thought, to occupy my entire attention. I was anxious to study and describe, in their parallel development and reciprocal action, the various elements of our French society, the Roman world, the Barbarians, the Christian Church, the Feudal System, the Papacy, Chivalry, Monarchy, the Commonalty, the Third Estate, and Reform. I desired not only to satisfy the scientific or philosophic curiosity of the public, but to accomplish a double end, real and practical. I proposed to demonstrate that the efforts of our time to establish a system of equal and legal justice in society, and also of political guarantees and liberties in the State, were neither new nor extraordinary,—that in the course of her history, more or less obscurely or unfortunately, France had at several intervals embraced this design, and that the generation of 1789, grasping it with enthusiasm, had committed both good and evil,—good, in resuming the glorious attempt of their ancestors,—evil in attributing to themselves the invention and the honour, and in believing that they were called upon to create, through their own ideas and wishes, a world entirely new. Thus, while promoting the interests of existing society, I was desirous of bringing back amongst us a sentiment of justice and sympathy for our early recollections and ancient customs; for that old French social system which had lived actively and gloriously for fifteen centuries, to accumulate the inheritance of civilization which we have gathered. It is a lamentable mistake, and a great indication of weakness, in a nation, to forget and despise the past. It may in a revolutionary crisis rise up against old and defective institutions; but when this work of destruction is accomplished, if it still continues to treat its history with contempt, if it persuades itself that it has completely broken with the secular elements of its civilization, it is not a new state of society which it can then form, it is the disorder of revolution that it perpetuates. When the generation who possess their country for a moment, indulge in the absurd arrogance of believing that it belongs to them, and them alone; and that the past, in face of the present, is death opposed to life; when they reject thus the sovereignty of tradition and the ties which mutually connect successive races, they deny the distinction and pre-eminent characteristic of human nature, its honour and elevated destiny; and the people who resign themselves to this flagrant error, also fall speedily into anarchy and decline; for God does not permit that nature and the laws of His works should be forgotten and outraged to such an extent with impunity.

During my course of lectures from 1828 to 1830, it was my prevailing idea to contend against this injurious tendency of the public mind, to bring it back to an intelligent and impartial appreciation of our old social system, to inspire an affectionate respect for the early history of France; and thus to contribute, as far as I could, to establish between the different elements of our ancient and modern society, whether monarchical, aristocratic, or popular, that mutual esteem and harmony which an attack of revolutionary fever may suspend, but which soon becomes once more indispensable to the liberty as well as to the prosperity of the citizens, to the strength and tranquillity of the State.

I had some reason to think that I succeeded to a great extent in my design. My audience, numerous and diversified, youths and experienced men, natives and foreigners, appeared to take a lively interest in the ideas I expounded. These notions assimilated with the general impressions of their minds, without demanding complete subservience, so as to combine the charms of sympathy and novelty. My listeners found themselves, not thrown back into retrograding systems, but urged forward in the path of just and liberal reflection. By the side of my historical lessons, but without concert, and in spite of wide differences of opinion between us, literary and philosophic instruction received from my two friends, MM. Villemain and Cousin, a corresponding character and impulse. Opposite breezes produced the same movement; we bestowed no thought on the events and questions of the day, and we felt no desire to bring them to the attention of the public by whom we were surrounded. We were openly and freely devoted to great general interests, great recollections, and great hopes for man and human associations; caring only to propagate our ideas, not indifferent as to their possible results, but not impatient to attain them; gratified by the intellectual advance in the midst of which we lived, and confident in the ultimate ascendency of the truth which we flattered ourselves we should possess and in the liberty we hoped to enjoy.

It would certainly have been profitable for us, and as I also believe for the country, if this intention could have been prolonged, and if our minds could have fortified themselves in their calm meditations before being once more engaged in the passions and trials of active life. But, as it happens almost invariably, the errors of men stepped in to interrupt the progress of ideas by precipitating the course of events. The Martignac Ministry adopted a moderate and constitutional policy. Two bills, honestly intended and ably discussed, had given effectual guarantees, the one, to the independence of elections, and the other, to the liberty of the press. A third, introduced at the opening of the session of 1829, secured to the elective principle a share in the administration of the departments and townships, and imposed on the central Government new rules and limitations for local affairs. These concessions might be considered too extensive or too narrow; but in either case they were real, and the advocates of public liberty could do nothing better than accept and establish them. But in the Liberal party who had hitherto supported the Cabinet, two feelings, little politic in their character, the spirit of impatience and the love of system, the desire for popularity and the severity of reason, were indisposed to be satisfied with those slow and imperfect conquests. The right-hand party, by refusing to vote, left the Ministry in contest with the wants of their allies. Despite the efforts of M. de Martignac, an amendment, more formidable in appearance than in reality, attacked in some measure the plan of the bill upon departmental administration. With the King, and also with the Chambers, the Ministry had reached the term of its credit; unable to obtain from the King what would give confidence to the Chambers, or from the Chambers what would satisfy the King, it voluntarily declared its impotence by hastily withdrawing the two bills, and still remained standing, although struck by a mortal wound.

How could it be replaced? The question remained in suspense for three months. Three men alone, M. Royer-Collard, M. de Villèle, and M. de Châteaubriand seemed capable of forming a new Cabinet that might last, although compounded of very different shades. The two first were entirely out of the question. Neither the King nor the Chambers contemplated the idea of making a Prime Minister of M. Royer-Collard. He perhaps had thought of it himself, more than once, for nothing was too bold to cross his mind in his solitary reveries; but these were merely inward lucubrations, not actually ambitious designs; if power had been offered to him he would assuredly have refused it; he had too little confidence in the future, and too much personal pride, to encounter such a risk of failure.

M. de Villèle, still suffering from the accusations first whispered against him in 1828, and which had remained in abeyance in the Chamber of Deputies, had formally refused to attend the session of 1829, and held himself in retirement at his estate near Toulouse; it was evident that he could not return to power, and act with the Chamber that had thrown him out. Neither the King nor himself would have consented, as I think, to encounter at that time the hazard of a new dissolution.

M. de Châteaubriand was at Rome. On the formation of the Cabinet of M. de Martignac he had accepted that embassy, and from thence, with a mixture of ambition and contempt he watched the uncertain policy and wavering position of the Ministers at Paris. When learned that they were beaten, and would in all probability be compelled to retire, he immediately commenced an active agitation. "You estimate correctly my surprise," he wrote to Madame Recamier, "at the news of the withdrawal of the two bills. Wounded self-love makes men children, and gives them very bad advice. What will be the end of all this? Will the Ministers endeavour to hold place? Will they retire partially or all together? Who will succeed them? How is a Cabinet to be composed? I assure you that, were it not for the pain of losing your society, I should rejoice at being here, out of the way, and at not being mixed up in all these enmities and follies, for I find that all are equally in the wrong.... Attend well to this; here is something more explicit: if by chance the portfolio of Foreign Affairs should be offered to me (and I have no reason to expect it), I should not refuse. I should come to Paris, I should speak to the King, I should arrange a Ministry without being included in it; for myself, I should propose, to attach me to my own work, a suitable position. I think, as you know, that it belongs to my ministerial reputation, as well as to revenge me for the injury I sustained from Villèle, that the portfolio of Foreign Affairs should be given to me for the moment. This is the only honourable mode in which I could rejoin the Administration. But that done, I should immediately retire, to the great satisfaction of all new aspirants, and pass the remainder of my life near you in perfect repose."

M. de Châteaubriand was not called to enjoy this haughty vengeance, or to exhibit such a demonstration of generosity. While he still dreamed of it in the Pyrenees, whither he had repaired to rest from the labours of the Conclave which gave Pius VIII. as successor to Leo X., the Prince de Polignac, brought over from London by the King, arrived in Paris on the 27th of July; and on the 9th of August, eight days after the closing of the session, his Cabinet was officially announced in the 'Moniteur.' What course would he propose to himself? What measures would he adopt? No one could tell; not even M. de Polignac and the King themselves any more than the public. But Charles X. had hoisted upon the Tuileries the flag of the Counter-Revolution.

Politics soon became the absorbing consideration of every mind. From all quarters a fierce struggle was foreseen in the approaching session; all parties hastened to congregate beforehand round the scene of action, seeking to draw some anticipation as to what would occur, and how to secure a place. On the 19th of October, 1829, the death of the learned chemist, M. Vauquelin, left open a seat in the Chamber of Deputies, in which he had represented the division of Lisieux and Pont-l'Évêque, which formed the fourth electoral district in the department of Calvados. Several influential persons of the country proposed to substitute me in his place. I had never inhabited or even visited that province. I had no property there of any kind. But since 1820, my political writings and lectures had given popularity to my name. The young portions of the community were everywhere favourably disposed towards me. The Moderates and active Liberals mutually looked to me to defend them, and their cause, should occasion arrive. As soon as the proposition became known at Lisieux and Pont-l'Évêque, it was cordially received. All the different shades of the Opposition, M. de La Fayette and M. de Châteaubriand, M. Dupont de l'Eure and the Duke de Broglie, M. Odillon Barrot and M. Bertin de Veaux, seconded my candidateship. Absent, but supported by a strong display of opinion in the district, I was elected on the 23rd of February, 1830, by a large majority.

At the same moment M. Berryer, whose age, as in my own case, had until then excluded him from the Chamber of Deputies, was elected by the department of the Higher Loire, where a seat had also become vacant.

On the day following that on which my election was known in Paris, I had to deliver my lecture at the Sorbonne. As I entered the hall, the entire audience rose and received me with a burst of applause. I immediately checked them, and said: "I thank you for your kind reception, by which I am sensibly affected. I request two favours of you; the first is to preserve always the same feelings towards me; the second is, never to evince them again in this manner. Nothing that passes without should resound within these walls. We come here to treat of pure, unmingled science, which is essentially impartial, disinterested, and estranged from all external occurrences, important or insignificant. Let us always maintain for learning this exclusive character. I hope that your sympathy will accompany me in the new career to which I am called; I will even presume to say that I reckon upon it. Your silent attention here is the most convincing proof I can receive."

CHAPTER VIII.: ADDRESS OF THE TWO HUNDRED AND TWENTY-ONE.: 1830.

MENACING, AND AT THE SAME TIME INACTIVE ATTITUDE OF THE MINISTRY.—
LAWFUL EXCITEMENT THROUGHOUT THE COUNTRY.—ASSOCIATION FOR THE
ULTIMATE REFUSAL OF THE NON-VOTED TAXES.—CHARACTER AND VIEWS OF
M. DE POLIGNAC.—MANIFESTATIONS OF THE MINISTERIAL PARTY.—NEW
ASPECT OF THE OPPOSITION.—OPENING OF THE SESSION.—SPEECH OF THE
KING.—ADDRESS OF THE CHAMBER OF PEERS.—PREPARATION OF THE ADDRESS
OF THE CHAMBER OF DEPUTIES.—PERPLEXITY OF THE MODERATE PARTY AND
OF M. ROYER-COLLARD.—DEBATE ON THE ADDRESS.—THE PART TAKEN IN IT
BY M. BERRYER AND MYSELF.—PRESENTATION OF THE ADDRESS TO THE
KING.—PROROGATION OF THE SESSION.—RETIREMENT OF MM. DE CHABROL
AND COURVOISIER.—DISSOLUTION OF THE CHAMBER OF DEPUTIES.—MY
JOURNEY TO NISMES FOR THE ELECTIONS.—TRUE CHARACTER OF THE
ELECTIONS.—INTENTIONS OF CHARLES X.

Whether, attention is arrested by the life of an individual or the history of a nation, there is no
spectacle more imposing than that of a great contrast between the surface and the interior, the
appearance and the reality of matters. To be excited under the semblance of immobility, to do
nothing while we expect much, to look on the calm while we anticipate the tempest,—this,
perhaps, of all human situations, is the most oppressive for the mind to endure, and the most
difficult to sustain for any length of time.

At the commencement of the year 1830, such was the common position of all,—of the
Government and the nation, of the ministers and citizens, of the supporters and opponents of
power. No one acted directly, and all prepared themselves for unknown chances. We pursued our
ordinary course of life, while we felt ourselves on the brink of a convulsion.

I proceeded quietly with my course at the Sorbonne. There, where M. de Villèle and the Abbé
Frayssinous had silenced me, M. de Polignac and M. de Guernon-Ranville permitted me to speak
freely. While enjoying this liberty, I scrupulously preserved my habitual caution, keeping every
lecture entirely divested of all allusion to incidental questions, and not more solicitous of
winning popular favour, than apprehensive of losing ministerial patronage. Until the meeting of
the Chamber, my new title of Deputy called for no step or demonstration, and I sought not for
any factitious opportunity. In some paragraphs of town and court gossip, several of the papers in
the interest of the extreme right asserted that meetings of Deputies had been held at the residence
of the late President of the Chamber. M. Royer-Collard, upon this, wrote immediately to the
'Moniteur:'—"It is positively false that any meeting of Deputies has taken place at my residence
since the closing of the session of 1829. This is all I have to say; I should feel ashamed of
formally denying absurd reports, in which the King is not more respected than the truth."
Without feeling myself restricted to the severe abstinence of M. Royer-Collard, I sedulously
avoided all demonstrative opposition; my friends and I were mutually intent on furnishing no
pretext for the mistakes of power.

But in the midst of this tranquil and reserved life, I was deeply occupied in reflecting on my new position, and on the part I was henceforward to assume in the uncertain fortune of my country. I revolved over in my mind every opposite chance, looking upon all as possible, and wishing to be prepared for all, even for those I was most desirous to avert. Power cannot commit a greater error than that of plunging imaginations into darkness. A great public terror is worse than a great positive evil; above all, when obscure perspectives of the future excite the hopes of enemies and blunderers, as well as the alarms of honest men and friends. I lived in the midst of both classes. Although no longer interested in the electoral object which had occasioned its institution in 1827, the society called, "Help thyself and Heaven will help thee" existed still, and I still continued to be a member. Under the Martignac Ministry I considered it advisable to remain amongst them, that I might endeavour to moderate a little the wants and impatience of the external opposition, which operated so powerfully on the opposition in Parliament. Since the formation of the Polignac Cabinet, from which everything was to be apprehended, I endeavoured to maintain a certain degree of interest in this assembly of all opposing parties, Constitutionalists, Republicans, and Buonapartists, which, in the moment of a crisis, might exercise itself such preponderating influence on the destiny of the country. At the moment, I possessed considerable popularity, especially with the younger men, and the ardent but sincere Liberals. I felt gratified at this, and resolved to turn it to profitable use, let the future produce what it might.

The temper of the public resembled my own, tranquil on the surface but extremely agitated at the heart. There was neither conspiracy, nor rising, nor tumultuous assembly; but all were on the alert, and prepared for anything that might happen. In Brittany, in Normandy, in Burgundy, in Lorraine, and in Paris, associations were publicly formed to resist payment of the taxes, if the Government should attempt to collect them without a legal vote of the legal Chambers. The Government prosecuted the papers which had advertised these meetings; some tribunals acquitted the responsible managers, others, and amongst them the Royal Court of Paris, condemned them, but to a very slight punishment, "for exciting hatred and contempt against the King's government, in having imputed to them the criminal intention either of levying taxes which had not been voted by the two Chambers, or of changing illegally the mode of election, or even of revoking the constitutional Charter which has been granted and confirmed in perpetuity, and which regulates the rights and duties of every public authority." The ministerial journals felt their position, and saw that their patrons were so reached by this sentence, that, in publishing it, they suppressed all observations.

In presence of this opposition, at once so decided and restrained, the Ministry remained timid and inactive. Evidently doubtful of themselves, they feared the opinion in which they were held by others. A year before this time, at the opening of the session of 1829, when the Cabinet of M. de Martignac still held power, and the department of Foreign Affairs had fallen vacant by the retirement of M. de la Ferronnays, M. de Polignac had endeavoured, in the debate on the address in the Chamber of Peers, to dissipate, by a profession of constitutional faith, the prejudices entertained against him. His assurances of attachment to the Charter were not, on his part, a simply ambitious and hypocritical calculation; he really fancied himself a friend to constitutional government, and was not then meditating its overthrow; but in the mediocrity of his mind, and the confusion of his ideas, he neither understood thoroughly the English society he wished to imitate, nor the French system he desired to reform. He believed the Charter to be compatible with the political importance of the old nobility, and with the definitive supremacy of the ancient Royalty; and he flattered himself that he could develop new institutions by making them assist in the preponderance of influences which it was his distinct object to limit or abolish. It is difficult to measure the extent of conscientious illusions in a mind weak but enthusiastic, ordinary, but with some degree of elevation, and mystically vague and subtle. M. de Polignac felt honestly surprised at not being acknowledged as a minister devoted to constitutional rule; but the public, without troubling themselves to inquire into his sincerity, had determined to regard him as the champion of the old system, and the standard-bearer of the counter-revolution. Disturbed by this reputation, and fearing to confirm it by his acts, M. de Polignac did nothing. His Cabinet, sworn to conquer the Revolution and to save the Monarchy, remained motionless and sterile. The Opposition insultingly taxed them with their impotence: they were christened "the Braggadocio Ministry," "the most helpless of Cabinets;" and to all this they gave no answer, except by preparing the expedition to Algiers, and by convoking the assembly of the Chambers, ever protesting their fidelity to the Charter, and promising themselves, as means of escape from their embarrassments, a conquest and a majority.

M. de Polignac was ignorant that a minister does not entirely govern by his own acts, and that he is responsible for others besides himself. While he endeavoured to escape from the character assigned to him, by silence and inaction,—his friends, his functionaries, his writers, his entire party, masters and servants, spoke and moved noisily around him. He expressed his anger when they discussed, as an hypothesis, the collection of taxes not voted by the Chambers; and at that same moment the Attorney-General of the Royal Court at Metz, M. Pinaud, said, in a requisition, "Article 14 of the Charter secures to the King a method of resisting electoral or elective majorities. If then, renewing the days of 1792 and 1793, the majority should refuse the taxes, would the King be called upon to deliver up his crown to the spectre of the Convention? No; but in that case he ought to maintain his right, and save himself from the danger by means respecting which it is proper to keep silence." On the 1st of January, the Royal Court of Paris, who had just given a proof of their firm adherence to the Charter, presented themselves, according to custom, at the Tuileries; the King received and spoke to them with marked dryness; and when arriving in front of the Dauphiness, the first President prepared to address his homage to her, "Pass on, pass on," exclaimed she brusquely; and while complying with her words, M. Seguier said to the Master of the Ceremonies, M. de Rochemore, "My Lord Marquis, do you think that the Court ought to inscribe the answer of the Princess in its records?" A magistrate high in favour with the Minister, M. Cotta, an honest but a light and credulous individual, published a work entitled, 'On the Necessity of a Dictatorship.' A publicist, a fanatical but sincere reasoner, M. Madrolle, dedicated to M. de Polignac a memorial, in which he maintained the necessity of remodelling the law of elections by a royal decree. "What are called coups d'état," said some important journals, and avowed friends of the Cabinet, "are social and regular in their nature when the King acts for the general good of the people, even though in appearance he may contravene the existing laws." In fact France was tranquil, and legal order in full vigour; neither on the part of authority nor on that of the people had any act of violence called for violence in return; and yet the most extreme measures were openly discussed. In all quarters people proclaimed the imminence of revolution, the dictatorship of the King, and the legitimacy of coups d'état.

In a moment of urgent danger, a nation may accept an isolated coup d'état as a necessity; but it cannot, without dishonour and decline, admit the principle of such measures as the permanent basis of its public rights and government. Now this was precisely what M. de Polignac and his friends pretended to impose on France. According to them, the absolute power of the old Royalty remained always at the bottom of the Charter; and to expand and display this absolute power, they selected a moment when no active plot, no visible danger, no great public disturbance, threatened either the Government of the King or the order of the State. The sole question at issue was, whether the Crown could, in the selection and maintenance of its advisers, hold itself entirely independent of the majority in the Chambers, or the country; and whether, in conclusion, after so many constitutional experiments, the sole governing power was to be concentrated in the Royal will. The formation of the Polignac Ministry had been, on the part of the King, Charles X., an obstinate idea even more than a cry of alarm, an aggressive challenge as much as an act of suspicion. Uneasy, not only for the security of his throne, but for what he considered the unalienable rights of his crown, he placed himself, to maintain them, in the most offensive of all possible attitudes towards the nation. He assumed defiance rather than defence. It was no longer a struggle between the different parties and systems of government, but a question of political dogma, and an affair of honour between France and her King.

In presence of a subject under this aspect, passions and intentions hostile to established order could not fail to resume hope and appear once more upon the stage. The sovereignty of the people was always at hand, available to be invoked in opposition to the sovereignty of the Monarch. Popular strokes of policy were to be perceived, ready to reply to the attempts of royal power. The party which had never seriously put faith in or adhered to the Restoration, had now new interpreters, destined speedily to become new leaders, and younger, as well as more rational and skilful than their predecessors. There were no conspiracies, no risings in any quarter; secret machinations and noisy riots were equally abandoned; everywhere a bolder and yet a more moderate line of conduct was adopted, more prudent, and at the same time more efficacious. In public discussion, appeal was made to examples from history and to the probabilities of the future. Without directly attacking the reigning power, lawful freedom in opposition was pushed to its extremest limits, too clearly to be taxed with hypocrisy, and too ingeniously to be arrested in this hostile proceeding. In the more serious and intelligent organs of the party, such as the 'National,' they did not absolutely propound anarchical theories, or revolutionary constitutions; they confined themselves to the Charter from which Royalty seemed on the point of escaping, either by carefully explaining the import, or by peremptorily demanding the complete and sincere execution; by making it clearly foreseen that compromising the national right would also compromise the reigning dynasty. They avowed themselves decided and prepared, not to anticipate, but to accept without hesitation the last trial evidently approaching, and the rapid progress of which they clearly indicated to the public from day to day.

The conduct to be held by the constitutional Royalists who had laboured in honest sincerity to establish the Restoration with the Charter, although less dangerous, was even more complex and difficult. How could they repulse the blow with which Royalty menaced the existing institutions, without inflicting on Royalty a mortal wound in return? Should they remain on the defensive, wait until the Cabinet committed acts, or introduced measures really hostile to the interests and liberties of France, and reject them when their character and object had been clearly developed in debate? Or should they take a bolder initiative, and check the Cabinet in its first steps, and thus prevent the unknown struggles which at a later period it would be impossible to direct or restrain? This was the great practical question, which, when the Chambers were convened, occupied, above all other considerations, those minds which were strangers to all preconcerted hostility, and to every secret desire of encountering new hazards.

Two figures have remained, since 1830, impressed on my memory; the King, Charles X., at the Louvre on the 2nd of March, opening the session of the Chambers; and the Prince de Polignac at the Palais Bourbon on the 15th and 16th of March, taking part in the discussion on the address of the Two Hundred and Twenty-One Deputies. The demeanour of the King was, as usual, noble and benevolent, but mingled with restrained agitation and embarrassment. He read his speech mildly, although with some precipitation, as if anxious to finish; and when he came to the sentence which, under a modified form, contained a royal menace, he accentuated it with more affectation than energy. As he placed his hand upon the passage, his hat fell; the Duke d'Orléans raised and presented it to him, respectfully bending his knee. Amongst the Deputies, the acclamations of the right-hand party were more loud than joyful, and it was difficult to decide whether the silence of the rest of the Chamber proceeded from sadness or apathy. Fifteen days later, at the Chamber of Deputies, and in the midst of the secret committee in which the address was discussed, in that vast hall, void of spectators, M. de Polignac was on his bench, motionless, and little attended even by his friends, with the air of a stranger surprised and out of place, thrown into a world with which he is scarcely acquainted, where he feels that he is unwelcome, and charged with a difficult mission, the issue of which he awaits with inert and impotent dignity. In the course of the debate, he was reproached with an act of the Ministry in reference to the elections, to which he replied awkwardly by a few short and confused words, as if not thoroughly understanding the objection, and anxious to resume his seat. While I was in the tribune, my eyes encountered his, and I was struck by their expression of astonished curiosity. It was manifest that at the moment when they ventured on an act of voluntary boldness, neither the King nor his minister felt at their ease; in the two individuals, in their respective aspects as in their souls, there was a mixture of resolution and weakness, of confidence and uncertainty, which at the same moment testified blindness of the mind and the presentiment of coming evil.

We waited with impatience the address from the Chamber of Peers. Had it been energetic, it would have added strength to ours. Whatever has been said, their address was neither blind nor servile, but it was far from forcible. It recommended respect for institutions and national liberties, and protested equally against despotism and anarchy. Disquietude and censure were perceptible through the reserve of words; but these impressions were dimly conveyed and stripped of all power. Their unanimity evinced nothing beyond their nullity. M. de Châteaubriand alone, while signifying his approbation, considered them insufficient. The Court declared itself satisfied. The Chamber seemed more desirous of discharging a debt of conscience, and of escaping from all responsibility in the evils which it foresaw, than of making a sound effort to prevent them. "If the Chamber of Peers had spoken out more distinctly," said M. Royer-Collard to me, shortly after the Revolution, "it might have arrested the King on the brink of the abyss, and have prevented the Decrees." But the Chamber of Peers had little confidence in their own power to charm away the danger, and feared to aggravate it by a too open display. The entire weight of the situation fell upon the Chamber of Deputies.

The perplexity was great,—great in the majority of sincere Royalists, in the Committee charged to draw up the Address, and in the mind of M. Royer-Collard who presided, both in the Committee and the Chamber, and exercised on both a preponderating influence. One general sentiment prevailed,—a desire to stay the King in the false path on which he had entered, and a conviction that there was no hope of succeeding in this object, but by placing before him an impediment which it would be impossible for him personally to misunderstand. It was evident, when he dismissed M. de Martignac and appointed M. de Polignac to succeed him, that he was not alone influenced by his fears as a King. In this act Charles X. had, above all considerations, been swayed by his passions of the old system. It became indispensable that the peril of this tendency should be clearly demonstrated to him, and that where prudence had not sufficed, impossibility should make itself felt. By expressing, without delay or circumlocution, its want of confidence in the Cabinet, the Chamber in no way exceeded its privilege; it expressed its own judgment, without denying to the King the free exercise of his, and his right of appealing to the country by a dissolution. The Chamber acted deliberately and honestly; it empty or ambiguous words, to assert the frank and strong measures of the constitutional system. There was no other method of remaining in harmony with the public feeling so strongly excited, and of restraining it by legitimate concessions. There was reason to hope that language at once firm and loyal would prove as efficacious as it was necessary; already, under similar circumstances, the King had not shown himself intractable, for two years before, in January, 1828, he had dismissed M. de Villèle, almost without a struggle, after the elections had produced a majority decidedly opposed to his Cabinet.

During five days, the Committee, in their sittings, and M. Royer-Collard in his private reflections, as well as in his confidential intercourse with his friends, scrupulously weighed all these considerations, as well as all the phrases and words of the Address. M. Royer-Collard was not only a staunch Royalist, but his mind was disposed to doubt and hesitation; he became bewildered in his resolves as he looked on the different aspects of a question, and always shrank from important responsibility. For two years he had observed Charles X. closely, and more than once during the Martignac Administration he had said to some of the more rational oppositionists, "Do not press the King too closely; no one can tell to what follies he might have recourse." But at the point which matters had now reached, called upon as he was to represent the sentiments and maintain the honour of the Chamber, M. Royer-Collard felt that he could not refuse to carry the truth to the foot of the throne; and he flattered himself that on appearing there, with a respectful and affectionate demeanour, he would be in 1830, as in 1828, if not well received, at least listened to without any fatal explosion.

The Address in fact bore this double character: never had language more unpresuming in its boldness, and more conciliating in its freedom, been held to a monarch in the name of his people. When the President read it to the Chamber for the first time, a secret satisfaction faction of dignity mingled in the most moderate hearts with the uneasiness they experienced. The debate was short and extremely reserved, almost even to coldness. On all sides, the members feared to commit themselves by speaking; and there was an evident desire to come to a conclusion. Four of the Ministers, MM. de Montbel, de Guernon-Ranville, de Chantelauze, and d'Haussez took part in the discussion, but almost exclusively on the general question. In the Chamber of Deputies, as in the Chamber of Peers, the leader of the Cabinet remained mute. It is on more lofty conditions that political aristocracies maintain or raise themselves. When they came to the last paragraphs, which contained the decisive phrases, the individual members of the different parties maintained the contest alone. It was then that M. Berryer and I ascended the tribune for the first time, both new to the Chamber, he as a friend and I as an opponent of the Ministry; he to attack and I to defend the Address. It gives me pleasure, I confess, to retrace and repeat today, the ideas and arguments by which I supported it at the time. "Under what auspices," I asked the Chamber, "and in the name of what principles and interests has the present Ministry been formed? In the name of power menaced, of the Royal prerogative compromised, of the interests of the Crown ill understood and sustained by their predecessors. This is the banner under which they have entered the lists, the cause they have promised to make triumphant. We had a right to expect from their entrance on office that authority should be exercised with vigour, the Royal prerogative in active operation, the principles of power not only proclaimed but practised, perhaps at the expense of the public liberty, but at least for the advantage of that power itself. Gentlemen, has this happened? Has power strengthened itself within the last seven months? Has it been exercised with activity, energy, confidence, and efficacy? Either I grossly deceive myself, or during these seven months power has suffered in confidence and energy, to the full extent of what the public have lost in security."

"But power has lost more than this. It is not entirely comprised in the positive acts it commits or the materials it employs; it does not always end in decrees and circulars. The authority over minds, the moral ascendency, that ascendency so suitable to free countries, for it directs without controlling public will,—in this is comprised an important component of power, perhaps the first of all in efficiency. But beyond all question, it is the re-establishment of this moral ascendency which is at this moment the most essential need of our country. We have known power extremely active and strong, capable of great and difficult undertakings; but whether from the inherent vice of its nature, or by the evil of its position, moral ascendency, that easy, regular, and imperceptible empire, has been almost entirely wanting. The King's government, more than any other, is called upon to possess this. It does not extract its right from force. We have not witnessed its birth; we have not contracted towards it those familiar associations, some of which always remain attached to the authorities at the infancy of which those who obey them were present. What has the actual Ministry done with that moral ascendency which belongs naturally, without premeditation or labour, to the King's government? Has it exercised it skilfully, and increased it in the exercise? Has it not, on the contrary, seriously compromised this great element, by placing it at issue with the fears to which it has given rise, and the passions it has excited?...

"Gentlemen, your entire mission is not to control, or at the least to oppose power; you are not here solely to retrieve its errors or injuries and to make them known to the country; you are also sent here to surround the government of the King—to enlighten it while you surround, and to support it while you enlighten.... Well, then, what is at this moment the position in the Chamber of the members who are the most disposed to undertake the character of those who are the greatest strangers to the spirit of faction, and unaccustomed to the habits of opposition? They are compelled to become oppositionists; they are made so in spite of themselves; they desire to remain always united to the King's government, and now they are forced to separate from it; they wish to support, and are driven to attack. They have been propelled from their proper path. The perplexity which disturbs them has been created by the Ministry in office; it will continue and redouble as long as they continue where they are."

I pointed out the analogous perturbation which existed everywhere, in society as in the Chambers; I showed how the public authorities, in common with the good citizens, were thrown out of their natural duties and position; the tribunals, more intent on restraining the Government itself than in repressing disorders and plans directed against it; the papers, exercising with the tolerance, and even with the approbation of the public, an unlimited and disorderly influence. I concluded by saying: "They tell us that France is tranquil, that order is not disturbed. It is true; material order is not disturbed; everything circulates freely and peaceably; no commotion deranges the current of affairs.... The surface of society is calm,—so calm that the Government may well be tempted to believe that the interior is perfectly secure, and to consider itself sheltered from all peril. Our words, gentlemen, the frankness of our words, comprises the sole warning that power can at this moment receive, the only voice that can reach it and dissipate its illusions. Let us take care not to diminish their force or to enervate our expressions; let them be respectful and even gentle, but let them at the same time be neither timid nor ambiguous. Truth already finds it difficult enough to penetrate into the palaces of kings; let us not send her there weak and trembling; let it be as impossible to misunderstand what we say, as to mistake the loyalty of our sentiments."

The Address passed as it was drawn up, with uneasy sadness, but with a profound conviction of its necessity. Two days after the vote, on the 18th of March, we repaired to the Tuileries to present it to the King. Twenty-one members alone joined the official deputation of the Chamber. Amongst those who had voted for the Address, some were little anxious of supporting by their presence, under the eyes of the King, such an act of opposition; others, from respect for the

Crown, had no wish to give to this presentation additional solemnity and effect. Our entire number amounted only to forty-six. We waited some time in the "Salon de la Paix," until the King returned from Mass. We stood there in silence; opposite to us, in the recesses of the windows, were the King's pages and some members of the royal establishment, inattentive and almost intentionally rude. The Dauphiness crossed the saloon her way to the chapel, rapidly and without noticing us. She might have been much colder still before I could have felt that I had any right either to be surprised or indignant at her demeanour. There are crimes whose remembrance silences all other thoughts, and misfortunes before which we bow with a respect almost resembling repentance, as if we ourselves had been the author of them.

When we were introduced into the hall of the throne, M. Royer-Collard read the address naturally and suitably, with an emotion which his voice and features betrayed. The King listened to him with becoming dignity and without any air of haughtiness or ill humour; his answer was brief and dry, rather from royal habit than from anger, and, if I am not mistaken, he felt more satisfied with his own firmness than uneasy for the future. Four days before, on the eve of the debate on the address, in his circle at the Tuileries, to which many Deputies were invited, I saw him bestow marked intention on three members of the Commission, MM. Dupin, Étienne, and Gautier. In two such opposite situations, it was the same man and almost the same physiognomy, identical in his manners as in his ideas, careful to please although determined to quarrel, and obstinate from want of foresight and mental routine, rather than from the passion of pride or power.

On the day after the presentation of the address, the 19th of March, the session was prorogued to the 1st of September. Two months later, on the 16th of May, the Chamber of Deputies was dissolved; the two most moderate members of the Cabinet, the Chancellor and the Minister of Finance, M. Courvoisier and M. de Chabrol, left the Council; they had refused their concurrence to the extreme measures already debated there, in case the elections should falsify the expectations of power. The most compromised and audacious member of the Villèle Cabinet, M. de Peyronnet, became Minister of the Interior. By the dissolution, the King appealed to the country, and at the same moment he took fresh steps to separate himself from his people.

Having returned to the private life from which he never again emerged, M. Courvoisier wrote to me on the 29th of September 1831, from his retirement at Baume-les-Dames: "Before resigning the Seals, I happened to be in conversation with M. Pozzo di Borgo on the state of the country, and the perils with which the throne had surrounded itself. What means, said he to me, are there of opening the King's eyes, and of drawing him from a system which may once again overturn Europe and France?—I see but one, replied I, and that is a letter from the hand of the Emperor of Russia.—He shall write it, said he; he shall write it from Warsaw, whither he is about to repair.—We then conversed together on the substance of the letter. M. Pozzo di Borgo often said to me that the Emperor Nicholas saw no security for the Bourbons, but in the fulfilment of the Charter."

I much doubt whether the Emperor Nicholas ever wrote himself to the King, Charles X.; but what his ambassador at Paris had said to the Chancellor of France, he himself repeated to the

Duke de Mortemart, the King's ambassador at St. Petersburg:—"If they deviate from the Charter, they will lead direct to a catastrophe; if the King attempts a coup-d'état, the responsibility will fall on himself alone." The councils of monarchs were not more wanting to Charles X., than the addresses of nations, to detach him from his fatal design.

As soon as the electoral glove was thrown down, my friends wrote to me from Nismes that my presence was necessary to unite them all, and to hold out in the College of the department any prospect of success. It was also desired that I should go, of my own accord, to Lisieux; but they added that if I was required elsewhere, they thought, even in my absence, they could guarantee my election. I trusted to this assurance, and set out for Nismes on the 15th June, anxious to sound myself, and on the spot, the real dispositions of the country; which we so soon forget when confined to Paris.

I have no desire to substitute for my impressions of that epoch my ideas of the present day, or to attribute to my own political conduct and to that of my friends an interpretation which neither could assume. I republish, without alteration, what I find in the confidential letters I wrote or received during my journey. These supply the most unobjectionable evidences of what we thought and wished at the time.

On the 26th of June, some days after my arrival at Nismes, I wrote as follows:—

"The contest is very sharp, more so than you can understand at a distance. The two parties are seriously engaged, and hourly oppose each other with increasing animosity. An absolute fever of egotism and stupidity possesses and instigates the administration. The opposition struggles, with passionate ardour, against the embarrassments and annoyances of a situation, both in a legal and moral sense, of extreme difficulty. It finds in the laws means of action and defence, which impart the courage necessary to sustain the combat, but without inspiring the confidence of success; for almost everywhere, the last guarantee is wanting, and after having fought long and bravely, we always run the risk of finding ourselves suddenly disarmed, and helpless. A similar anxiety applies to the moral position: the opposition despises the ministry, and at the same time looks upon it as its superior; the functionaries are in disrepute, but still they take precedence; a remembrance of imperial greatness and power yet furnishes them with a pedestal; they are looked on disdainfully, with a mingled sensation of fear and anger. In this state of affairs there are many elements of agitation, and even of a crisis. Nevertheless, no sooner does an explosion appear imminent, or even possible, than every one shrinks from it in apprehension. In conclusion, all parties at present look for their security in order and peace. There is no confidence except in legitimate measures."

On the 9th of July, I received the following from Paris:—

"The elections of the great colleges have commenced. If we gain any advantage there, it will be excellent; above all, for the effect it may produce on the King's mind, who can expect nothing more favourable to him than the great colleges. At present, there are no indications of a coup d'état. The 'Quotidienne' announces this morning that it looks upon the session as opened, admitting at the same time that the Ministry will not have a majority. It appears delighted at there being no prospect of an address exactly similar to that of the Two Hundred and Twenty-one."

And again, on the 12th of July:—

"Today the 'Universel' exclaims against the report of a coup d'état, and seems to guarantee the regular opening of the session by a speech from the King. This speech, which will annoy you, will have the advantage of opening the session on a better understanding. But the great point is to have a session; violent extremes become much more improbable when we are constitutionally employed. But you will find it very difficult to draw up a new address; whatever it may be, the right and the extreme left will look upon it in the light of a retractation,—the right as a boast, the left as a complaint. You will have to defend yourselves against those who wish purely and simply a repetition of the former address, and who hold to it as the last words of the country. Having acquired a victory at the elections, and the alternative of dissolution being no longer available to the King, we shall have evidently a new line of conduct to adopt. Besides, what interest have we in compelling the King to make a stand? France has every thing to gain by years of regular government; let us be careful not to precipitate events."

I replied on the 16th of July:—"I scarcely know how we are to extricate ourselves from the new address. It will be an extremely difficult matter, but in any case we are bound to meet this difficulty, for evidently we must have a session. We should be looked upon as children and madmen if we were merely to recommence what we have taken in hand for four months. The new Chamber ought not to retreat; but it should adopt a new course. Let us have no coup d'état, and let constitutional order be regularly preserved. Whatever may be the ministerial combinations, real and ultimate success will be with us."

"Amongst the electors by whom I am surrounded here, I have met with nothing but moderate, patient, and loyal dispositions. M. de Daunant has just been elected, on the 13th of July instant, by the Divisional College of Nismes; he had 296 votes against 241 given in favour of M. Daniel Murjas, president of the college. When the result was announced, the official secretary proposed to the assembly to pass a vote of thanks to the president, who, notwithstanding his own candidateship, had presided with most complete impartiality and loyalty. The vote was carried on the instant, in the midst of loud cries of "Long live the King!" and the electors, as they retired, found in all quarters the same tranquillity and gravity which they had themselves preserved in the discharge of their own duties."

On the 12th of July, when news of the capture of Algiers arrived, I wrote thus:—"And so the African campaign is over, and well over; ours, which must commence in about two months, will be rather more difficult; but no matter; I hope this success will not stimulate power to the last madness, and I prefer our national honour to all parliamentary considerations."

I do not pretend to assert that the foregoing sentiments were those of all who, whether in the Chambers or in the country, had approved the Address of the Two Hundred and Twenty-one, and who, at the elections, voted for its support. The Restoration had not achieved such complete conquests in France. Inactive, but not resigned, the secret societies were ever in existence; ready, when opportunity occurred, to resume their work of conspiracy and destruction. Other adversaries, more legitimate but not less formidable, narrowly watched every mistake of the King and his Government, and sedulously brought them under public comment, expecting and prognosticating still more serious errors, which would lead to extreme consequences. Amongst the popular masses, a deeply rooted instinct of suspicion and hatred to all that recalled the old system and the invasion of the foreigners, continued to supply arms and inexhaustible hopes to the enemies of the Restoration. The people resemble the ocean, motionless and almost immutable at the bottom, however violent may be the storms which agitate the surface. Nevertheless, the spirit of legality and sound political reason had made remarkable progress; even during the ferment of the elections, public feeling loudly repudiated all idea of a new revolution. Never was the situation of those who sincerely wished to support the King and the Charter more favourable or powerful; they had given evidences of persevering firmness by legitimate opposition, they had lately maintained with reputation the principles of representative government, they enjoyed the esteem and even the favour of the public; the more violent party, through necessity, and the country, with some hesitation, mingled with honest hope, followed in their rear. If at this critical moment they could have succeeded with the King as with the Chambers and the country,—if Charles X., after having by the dissolution pushed his royal prerogative to the extreme verge, had listened to the strongly manifested wishes of France, and selected his advisers from amongst those of the constitutional Royalists who stood the highest in public consideration, I say, with a feeling of conviction which may appear foolhardy, but which I maintain to this hour, that there was every reasonable hope of surmounting the last decisive trial; and that the country taking confidence at once in the King and in the Charter, the Restoration and constitutional government would have been established together.

But the precise quality in which Charles X. was deficient, was that expansive freedom of mind which conveys to a monarch a perfect intelligence of the age in which he lives, and endows him with a sound appreciation of its resources and necessities. "There are only M. de La Fayette and I who have not changed since 1789," said he, one day; and he spoke truly. Through all the vicissitudes of his life he ever remained what his youthful training had made him at the Court of Versailles and in the aristocratic society of the eighteenth century—sincere and light, confident in himself and in his own immediate circle, unobservant and irreflective, although of an active spirit, attached to his ideas and his friends of the old system as to his faith and his standard. Under the reign of his brother Louis XVIII., and during the scission of the monarchical party, he became the patron and hope of that Royalist opposition which boldly availed itself of constitutional liberties, and presented in his own person a singular mixture of persevering intimacy with his old companions, and of a taste for the new popularity of a Liberal. When he found himself on the throne, he made more than one coquettish advance to this popular disposition, and sincerely flattered himself that he governed according to the Charter, with his old friends and his ideas of earlier times. M. de Villèle and M. de Martignac lent themselves to his views in this difficult work; and after their fall, which he scarcely opposed, Charles X. found himself left to his natural tendencies, in the midst of advisers little disposed to contradict, and without the power of restraining him. Two fatal mistakes then established themselves in his mind; he fancied that he was menaced by the Revolution, much more than was really the fact; and he ceased to believe in the possibility of defending himself, and of governing by the legal course of the constitutional system. France had no desire for a new revolution. The Charter contained, for a prudent and patient monarch, certain means of exercising the royal authority and of securing the Crown. But Charles X. had lost confidence in France and in the Charter. When the Address of the Two Hundred and Twenty-one Deputies came triumphant through the elections, he believed that he was driven to his last entrenchment, and reduced to save himself without the Charter, or to perish by a revolution.

A few days before the Decrees of July, the Russian ambassador, Count Pozzo di Borgo, had an audience of the King. He found him seated before his desk, with his eyes fixed on the Charter, opened at Article 14. Charles X. read and re-read that article, seeking with honest inquietude the interpretation he wanted to find there. In such cases, we always discover what we are in search of; and the King's conversation, although indirect and uncertain, left little doubt on the Ambassador's mind as to the measures in preparation.

The Viscount de Châteaubriand to M. Guizot.

Val-de-Loup, May 12th, 1809.

Sir,

I return you a thousand thanks. I have read your articles with extreme pleasure. You praise me with so much grace, and bestow on me so many commendations, that you may easily afford to diminish the latter. Enough will always remain to satisfy my vanity as an author, and assuredly more than I deserve.

I find your criticisms extremely just; one in particular has struck me by its refined taste. You say that the Catholics cannot, like the Protestants, admit a Christian mythology, because we have not been trained and accustomed to it by great poets. This is most ingenious; and if my work should be considered good enough to induce people to say that I am the first to commence this mythology, it might be replied that I come too late, that our taste is formed upon other models, etc. etc. etc.... Nevertheless there will always be Tasso, and all the Latin Catholic poems of the Middle Ages. This appears to me the only solid objection that can be raised against your remark.

In truth, and I speak with perfect sincerity, the criticisms which, before yours, have appeared on my work, make me feel to a certain extent ashamed of the French. Have you observed that no one seems to have comprehended its design? That the rules of epic composition are so generally forgotten, that a work of thought and immense labour is judged as if it were the production of a day, or a mere romance? And all this outcry is against the marvellous! Would it not imply that I am the inventor of this style? that it has been hitherto unheard of, and is singular and new? And yet we have Tasso, Milton, Klopstock, Gessner, and even Voltaire! And if we are not to employ the marvellous in a Christian subject, there can no longer be an epic in modern poetry, for the marvellous is essential to that style of composition, and I believe no one would be inclined to introduce Jupiter in a subject taken from our own history. All this, like every thing else in France, is insincere. The question to be decided was, whether my work was good or bad as an epic poem; all was comprised in this point, without attempting to ascertain whether it was or was not contrary to religion; and a thousand other arguments of the same kind.

I cannot deliver an opinion on my own work; I can only convey to you that of others. M. Fontanes is entirely in favour of 'The Martyrs.' He finds this production much superior to what I have written before, in plan, style, and characters.

What appears singular to me is, that the third Book, which you condemn, seems to him one of the best of the whole! With regard to style, he thinks that I have never before reached so high a point as in the description of the happiness of the just, in that of the light of Heaven, and in the passage on the Virgin. He tolerates the length of the two dialogues between the Father and Son, on the necessity of establishing the epic machinery. Without these dialogues there could be no more narrative or action; the narrative and action are accounted for by the conversation of the uncreated beings.

I mention this, Sir, not to convince, but to show you how sound judgments can see the same object under different aspects. With you I dislike the description of torture, but I consider it absolutely necessary in a work upon Martyrs. It has been consecrated by all history and every art. Christian painting and sculpture have selected these subjects; herein lies the real controversy of the question. You, Sir, who are well acquainted with the details, know to what extent I have softened the picture, and how much I have suppressed of the Acta Martyrum, particularly in holding back physical agony, and in opposing agreeable images to harrowing torments. You are too just not to distinguish between the objections of the subject and the errors of the poet.

For the rest, you, Sir, well know the tempest raised against my work, and the source from whence they proceed. There is another sore not openly displayed, and which lies at the root of all this anger. It is that Hierocles massacres the Christians in the name of philosophy and liberty. Time will do me justice if my book deserves it, and you will greatly accelerate this judgment by publishing your articles, if you could be induced to modify them to a certain extent. Show me my faults and I will correct them. I only despise those writers, who are as contemptible in their language as in the secret reasons which prompt them to speak. I can neither find reason nor honour in the mouths of those literary mountebanks in the hire of the Police, who dance in the kennels for the amusement of lacqueys.

I am in my cottage, where I shall be delighted to hear from you. It would give me the greatest pleasure to receive you here, if you would be so kind as to visit me. Accept the assurance of my profound esteem and high consideration.

De Châteaubriand.

The Viscount de Châteaubriand to M. Guizot.

Val-de-Loup, May 30th, 1809.

Sir,

Far from troubling me, you have given me the greatest pleasure in doing me the favour to communicate your ideas. This time I shall condemn the introduction of the marvellous in a Christian subject, and am willing to believe with you, that it will never be adopted in France. But I cannot admit that 'The Martyrs' are founded on a heresy. The question is not of a redemption, which would be absurd, but of an expiation, which is entirely consistent with faith. In all ages, the Church has held that the blood of a martyr could efface the sins of the people, and deliver them from their penalties. Undoubtedly you know, better than I do, that formerly, in times of war and calamity, a monk was confined in a tower or a cell, where he fasted and prayed for the salvation of all. I have not left my intention in doubt, for in the third Book I have caused it to be positively declared to the Eternal that Eudore will draw the blessings of Heaven upon the Christians through the merits of the blood of the Saviour. This, as you see, is precisely the orthodox phrase, and the exact lesson of the catechism. The doctrine of expiation, so consolatory in other respects, and consecrated by antiquity, has been acknowledged in our religion: its mission from Christ has not destroyed it. And I may observe, incidentally, that I hope the sacrifice of some innocent victim, condemned in the Revolution, will obtain from Heaven the pardon of our guilty country. Those whom we have slaughtered are, perhaps, praying for us at this very moment. Surely you cannot wish to renounce this sublime hope, which springs from the tears and blood of Christians.

In conclusion, the frankness and sincerity of your conduct make me forget for a moment the baseness of the present age. What can we think of a time when an honest man is told, "You will pronounce on such a work, such an opinion; you will praise or blame it, not according to your conscience, but according to the spirit of the journal in which you write"! We are too happy to find critics like you, who stand up against such conventional baseness, and preserve the tradition of honour for human nature. As a conclusive estimate, if you carefully examine 'The Martyrs,' undoubtedly you will find much to reprehend; but taking all points into consideration, you will see that in plan, characters, and style, it is the best and least defective of my feeble writings.

I have a nephew in Russia, named Moreau, the grandson of a sister of my mother; I am scarcely acquainted with him, but I believe him to be an honourable man. His father, who was also in Russia, returned to France about a year ago. I have been delighted with the opportunity which has procured for me the honour of becoming acquainted with Mademoiselle de Meulan; she has appeared to me, as in all that she writes, full of mind, good taste, and sense. I much fear that I inconvenienced her by the length of my visit; I have the fault of remaining wherever I find amiable acquaintances, and especially when I meet exalted characters and noble sentiments.

I repeat most sincerely the assurance of my high esteem, gratitude, and devotion. I look forward with impatience to the moment when I can either receive you in my hermitage, or visit you in your solitude.

Accept, I pray you, my sincerest compliments.

De Châteaubriand.

The Viscount de Châteaubriand to M. Guizot.

Val-de-Loup, June 12th, 1809.

Sir,

I happened to be absent from my valley for several days, which has prevented me from replying sooner to your letters. Behold me thoroughly convinced of heresy. I admit that the word redeemed escaped me inadvertently, and in truth contrary to my intention. But there it is, and I shall efface it from the next edition.

I have read your first two articles, and repeat my thanks them. They are excellent, and you praise me far beyond what I deserve. What has been said with respect to the Church of the Holy Sepulchre is quite correct. The description could only have been given by one who knows the localities. But the Holy Sepulchre itself might easily have escaped the fire without a special miracle. It forms, in the middle of the circular nave of the church, a kind of catafalque of white marble: the cupola of cedar, in falling, might have crushed it, but could not have set it on fire. It is nevertheless a very extraordinary circumstance, and one worthy of much longer details than can be confined within the limits of a letter.

I wish much that I could relate these particulars to you, personally, in your retirement. Unfortunately, Madame de Châteaubriand is ill, and I cannot leave her. But I do not give up the idea of paying you a visit, nor of receiving you here in my hermitage. Honourable men ought, particularly at present, to unite for mutual consolation. Generous ideas and exalted sentiments become every day so rare that we ought to be too happy when we encounter them. I should be delighted if my society could prove agreeable to you, as also to M. Stapfer, to whom I beg you will convey my warmest thanks.

Accept once more, I pray you, the assurance of my high consideration and sincere devotion, and if you will permit me to add, of a friendship which is commenced under the auspices of frankness and honour.

De Châteaubriand.

The best of Jerusalem is that of Danville; but his little treatise is very scarce. In general, all travellers are very exact as to Palestine; there is a letter in the 'Lettres Édifiantes' ('Missions to the Levant'), which leaves nothing to be desired. With regard to M. de Volney, he is valuable on the government of the Turks, but it is evident that he has not been at Jerusalem. It is probable that he never went beyond Ramleh or Rama, the ancient Arimathea. You may also consult the 'Theatrum Terræ Sanctæ' of Adrichomius.

No. II.

Count de Lally-Tolendal to M. Guizot.
Brussels, April 27th, 1811.
Sir,

You will be unable to account for my silence, as I found it difficult to understand the tardy arrival of the prospectuses you had promised me in your letter of the fourth of this month. I must explain to you that the porter here had confounded that packet with the files of unimportant printed papers addressed to a Prefecture, and if the want of a book had not induced me to visit the private study of the Prefect, I should perhaps have not yet discovered the mistake. I thank you for the confidence with which you have treated me on this occasion. You are aware that no one renders you more than I do, the full justice to which you are entitled, and you also know that I accord it equally from inclination and conviction. My generation has passed away, yours is in full action, and a third is on the point of rising. I see you placed between two, to console the first, to do honour to the second, and to form the third. Endeavour to make the last like yourself; by which I do not mean that I wish all the little boys to know as much as you do, or all the little girls to resemble in everything, your more than amiable partner. We must not desire what we cannot obtain, and I should too much regret my own decline if such an attractive age were about to commence. But restrain my idea within its due limits, and dictate like Solon the best laws which the infancy of the nineteenth century can bear or receive; this will abundantly suffice. Today the mox progeniem daturos vitiosiorem would make one's hair stand on end.

Madame de la Tour du Pin, a Baroness of the Empire for two years, a Prefectess of the Dyle for three, and a religious mother for twenty, will recommend your journal with all the influence of her two first titles, and subscribes to it with all the interest that the last can inspire. I, who have no other pretension, and desire no other, than that of a father and a friend, request your permission to subscribe for my daughter, who, commencing the double education of a little Arnaud and a little Léontine, will be delighted to profit by your double instruction. I believe also that the grandfather himself will often obtain knowledge, and always pleasure, from the same source. It seems to me that no association could be more propitious to the union of the utile dulci. If I were to allow free scope to my pen, I feel assured that I should write thus like a madman to one of the two authors: "Not being able to make myself once more young, to adore your merits, I become an old infant, to receive your lessons. I kiss from a distance the hand of my youthful nurse, with the most profound respect, but not sufficiently abstracted from some of those emotions which have followed my first childhood, and which my second education ought to correct. Is it possible to submit to your rod with more ingenuousness? At least I confess my faults. As I am bound to speak the truth, I dare not yet add, this can never happen to me again. But the strong resolution will come with weak age; and the more I can transform myself, the nearer I shall approach perfection."

Will you be so kind as to present my respects to Madame and Mademoiselle de Meulan. Have you not a very excellent and amiable young man (another of the few who are consoled by elevation and purity of mind), the nephew of M. Hocher, residing under the same roof with yourself? If so, I beg you to recall me to his remembrance, and through him to that of his uncle, from whom I expect, with much anxiety, an answer upon a matter of the greatest interest to the uncle of my son-in-law, in the installation of the Imperial Courts. But nothing has arrived by the post.

I shall say nothing to you of our good and estimable friends of the Place Louis Quinze, for I am going to write to them directly.

But it has just occurred to me to entreat a favour of you before I close my letter. When, in your precepts to youth, you arrive at the chapter and age which treats of the choice of a profession, I implore you to insert something to this effect: "If your vocation leads you to be a publisher or editor of any work, moral, political, or historical, it matters not which, do not consider yourself at liberty to mutilate an author without his previous knowledge, and above all, one who is tenacious of the inviolability of his text more from conscience than self-love. If you mutilate him on your own responsibility, which is tolerably bold, do not believe that you are permitted to substitute a fictitious member of your own construction for the living one you have lopped off; and be cautious lest, without being aware of it, you replace an arm of flesh by a wooden leg. But break up all your presses rather than make him say, under the seal of his own signature, the contrary of what he has written, thought, or felt. To do this is an offence almost amounting to a moral crime." I write more at length on this topic to my friends of the Place Louis Quinze, and I beg you to speak to none but them of my enigma, which assuredly you have already solved; I hope that what has now offended and vexed me will not happen again. In saying what was necessary, I used very guarded expressions. I do not wish a rupture, the vengeance of which might fall on cherished memories or living friends. My letter has taken a very serious turn; I little thought, when I began, that it would lead me to this conclusion. I feel that I am in conversation with you, and carried away by full confidence. It is most gratifying to me to have added an involuntary proof of this sentiment to the spontaneous expression of all those with which you have so deeply inspired me, and the assurance of which I have the honour to repeat, accompanied by my sincere salutations.

Lally-Tolendal.

P.S. Allow me to enclose the addresses for the two subscriptions.

No. III.

Discourse delivered by M. Guizot, on the opening of his first Course of Lectures on Modern History. December 11th, 1812.

A statesman equally celebrated for his character and misfortunes, Sir Walter Raleigh, had published the first part of a 'History of the World;' while confined in the Tower, he employed himself in finishing the second. A quarrel arose in one of the courts of the prison; he looked on attentively at the contest, which became sanguinary, and left the window with his imagination strongly impressed by the scene that had passed under his eyes. On the morrow a friend came to visit him, and related what had occurred. But great was his surprise when this friend, who had been present at and even engaged in the occurrence of the preceding day, proved to him that this event, in its result as well as in its particulars, was precisely the contrary of what he had believed he saw. Raleigh, when left alone, took up his manuscript and threw it in the fire; convinced that, as he had been so completely deceived with respect to the details of an incident he had actually witnessed, he could know nothing whatever of those he had just described with his pen.

Are we better informed or more fortunate than Sir Walter Raleigh? The most confident historian would hesitate to answer this question directly in the affirmative. History relates a long series of events, and depicts a vast number of characters; and let us recollect, gentlemen, the difficulty of thoroughly understanding a single character or a solitary event. Montaigne, after having passed his life in self-study, was continually making new discoveries on his own nature; he has filled a long work with them, and ends by saying, "Man is a subject so diversified, so uncertain and vain, that it is difficult to pronounce any fixed and uniform opinion on him." He is, in fact, an obscure compound of an infinity of ideas and sentiments, which change and modify themselves reciprocally, and of which it is as difficult to disentangle the sources as to foresee the results. An uncertain produce of a multiplicity of circumstances, sometimes impenetrable, always complicated, often unknown to the person influenced by them, and not even suspected by those who surround him, man scarcely learns how to know himself, and is never more than guessed at by others. The simplest mind, if it attempted to examine and describe itself, would impart to us a thousand secrets, of which we have not the most remote suspicion. And how many different men are comprised in an event! how many whose characters have influenced that event, and have modified its nature, progress, and effects! Bring together circumstances in perfect accordance; suppose situations exactly similar: let a single actor change, and all is changed. He is urged by fresh motives, and desires new objects. Take the same actors, and alter but one of those circumstances independent of human will, which are called chance or destiny; and all is changed again. It is from this infinity of details, where everything is obscure, and nothing isolated, that history is composed; and man, proud of what he knows, because he forgets to think of how much he is ignorant, believes that he has acquired a full knowledge of history when he has read what some few have told him, who had no better means of understanding the times in which they lived, than we possess of justly estimating our own.

What then are we to seek and find in the darkness of the past, which thickens as it recedes from us? If Cæsar, Sallust, or Tacitus have only been able to transmit doubtful and imperfect notions, can we rely on what they relate? And if we are not to trust them, how are we to supply ourselves with information? Shall we be capable of disembarrassing our minds of those ideas and manners, and of that new existence, which a new order of things has produced, to adopt momentarily in our thoughts other manners and ideas, and a different character of being? Must we learn to become Greeks, Romans, or Barbarians, in order to understand these Romans, Barbarians, or Greeks, before we venture to judge them? And even if we could attain this difficult abnegation of an actual and imperious reality, should we become then as well acquainted with the history of the times of which they tell us, as were Cæsar, Sallust, or Tacitus? After being thus transported to the midst of the world they describe, we should find gaps in their delineations, of which we have at present no conception, and of which they were not always sensible themselves. That multiplicity of facts which, grouped together and viewed from a distance, appear to fill time and space, would present to us, if we found ourselves placed on the ground they occupy, as voids which we should find it impossible to fill up, and which the historians leave there designedly, because he who relates or describes what he sees, to others who see equally with himself, never feels called upon to recapitulate all that he knows.

Let us therefore refrain from supposing that history can present to us, in reality, an exact picture of the past; the world is too extensive, the night of time too obscure, and man too weak for such a portrait to be ever a complete reflection.

But can it be true that such important knowledge is entirely interdicted to us?—that in what we can acquire, all is a subject of doubt and error? Does the mind only enlighten itself to increase its wavering? Does it develope all its strength, merely to end in a confession of ignorance?—a painful and disheartening idea, which many men of superior intellect have encountered in their course, but by which they ought never to have been impeded!

Man seldom asks himself what he really requires to know, in his ardent pursuit of knowledge; he need only cast a glance upon his studies, to discover two divisions, the difference between which is striking, although we may be unable to assign the boundaries that separate them. Everywhere we perceive a certain innocent but futile labour, which attaches itself to questions and inquiries equally inaccessible and without results—which has no other object than to satisfy the restless curiosity of minds, the first want of which is occupation; and everywhere, also, we observe useful, productive, and interesting inquiry, not only advantageous to those who indulge in it, but beneficial to human nature at large. What time and talent have men wasted in metaphysical lucubrations! They have sought to penetrate the internal nature of things, of the mind, and of matter; they have taken purely vague combinations of words for substantial realities; but these very researches, or others which have arisen out of them, have enlightened us upon the order of our faculties, the laws by which they are governed, and the progress of their development; we have acquired from thence a history, a statistic of the human mind; and if no one has been able to tell us what it is, we have at least learned how it acts, and how we ought to act to strengthen its justice and extend its range.

Was not the study of astronomy for a long time directed to the dreams of astrology? Gassendi himself began to investigate it with that view; and when science cured him of the prejudices of superstition, he repented that he so openly declared his conversion, because, he said, many persons formerly studied astronomy to become astrologers, and he now perceived that they ceased to learn astronomy, since he had condemned astrology. Who then can prove to us that, without the restlessness of anticipation which had led men to seek the future in the stars, the science, by which today our ships are directed, would ever have reached its present perfection?

It is thus that we shall ever find, in the labours of man, one half fruitless, by the side of another moiety profitable; we shall then no longer condemn the curiosity which leads to knowledge; we shall acknowledge that, if the human mind often wanders in its path, if it has not always selected the most direct road, it has finally arrived, by the necessity of its nature, at the discovery of important truths; but, with progressive enlightenment, we shall endeavour not to lose time, to go straight to the end by concentrating our strength on fruitful inquiries and profitable results; and we shall soon convince ourselves that what man cannot do is valueless, and that he can achieve all that is necessary.

The application of this idea to history will soon remove the difficulty which its uncertainty raised at the outset. For example, it is of little consequence to us to know the exact personal appearance or the precise day of the birth of Constantine; to ascertain what particular motives or individual feelings may have influenced his determination or conduct on any given occasion; to be acquainted with all the details of his wars and victories in the struggles with Maxentius or Licinius: these minor points concern the monarch alone; and the monarch exists no longer. The anxiety some scholars display in hunting them out is merely a consequence of the interest which attaches to great names and important reminiscences. But the results of the conversion of Constantine, his administrative system, the political and religious principles which he established in his empire,—these are the matters which it imports the present generation to investigate; for they do not expire with a particular age, they form the destiny and glory of nations, they confer or take away the use of the most noble faculties of man; they either plunge them silently into a state of misery alternately submissive and rebellious, or establish for them the foundation of a lasting happiness.

It may be said, to a certain extent, that there are two pasts, the one entirely extinct and without real interest, because its influence has not extended beyond its actual duration; the other enduring for ever by the empire it has exercised over succeeding ages, and by that alone preserved to our knowledge, since what remains of it is there to enlighten us upon what has perished. History presents us, at every epoch, with some predominant ideas, some great events which have decided the fortune and character of a long series of generations. These ideas and events have left monuments which still remain, or which long remained, on the face of the world; an extended trace, in perpetuating the memory and effect of their existence, has multiplied the materials suitable for our guidance in the researches of which they are the object; reason itself can here supply us with its positive data to conduct us through the uncertain labyrinth of facts. In a past event there may have been some particular circumstance at present unknown, which would completely alter the idea we have formed of it. Thus, we shall never discover the reason which delayed Hannibal at Capua, and saved Rome; but in an effect which has endured for a long time, we easily ascertain the nature of its cause. The despotic authority which the Roman Senate exercised for ages over the people, explains to us the ideas of liberty within which the Senators restricted themselves when they expelled their kings. Let us then follow the path in which we can have reason for our guide; let us apply the principles, with which she furnishes us, to the examples borrowed from history. Man, in the ignorance and weakness to which the narrow limits of his life and faculties condemn him, has received reason to supply knowledge, as industry is given to him in place of strength.

Such, gentlemen, is the point of view under which we shall endeavour to contemplate history. We shall seek, in the annals of nations, a knowledge of the human race; we shall try to discover what, in every age and state of civilization, have been the prevailing ideas and principles in general adoption, which have produced the happiness or misery of the generations subjected to their power, and have influenced the destiny of those which succeeded them. The subject is one of the most abundant in considerations of this nature. History presents to us periods of development, during which man, emerging from a state of barbarism and ignorance, arrives gradually at a condition of science and advancement, which may decline, but can never perish, for knowledge is an inheritance that always finds heirs. The civilization of the Egyptians and Phœnicians prepared that of the Greeks; while that of the Romans was not lost to the barbarians who established themselves upon the ruins of the Empire. No preceding age has ever enjoyed the advantage we possess, of studying this slow but real progression: while looking back on the past, we can recognize the route which the human race has followed in Europe for more than two thousand years. Modern history alone, from its vast scope, from the variety and extent of its duration, offers us the grandest and most complete picture which we could possibly possess of the civilization of a certain portion of the globe. A rapid glance will suffice to indicate the character and interest of the subject.

Rome had conquered what her pride delighted to call the world. Western Asia, from the frontiers of Persia, the North of Africa, Greece, Macedonia, Thrace, all the countries situated on the right bank of the Danube, from its source to its mouth, Italy, Gaul, Great Britain, and Spain, acknowledged her authority. That authority extended over more than a thousand leagues in breadth, from the Wall of Antoninus and the southern boundaries of Dacia, to Mount Atlas;—and beyond fifteen hundred leagues in length, from the Euphrates to the Western Ocean. But if the immense extent of these conquests at first surprises the imagination, the astonishment diminishes when we consider how easy they were of accomplishment, and how uncertain of duration. In Asia, Rome had only to contend with effeminate races; in Europe, with ignorant savages, whose governments, without union, regularity, or vigour, were unable to contend with the strong constitution of the Roman aristocracy. Let us pause a moment to reflect on this. Rome found it more difficult to defend herself against Hannibal than to subjugate the world; and as soon as the world was subdued, Rome began to lose, by degrees, all that she had won by conquest. How could she maintain her power? The comparative state of civilization between the victors and the vanquished had prevented union or consolidation into one substantial and homogeneous whole; there was no extended and regular administration, no general and safe communication; the provinces were only connected with Rome by the tribute they paid; Rome was unknown in the provinces, except by the tribute she exacted. Everywhere, in Asia Minor, in Africa, in Spain, in Britain, in the North of Gallia, small colonies defended and maintained their independence; all the power of the Emperors was inadequate to compel the submission of the Isaurians. The whole formed a chaos of nations half vanquished and semi-barbarous, without interest or existence in the State of which they were considered a portion, and which Rome denominated the Empire.

No sooner was this Empire conquered, than it began to dissolve, and that haughty city which looked upon every region as subdued where she could, by maintaining an army, appoint a proconsul, and levy imposts, soon saw herself compelled to abandon, almost voluntarily, the possessions she was unable to retain. In the year of Christ 270, Aurelian retired from Dacia, and tacitly abandoned that territory to the Goths; in 412, Honorius recognized the independence of Great Britain and Armorica; in 428, he wished the inhabitants of Gallia Narbonensis to govern themselves. On all sides we see the Romans abandoning, without being driven out, countries whose obedience, according to the expression of Montesquieu, weighed upon them, and which, never having been incorporated with the Empire, were sure to separate from it on the first shock.

The shock came from a quarter which the Romans, notwithstanding their pride, had never considered one of their provinces. Even more barbarous than the Gauls, the Britons, and the Spaniards, the Germans had never been conquered, because their innumerable tribes, without fixed residences or country, ever ready to advance or retreat, sometimes threw themselves, with their wives and flocks, upon the possessions of Rome, and at others retired before her armies, leaving nothing for conquest but a country without inhabitants, which they re-occupied as soon as the weakness or distance of the conquerors afforded them the opportunity. It is to this wandering life of a hunting nation, to this facility of flight and return, rather than to superior bravery, that the Germans were indebted for the preservation of their independence. The Gauls and Spaniards had also defended themselves courageously; but the one, surrounded by the ocean, knew not where to fly from enemies they could not expel; and the other, in a state of more advanced civilization, attacked by the Romans, to whom the Narbonnese province afforded, in the very heart of Gaul itself, an impregnable base, and repulsed by the Germans from the land into which they might have escaped, were also compelled to submit. Drusus and Germanicus had long before penetrated into Germany; they withdrew, because the Germans always retreating before them, they would, by remaining, have only occupied territory without subjects.

When, from causes not connected with the Roman Empire, the Tartar tribes who wandered through the deserts of Sarmatia and Scythia, from the northern frontiers of China, marched upon Germany, the Germans, pressed by these new invaders, threw themselves upon the Roman provinces, to conquer possessions where they might establish themselves in perpetuity. Rome then fought in defence; the struggle was protracted; the skill and courage of some of the Emperors for a long time opposed a powerful barrier; but the Barbarians were the ultimate conquerors, because it was imperative on them to win the victory, and their swarms of warriors were inexhaustible. The Visigoths, the Alani, and the Suevi established themselves in the South, of Gaul and Spain; the Vandals passed over into Africa; the Huns occupied the banks of the Danube; the Ostrogoths founded their kingdom in Italy; the Franks in the North of Gaul; Rome ceased to call herself the mistress of Europe; Constantinople does not apply to our present subject.

Those nations of the East and the North who transported themselves in a mass into the countries where they were destined to found States, the more durable because they conquered not to extend but to establish themselves, were barbarians, such as the Romans themselves had long remained. Force was their law, savage independence their delight; they were free because none of them had ever thought or believed that men as strong as themselves would submit to their domination; they were brave because courage with them was a necessity; they loved war because war brings occupation without labour; they desired lands because these new possessions supplied them with a thousand novel sources of enjoyment, which they could indulge in while giving themselves up to idleness. They had chiefs because men leagued together always have leaders, and because the bravest, ever held in high consideration, soon become the most powerful, and bequeath to their descendants a portion of their own personal influence. These chiefs became kings; the old subjects of Rome, who at first had only been called upon to receive, to lodge, and feed their new masters, were soon compelled to surrender to them a portion of their estates; and as the labourer, as well as the plant, attaches himself to the soil that nourishes him, the lands and the labourers became the property of these turbulent and lazy owners. Thus feudalism was established,—not suddenly, not by an express convention between the chief and his followers, not by an immediate and regular division of the conquered country amongst the conquerors, but by degrees, after long years of uncertainty, by the simple force of circumstances, as must always happen when conquest is followed by transplantation and continued possession.

We should be wrong in supposing that the barbarians were destitute of all moral convictions. Man, in that early epoch of civilization, does not reflect upon what we call duties; but he knows and respects, amongst his fellow-beings, certain rights, some traces of which are discoverable even under the empire of the most absolute force. A simple code of justice, often violated, and cruelly avenged, regulates the simple intercourse of associated savages. The Germans, unacquainted with any other laws or ties, found themselves suddenly transported into the midst of an order of things founded on different ideas, and demanding different restrictions. This gave them no trouble; their passage was too rapid to enable them to ascertain and supply what was deficient in their legislature and policy. Bestowing little thought on their new subjects, they continued to follow the same principles and customs which recently, in the forests of Germany, had regulated their conduct and decided their quarrels. Thus the conquered people were, at first, more forgotten than vanquished, more despised than oppressed; they constituted the mass of the nation, and this mass found itself controlled without being reduced to servitude, because they were not thought of, and because the conquerors never suspected that they could possess rights which they feared to defend. From thence sprang, in the sequel, that long disorder at the commencement of the Middle Ages, during which everything was isolated, fortuitous, and partial; hence also proceeded the absolute separation between the nobles and the people, and those abuses of the feudal system which only became portions of a system when long possession had caused to be looked upon as a right, what at first was only the produce of conquest and chance.

The clergy alone, to whom the conversion of the victors afforded the means of acquiring a power so much the greater that its force and extent could only be judged by the opinion it directed, maintained their privileges, and secured their independence. The religion which the Germans embraced became the only channel through which they derived new ideas, the sole point of contact between them and the inhabitants of their adopted country. The clergy, at first, thought only of their own interest; in this mode of communication, all the immediate advantages of the invasion of the barbarians were reaped by them for themselves. The liberal and beneficent influences of Christianity expanded slowly; that of religious animosity and theological dispute was the first to make itself felt. It was only in the class occupied by those dissensions, and excited by those rancorous feelings, that energetic men were yet to be found in the Roman Empire; religious sentiments and duties had revived, in hearts penetrated with their importance, a degree of zeal long extinguished. St. Athanasius and St. Ambrose had alone resisted Constantine and Theodosius; their successors were the sole opponents who withstood the barbarians. This gave rise to the long empire of spiritual power, sustained with devotion and perseverance, and so weakly or fruitlessly assailed. We may say now, without fear, that the noblest characters, the men most distinguished by their ability or courage, throughout this period of misfortune and calamity, belonged to the ecclesiastical order; and no other epoch of history supplies, in such a remarkable manner, the confirmation of this truth, so honourable to human nature, and perhaps the most instructive of all others,—that the most exalted virtues still spring up and develope themselves in the bosom of the most pernicious errors.

To these general features, intended to depict the ideas, manners, and conditions of men during the Middle Ages, it would be easy to add others, not less characteristic, and infinitely more minute. We should find poetry and literature, those beautiful and delightful emanations of the mind, the seeds of which have never been choked by all the follies and miseries of humanity, take birth in the very heart of barbarism, and charm the barbarians themselves by a new species of enjoyment. We should find the source and true character of that poetical, warlike, and religious enthusiasm which created chivalry and the crusades. We should probably discover, in the wandering lives of the knights and crusaders, the reflected influence of the roving habits of the German hunters, of that propensity to remove, and that superabundance of population, which ever exist where social order is not sufficiently well regulated for man to feel satisfied with his condition and locality; and before laborious industry has taught him to compel the earth to supply him with certain and abundant subsistence. Perhaps, also, that principle of honour which inviolably attached the German barbarians to a leader of their own choice, that individual liberty of which it was the fruit, and which gives man such an elevated idea of his own individual importance; that empire of the imagination which obtains such control over all young nations, and induces them to attempt the first steps beyond physical wants and purely material incitements, might furnish us with the causes of the elevation, enthusiasm, and devotion which, sometimes detaching the nobles of the Middle Ages from their habitual rudeness, inspired them with the noble sentiments and virtues that even in the present day command our admiration. We should then feel little surprised at seeing barbarity and heroism united, so much energy combined with so much weakness, and the natural coarseness of man in a savage state blended with the most sublime aspirations of moral refinement.

It was reserved for the latter half of the fifteenth century to witness the birth of events destined to introduce new manners and a fresh order of politics into Europe, and to lead the world towards the direction it follows at present. Italy, we may say, discovered the civilization of the Greeks; the letters, arts, and ideas of that brilliant antiquity inspired universal enthusiasm. The long quarrels of the Italian Republics, after having forced men to display their utmost energy, made them also feel the necessity of a period of repose ennobled and charmed by the occupations of the mind. The study of classic literature supplied the means; they were seized with ardour. Popes, cardinals, princes, nobles, and men of genius gave themselves up to learned researches; they wrote to each other, they travelled to communicate their mutual labours, to discover, to read, and to copy ancient manuscripts. The discovery of printing came to render these communications easy and prompt; to make this commerce of the mind extended and prolific. No other event has so powerfully influenced human civilization. Books became a tribune from which the world was addressed. That world was soon doubled. The compass opened safe roads across the monotonous immensity of the seas. America was discovered; and the sight of new manners, the agitation of new interests which were no longer the trifling concerns of one town or castle with another, but the great transactions of mighty powers, changed entirely the ideas of individuals and the political intercourse of States.

The invention of gunpowder had already altered their military relations; the issue of battles no longer depended on the isolated bravery of warriors, but on the power and skill of leaders. It has not yet been sufficiently investigated to what extent this discovery has secured monarchical authority, and given rise to the balance of power.

Finally, the Reformation struck a deadly blow against spiritual supremacy, the consequences of which are attributable to the bold examination of the theological questions and political shocks which led to the separation of religious sects, rather than to the new dogmas adopted by the Reformers as the foundation of their belief.

Figure to yourselves, gentlemen, the effect which these united causes were calculated to produce in the midst of the fermentation by which the human species was at that time excited, in the progress of the superabundant energy and activity which characterized the Middle Ages. From that time, this activity, so long unregulated, began to organize itself and advance towards a defined object; this energy submitted to laws; isolation disappeared; the human race formed itself into one great body; public opinion assumed influence; and if an age of civil wars, of religious dissensions, presents the lengthened echo of that powerful shock which towards the end of the fifteenth century staggered Europe, under so many different forms, it is not the less to the ideas and discoveries which produced that blow that we are indebted for the two centuries of splendour, order, and peace during which civilization has reached the point where we find it in the present day.

This is not the place to follow the march of human nature during these two centuries. That history is so extensive, and composed of so many relations, alternately vast and minute, but always important; of so many events closely connected, brought about by causes so mixed together, and causes in their turn productive of such numerous effects, of so many different labours, that it is impossible to recapitulate them within a limited compass. Never have so many powerful and neighbouring States exercised upon each other such constant and complicated influence; never has their interior structure presented so many ramifications to study; never has the human mind advanced at once upon so many different roads; never have so many events, actors, and ideas been engaged in such an extended space, or produced such interesting and instructive results. Perhaps on some future occasion we may enter into this maze, and look for the clew to guide us through it. Called upon, at present, to study the first ages of modern history, we shall seek for their cradle in the forests of Germany, the country of our ancestors; after having drawn a picture of their manners, as complete as the number of facts which have reached our knowledge, the actual state of our information, and my efforts to reach that level will permit, we shall then cast a glance upon the condition of the Roman Empire at the moment when the barbarians invaded it to attempt establishment; after that we shall investigate the long struggles which ensued between them and Rome, from their irruption into the West and South of Europe, down to the foundation of the principal modern monarchies. This foundation will thus become for us a resting-point, from whence we shall depart again to follow the course of the history of Europe, which is in fact our own; for if unity, the fruit of the Roman dominion, disappeared with it, there are always, nevertheless, between the different nations which rose upon its ruins, relations so multiplied, so continued, and so important, that from them, in the whole of modern history taken together, an actual unity results which we shall be compelled to acknowledge. This task is enormous; and when we contemplate its full extent, it is impossible not to recoil before the difficulty. Judge then, gentlemen, whether I ought not to tremble at such an undertaking; but your indulgence and zeal will make up for the weakness of my resources: I shall be more than repaid if I am able to assist you in advancing even a few steps on the road which leads to truth!

No. IV.

The Abbé de Montesquiou to M. Guizot.

March 31st, 1815.

I am not, my dear Sir, so lost to my friends that I have forgotten their friendship: yours has had many charms for me. I do not reproach myself with the poor trick I have played you. Your age does not run a long lease with mine. We can only show the public the objects worthy of their confidence; and I congratulate myself with having left them an impression of you which will not readily be effaced. I have been less fortunate on my own account, and can only deplore that fatality which has triumphed over my convictions, my repugnances, and the immeasurable consolations which friendship has bestowed on me. Let my example be profitable to you on some future occasion. Give to public affairs the period of your strength, but not that which requires repose alone; the interval will be long enough, at your time of life, to enable you to arrive at much distinction. I shall enjoy it with the interest which you know I feel, and with all the warm feelings with which your attachment has inspired me. Present my respects to Madame Guizot; it is to her I offer my apologies for having disturbed her tranquillity. But I hope her infant will profit by the strong food we have already administered to it. Allow me to request some token of remembrance from her as well as from yourself, for all the sentiments of respect and friendship I have vowed to you for life.

The Abbé de Montesquiou to M. Guizot.

Plaisance, June 8th, 1816.

I was expecting to hear from you, my dear friend, with much impatience, and I now thank you sincerely for having written to me. It was not that I doubted your philosophy; you know that those who precede their age learn too soon the uncertainty of all human affairs; but I feared lest your taste for your early avocations might induce you to abandon public affairs, for which you have evinced such ready ability; and we are not rich enough to make sacrifices. I feel very happy at being satisfied on this point, and leave the rest to the caprices of that destiny which can scarcely be harsh towards you. You will be distinguished at the Council, as you have been in all other situations; and it must naturally follow, that the better you are known, your career will become the more brilliant and secure. Youth, which feels its power, ought always to say, with the Cardinal de Bernis, "My Lord, I shall wait." The more I see of France, the more I am impressed with the truth, that those who believe they have secured the State by compromising the royal authority in these distant departments, have committed a mistake. All that are honest and rational are royalists; but, thanks to our own dissensions, they no longer know how to show themselves such. They thought until then, that to serve the King was to do what he required through the voice of his ministers, and they have been lately told that this was an error, but they have been left in ignorance as to who are his Majesty's real organs. The enemies to our repose profit by this. The most absurd stories are propagated amongst the people, and all are the people at so great a distance. I can imagine that the character of these disturbers varies in our different provinces. In this, where we have no large towns, and no aristocracy, we lie at the mercy of all who pretend to know more than ourselves. Great credit thus attaches to the Half-pays, who, belonging more to the people than to any other class, and not being able to digest their last disappointment, trade upon it in every possible manner, and are always believed because they are the richest in their immediate locality. The gentlemen Deputies come next upon the list, estimating themselves as little proconsuls, disposing of all places, and setting aside prefects. Thus you see how little authority remains with the King, whose agents are masters and do nothing in his name. As to the administration of justice, you may readily suppose that no one thinks of it. The people are in want of bread; their harvest rots under continual rains; the roads are horrible, the hospitals in the greatest misery; nothing remains but dismissals, accusations, and deputations. If you could change them for a little royal authority, we might still see the end of our sufferings; but make haste, for when the month of October has arrived it will be too late.

Adieu, my dear friend, present my respects to Madame Guizot, and receive the fullest assurance of my good wishes.

No. V.

Fragments selected from a Pamphlet by M. Guizot, entitled 'Thoughts upon the Liberty of the Press,' 1814.

Many of the calamities of France, calamities which might be indefinitely prolonged if they were not attacked at their source, arise, as I have just said, from the ignorance to which the French people have been condemned as to the affairs and position of the State, to the system of falsehood adopted by a Government which required everything to be concealed, and to the indifference and suspicion with which this habitual deceit and falsehood had inspired the citizens. It is truth, therefore, which ought to appear in broad daylight; it is obscurity which ought to be dissipated, if we wish to re-establish confidence and revive zeal. It will not suffice that the intentions of Government should be good, or its words sincere; it is requisite that the people should be convinced of this, and should be supplied with the means of satisfying themselves. When we have been for a long time tricked by an impostor, we become doubtful even of an honest man; and all our proverbs on the melancholy suspicion of old age are founded on this truth ...

The nation, so long deceived, expects the truth from every quarter; at present, it has a hope of accomplishing this object. It demands it with anxiety from its representatives, its administrators, and from all who are believed capable of imparting it. The more it has been withheld up to this period, the more precious it will be considered. There will be this advantage, that it will be hailed with transport by the people as soon as they satisfy themselves that it may be trusted; and there will be a corresponding evil,—they will listen to it without fear, when they discover that they are left in freedom to deliver their opinions, and to labour openly in its support. No one questions the embarrassments which truth will dissipate, or the references it will supply. A nation from whom it has been sedulously withheld, soon believes that something hostile is in agitation, and recoils back into mistrust. But when the truth is openly manifested, when a Government displays a noble confidence in its own sentiments and in the good feeling of its subjects, this confidence excites theirs in return, and calls up all their zeal.... The French, certain to understand, and quick to utter truth, will soon abandon that injurious tendency to suspicion which leads them from all esteem for their head, and all devotion to the State. The most indifferent spirits will resume an interest in public affairs, when they discover that they can take a part in them; the most apprehensive will cease their fears when they cease to live in clouds; they will no longer be continually occupied in calculating how much they should reject out of the speeches that are addressed to them, the recitals delivered and the portions presented for investigation; or how much artifice, dangerous intention, or afterthought remains hidden in all that proceeds from the throne.... An extended liberty of the press can alone, while restoring confidence, give back that energy to the King and the people which neither can dispense with: it is the life of the soul that requires to be revived in the nation in which it has been extinguished by despotism; that life lies in the free action of the press, and thought can only expand and develope itself in full publicity. No one in France can longer dread the oppression under which we have lived for ten years; but if the want of action which weakness engenders were to succeed that which tyranny imposes;—if the weight of a terrible and mute agitation should be replaced only by the languor of repose, we should never witness a renewal in France of that national activity, that brave and generous disposition which makes many sacrifices to duty;—finally, of that confidence in the sovereign, the necessity of which will be more acknowledged every day. We should merely obtain from the nation a barren tranquillity, the insufficiency of which would compel recourse to measures evil in themselves, and very far removed from the paternal intentions of the King.

Let us, on the contrary, adopt a system of liberty and frankness; let truth circulate freely from the throne to the people, and from the people to the throne; let the paths be opened to those who ought to speak freely, and to others who desire to learn; we shall then see apathy dissipate, suspicion vanish, and loyalty become general and spontaneous, from the certainty of its necessity and usefulness.

Unfortunately, during the twenty-five years which have recently elapsed, we have so deplorably abused many advantages, that, at present, to name them suffices to excite the most deplorable apprehensions. We are not inclined to take into consideration the difference of the times, of situation, of the march of opinion, or of the temperament of men's minds: we look upon as always dangerous what has once proved fatal; we think and act as mothers might do, who, because they saw the infant fall, would prevent the youth from walking.... This inclination is general; we retrace it under every form; and those who have closely observed it will have little trouble in satisfying themselves that perfect liberty of the press, at least with regard to political questions, would, in the present day, be almost without danger. Those who fear it fancy themselves still at the beginning of the Revolution—at that epoch when all passions sought only to display themselves, when violence was the popular characteristic, and reason obtained only a contemptuous smile. Nothing can be more dissimilar than that time and the present; and, from the very cause that unlicensed freedom then gave rise to the most disastrous evils, we may infer, unless I deceive myself, that very few would now spring from the same source.

Nevertheless, as many people appear to dread such a result; as I am unwilling to affirm that the experiment might not be followed by certain inconveniences, more mischievous from the fear they would inspire than from the actual consequences they might introduce;—as in the state in which we find ourselves, without a guide in the experience of the past, or certain data for the future, it is natural that we should advance cautiously; and as the spirit of the nation seems to indicate that in every respect circumspection is necessary, the opinions of those who think that some restrictions should be imposed, ought, perhaps, to prevail. For twenty-five years the nation has been so utterly a stranger to habits of true liberty, it has passed through so many different forms of despotism, and the last was felt to be so oppressive, that, in restoring freedom, we may dread inexperience more than impetuosity; it would not dream of attack, but it might prove unequal to defence; in the midst of the necessity for order and peace which is universally felt, in the midst of a collision of opposing interests which must be carefully dealt with, Government may wish, and with reason, to avoid the appearance of clashing and disturbance, which might probably be without importance, but the danger of which would be exaggerated by imagination.

The question then reduces itself to this:—What are, under existing circumstances, the causes which call for a certain restraint in the liberty of the press? and by what restrictions, conformable to the nature of these causes, can we modify without destroying its freedom? and how shall we gradually remove these qualifications, for the present considered necessary?

All liberty is placed between oppression and license: the liberty of man in the social state is necessarily restrained by certain laws, the abuse or oblivion of which are equally dangerous; but the circumstances which expose society to either of these perils are different. In a well-established government, solidly constituted, the danger against which the friends of liberty have to contend is oppression: all is there combined for the maintenance of law; all tends to support vigorous discipline, against which every individual labours to retain the share of freedom which is his due; the function of government is to support order; that of the governed to watch over liberty.

The state of things is entirely different in a government only commencing. If it follows a period of misfortune and disturbance, during which morality and reason have been equally perverted,— when passions have been indulged without curb, when private interests have been paraded without shame,—then oppression falls within the number of dangers which are only to be anticipated, while license is that which must be directly opposed. Our Government has not yet attained its full strength; it is not yet possessed of all the means which are to be placed at its disposal to maintain order and rule: before acquiring all, it will be careful not to abuse any; and the governed, who are still without some of the advantages of order, wish to possess all those of confusion. They are not yet sufficiently sure of their own tranquillity, to abstain from attacking that of others. Every one is ready to inflict the blow he is exposed to receive; we offend with impunity the laws which have not yet foreseen all the methods that may be adopted to elude them; we brave without danger the authorities which cannot yet appeal, in their own support, to the experience of the happiness enjoyed under their auspices. It is, then, against particular attempts that constant watch should be kept; thus it becomes necessary to protect liberty from the outrages of license, and sometimes to prevent a strong government from being reduced to defence when uncertain of commanding obedience.

Thus, unrestricted liberty of the press, without detrimental consequences in a state of government free, happy, and strongly constituted, might prove injurious under a system only commencing, and in which the citizens have still to acquire liberty and prosperity. In the first case there is no danger in allowing freedom of thought and utterance to all, because, if the order of things is good, the great majority of the members of society will be disposed to support it, and also because the nation, enlightened by its actual happiness, will not be easily drawn to the pursuit of something always represented as better, but ever uncertain of acquirement. In the second case, on the contrary, the passions and interests of many individuals, differing in themselves, and all, more or less, abstracted from any feeling for the public good, are neither instructed by prosperity nor enlightened by experience; there exist therefore in the nation very few barriers against the plotters of evil, while in the government there are many gaps through which disorder may introduce itself: every species of ambition revives, and none can tell on what point to settle; all seek their place, without being sure of finding it; common sense, which invents nothing, but knows how to select, has no fixed rule upon which to act; the bewildered multitude, who are directed by nothing and have not yet learned to direct themselves, know not what guide to follow; and in the midst of so many contradictory ideas, and incapable of separating truth from falsehood, the least evil that can happen is, that they may determine to remain in their ignorance and stupidity. While information is still so sparingly disseminated, the license of the press becomes an important obstacle to its progress; men, little accustomed to reason upon certain matters, and poor in positive knowledge, adopt too readily the errors which are propagated from every quarter, and find it difficult to distinguish readily the truth when presented to them; thence originate a host of false and crude notions, a multiplicity of judgments adopted without examination, and a pretended acquirement, the more mischievous as, occupying the place which reason alone should hold, it for a long time interdicts her approach.

The Revolution has proved to us the danger arising from knowledge so erroneously obtained. From this danger we are now called on to protect ourselves. It is better to confess the fact: we have learned wisdom from misfortune; but the despotism of the last ten years has extinguished, for the greater part of the French people, the light we might thence have derived. Some individuals, undoubtedly, have continued to reflect, to observe, and to study—they have been instructed by the very despotism which oppressed them; but the nation in general, crushed and unfortunate, has found itself arrested in the development of its intellectual faculties. When we look closely into the fact, we feel surprised and almost ashamed of our national thoughtlessness and ignorance; we feel the necessity of emerging from it. The most oppressive yoke alone was able to reduce, and could again reduce it for a certain time to silence and inaction; but it requires to be propped and guided, and, after so much experimental imprudence, for the interest even of reason and knowledge, the liberty of the press, which we have never yet enjoyed, ought to be attempted with caution.

Regarded in this point of view, the restrictions which may be applied will less startle the friends of truth and justice; they will see in them nothing more than a concession to existing circumstances, dictated solely by the interest of the nation; and if care is taken to limit this concession so that it may never become dangerous; if, in establishing a barrier against license, a door is always left open for liberty; if the object of these restrictions is evidently to prepare the French people to dispense with them, and to arrive hereafter at perfect freedom; if they are so combined and modified that the liberty may go on increasing until the nation becomes more capable of enjoying it profitably;—finally, if, instead of impeding the progress of the human mind, they are only calculated to assure it, and to direct the course of the most enlightened spirits;—so far from considering them as an attack upon the principles of justice, we shall see in them a measure of prudence, a guarantee for public order, and a new motive for hoping that the overthrow of that order will never again occur to disturb or retard the French nation in the career of truth and reason.

No. VI.

Report to the King, and Royal Decree for the Reform of Public Instruction, February 17th, 1815.

Louis, by the grace of God, King of France and Navarre, to all who may receive these presents, they come greeting.

Having had an account delivered to us, of the state of public instruction in our kingdom, we have observed that it rested upon institutions destined to advance the political views of the Government which had formed them, rather than to extend to our subjects the advantages of moral education, conformable with the necessities of the age. We have rendered justice to the wisdom and zeal of all who were appointed to watch over and direct instruction. We have seen with satisfaction that they have never ceased to struggle against the obstacles which the times opposed to them, and also to the institutions which they were called to put in force. But we have felt the necessity of reforming these institutions, and of bringing back national education to its true object; which is, to disseminate sound doctrines, to maintain good manners, and to train men who, by their knowledge and virtue, may communicate to society the profitable lessons and wise examples they have received from their masters.

We have maturely considered these institutions, which we now propose to reform; and it appears to us that a system of single and absolute authority is incompatible with our paternal intentions and with the liberal spirit of our government;

That this authority, essentially occupied in the direction of the whole, was to a certain extent condemned to be in ignorance or neglectful of those details of daily examination, which can only be intrusted to local supervisors better informed as to the necessities, and more directly interested in the prosperity of the establishments committed to their charge;

That the right of nomination to all these situations, concentrated in the hands of a single person, left too much opening for error, and too much influence to favour, weakening the impulse of emulation, and reducing the teachers to a state of dependence ill suited to the honourable post they occupied, and to the importance of their functions;

That this dependence and the too frequent removals which are the inevitable result, rendered the position of the teachers uncertain and precarious; was injurious to the consideration they ought to enjoy to induce them to work zealously in their laborious vocations; and prevented, between them and the relations of their pupils, that confidence which results from long service and old habits; and thus deprived them of the most gratifying reward they could attain—the respect and affection of the countries to which they have dedicated their talents and their lives;

Finally, that the tax of one-twentieth of the costs of instruction, levied upon all the pupils of the lyceums, colleges, and schools, and applied to expenses from which those who pay it derive no immediate advantage, and which charges may be considerably reduced, are in opposition to our desire of favouring good and profitable studies, and of extending the benefits of education to all classes of our subjects.

Wishing to enable ourselves, as soon as possible, to lay before the two Chambers the bills which are intended to establish the system of public instruction throughout France, and to provide for the necessary expenses, we have resolved to establish provisionally the reforms best adapted to supply the experience and information which we still require, to accomplish this object; and in place of the tax of one-twentieth on the costs of instruction, the abolition of which we are not inclined to defer, it has pleased us to appropriate, from our Civil List, the sum of one million, which will be employed during the present year, 1815, for the use of public instruction in this our kingdom.

For these reasons, and on the report of our Minister the Secretary of State for the Department of the Interior, and by and with the advice of our Council of State, we have decreed, and do decree, as follows:—

Title I.

General Arrangements.

Article 1. The divisions arranged under the name of Academies by the decree of the 17th of May, 1808, are reduced to seventeen, conformably to the table at present annexed. They will assume the title of Universities.

The Universities will be named after the Head Town assigned to each.

The Lyceums at present established will be called Royal Colleges.

2. Each University will be composed, first, of a council, presided over by a rector; secondly, of faculties; thirdly, of colleges; fourthly, of district colleges.

3. The mode of teaching and discipline in all the Universities will be regulated and superintended by a Royal Council of Public Instruction.

4. The Normal School of Paris will be common to all the Universities; it will provide, at the expense of the State, the number of professors and masters which may be required to give instruction in science and literature.

Title II.

Respecting the Universities.

Section 1.

The Councils of the Universities.

5. The Council of each University will consist of a presiding rector, of the deans of faculty, of the provost of the royal college of the Head Town, or of the oldest provost if there are more than one royal college; and of at least three of the principal inhabitants, selected by our Royal Council of Public Instruction.

6. The bishop and prefect will be members of this council, and will have votes in the meetings, above the rector.

7. The council of the University can visit, whenever they consider it proper to do so, the royal and district colleges, the institutes, boarding-schools, and other seminaries of instruction, through two appointed inspectors; who will report on the state of teaching and discipline within the jurisdiction of the University, according to the instructions delivered to them.

The number of inspectors for the University of Paris may amount to six.

8. The council will select each of these inspectors from two candidates recommended by the

rector.

9. The council will also select, each from two candidates recommended by the rector, the provosts, the censors or inspectors of studies, the professors of philosophy, rhetoric, and higher mathematics, the chaplains, and bursars of the royal colleges.

10. The inspectors of the Universities will be selected from the provosts, the superintendent-masters, the professors of philosophy, rhetoric, and mathematics of the royal colleges, and from the head masters of the district colleges; the superintendent-masters in the royal colleges will be chosen from the professors of philosophy, rhetoric, or superior mathematics in the same colleges.

11. The council of the University can revoke, if they see cause, any appointment they may make: in these cases their resolutions must be notified and accounted for, and cannot take effect until sanctioned by our Royal Council of Public Instruction.

12. No one can establish an institution or a boarding-school, or become head of an institution or a boarding-school already established, without having been previously examined and duly qualified by the council of the University, and unless their qualification has been approved of by the Royal Council of Public Instruction.

13. The council of the University will examine and decide on the accounts of the faculties, and of the royal colleges; they will also examine the accounts of general expenditure handed in by the rector, and, after having decided on them, will transmit the same to our Royal Council of Public Instruction.

14. The council will keep a registry of its proceedings, and will forward a copy once a month to our Royal Council.

15. In public ceremonies, the council will rank after the Council of Prefecture.

Section 2.

Of the Rectors of Universities.

16. The rectors of the Universities are appointed by us, each selected from three candidates presented by our Royal Council of Public Instruction, and chosen from rectors already appointed, from inspectors-general of study, of whom we shall speak hereafter, from the professors of faculty, the professors of the Universities, the provosts, the censors, and the professors of philosophy, rhetoric, and superior mathematics in the royal colleges.

17. The rectors of the Universities appoint the professors, doctors of faculty, and masters in all the colleges, with the exception of the professors of philosophy, rhetoric, and superior mathematics in the royal colleges, who are appointed as already named in Article 9.

18. The rectors will select the candidates from amongst the professors, doctors of faculty, and masters already employed in the old or new establishments of education, or from the pupils of the Normal School, who, having completed their courses, have received the degree of Professor-Substitute.

19. The professors and doctors of faculty thus appointed can only be removed by the council of the University upon the explained proposition of the rector.

20. The professors and doctors of faculty, appointed by one or more rectors, not being those of the Universities in which they are actually employed, can choose the University and select the

employment they may prefer; but they are bound to notify their decision, one month before the commencement of the scholastic year, to the rector of the University to which they belong.

21. The pupils of the Normal School selected by rectors not belonging to the University from whence they were sent, have the same privilege of option, on giving similar notice.

22. The rector of the University will preside, whenever he thinks proper, at the examinations which precede the conferring of degrees in the different faculties.

23. The rector has the entire charge of correspondence.

24. He will lay before the council of the University all matters that require to be submitted to them, appoint the reporters, if necessary, regulate the order of discussion, and sign the resolutions.

25. If opinions are equally divided, he has the casting vote.

Section 3.

Of the Faculties.

26. The number and composition of the Faculties in each University are settled by us, on the proposition of our Royal Council of Public Instruction.

27. The faculties are placed immediately under the authority, direction, and supervision of that Council.

28. The Council appoints their deans, each from two candidates, who will be nominated for selection.

29. It appoints the professors for life, each from four candidates, two of whom must be presented by the faculty in which a chair has become vacant, and the other two by the council of the University.

30. Over and above the special teaching with which they are charged, the faculties will confer, after examination, and according to the established rules, the degrees which are or may become necessary for the various ecclesiastical, political, and civil functions and professions.

31. The diplomas of degrees are issued in our name, signed by the dean, and countersigned by the rector, who can refuse his visa if he has reason to think that the prescribed conditions have not been correctly observed.

32. In the Universities which as yet have no faculties of science or literature, the degree of Bachelor in Letters may be conferred after the prescribed examinations by the provost, the inspector of studies, and the professors of philosophy and rhetoric of the royal college of the Head Town of the district. The inspector of studies will perform the functions of dean; he will sign the diplomas, and will take his place in the sittings of the councils of the University, after the provost.

Section 4.

Of the Royal and District Colleges.

33. The Royal Colleges are governed by a provost, and the District Colleges by a principal.

34. The provosts and principals will execute and cause to be executed the regulations regarding instruction, discipline, and compatibility.

35. The administration of the royal college of the Head Town is placed under the immediate

superintendence of the rector and the council of the University.

36. All the other colleges, royal or provincial, are placed under the immediate superintendence of a committee of administration composed of the sub-prefect, the mayor, and at least three of the principal inhabitants of the place, appointed by the council of the University.

37. This committee will propose, in each case, two candidates to the rector, who will select from them the principals of the local colleges.

38. The principals, thus appointed, can only be removed by the council of the University, upon the proposition of the committee, and by the decision of the rector.

39. The Committee of Administration will examine and decide on the accounts of the local colleges.

40. The Committee will also examine and decide on the accounts of the royal colleges, except only on those of the royal college of the Head Town, and will transmit them to the council of the University.

41. The Committee will also keep a register of its proceedings, and transmit the same once in every month to the council of the University.

42. The president of this Committee will be the sub-prefect, or, in his absence, the mayor.

43. The bishops and prefects are members of all the Committees in their diocese or department; and when present they will have votes above the presidents.

44. The heads of institutions and masters of boarding-schools established within the boundaries of cities or towns in which there are either royal or local colleges, are required to send their boarders as day-scholars to the classes of the said colleges.

45. The second Ecclesiastical School which has been or may be established in each department, in virtue of our decree of ..., is excepted from this obligation: but the said school cannot receive day-scholars of any description.

Title III.

Of the Normal School.

46. Each University will send, every year, to the Normal School at Paris, a number of pupils proportioned to the necessities of education.

This number will be regulated by our Royal Council of Public Instruction.

47. The council of the University will select these pupils from those who, having finished their courses in rhetoric and philosophy, are intended, with the consent of their relatives, for public teachers.

48. The pupils sent to the Normal School will remain there three years, after which they will be examined by our Royal Council of Public Instruction, who will deliver to them, on approbation, the brevet of Professor-Substitute.

49. The pupils who have received this brevet, if not summoned by the rector of other Universities, will return to that to which they originally belonged, where they will be placed by the rector, and advanced according to their capacity and services.

50. The head master of the Normal School will hold the same rank, and exercise the same prerogatives, with the rectors of the Universities.

Title IV.

Of the Royal Council of Public Instruction.

51. Our Royal Council of Public Instruction will be composed of a president and eleven councillors appointed by us.

52. Two of this number will be selected from the clergy, two from our State Council, or from the Courts, and the seven others from individuals who have become eminent for their talents or services in the cause of public instruction.

53. The president of our Royal Council is alone charged with the correspondence; he will introduce all subjects of discussion to the Council, name the reporters, if necessary, establish the order of debate, sign and despatch the resolutions, and see them carried into effect.

54. In case of an equal division of opinions, he will have the casting vote.

55. Conformably with Article 3 of the present decree, our Royal Council will prepare, arrange, and promulgate the general regulations concerning instruction and discipline.

56. The Council will prescribe the execution of these rules to all the Universities, and will watch over them through Inspectors-General of Studies, who will visit the Universities whenever directed by the Council to do so, and will report on the state of all the schools.

57. The number of the Inspectors will be twelve; that is to say, two for the faculties of law, two for those of medicine, and the remaining eight for the faculties of science and literature and for the royal and local colleges.

58. The Inspectors-General of Studies will be appointed by us, each being selected from three candidates proposed by our Royal Council of Public Instruction, and who will have been chosen from amongst the rectors and inspectors of the Universities, the deans of faculty, the provosts, the censors of study, and the professors of philosophy, rhetoric, and superior mathematics in the royal colleges.

59. On the report of the Inspectors-General of Studies, our Royal Council will give such instructions to the councils of the Universities as may appear essential; they will detect abuses, and provide the necessary reforms.

60. The Council will furnish us with an annual account of the state of public instruction throughout our kingdom.

61. It will propose all such measures as may be considered suitable to advance instruction, and for which it may be requisite to appeal to our authority.

62. It will induce and encourage the production of such books as may still be wanting for general purposes of education, and will decide on those which are to be preferred.

63. It will remove, if necessary, the deans of faculty, and will propose to us the removal of the rectors of Universities.

64. It will examine and decide on the accounts of the general administration of the Universities.

65. The Normal School is placed under the special authority of the Royal Council; the Council can either appoint or remove the administrators and masters of that establishment.

66. The Council holds the same rank with our Court of Appeal and Court of Accounts, and will take place, in all public ceremonies, immediately after the last-named.

67. It will keep a registry of all its proceedings, and will deposit a copy with our Minister the Secretary of State for the department of the Interior, who will furnish us with an account of the same, and on whose report we shall exercise the right of reforming or annulling them.

Title V.

Of Receipts and Expenses.

68. The tax of one-twentieth on the expenses of studies, imposed upon the pupils of colleges and schools, is abolished from the date of the publication of the present decree.

69. Excepting always: 1. The charges for terms, examinations, and degrees, applied to the benefit of the faculties; 2. The subscriptions paid by the pupils of the royal and local colleges for the advantage of those establishments; 3. The annual contributions of the heads of seminaries and boarding-schools, for the use of the Universities.

70. The townships will continue to supply the funds for scholars on the foundation, and the sums they have hitherto contributed under the title of help to their colleges: with this object, the total of these sums, as also of the burses, will be included in their respective budgets with the fixed expenses; and no deviation whatever from this will take place, unless previously submitted to our Royal Council of Instruction.

71. The townships will also continue to supply and keep in repair the buildings requisite for the Universities, the faculties, and colleges.

72. The councils of the Universities will settle the budgets for the colleges and faculties.

73. The faculties and royal colleges, of which the receipts exceed the expenses, will apply the surplus to the treasury of the University.

74. The councils of the universities will receive the annual contributions of the heads of seminaries and boarding schools.

75. They will manage the property belonging to the University of France situated in the district of each provincial university, and will collect the revenue.

76. In case the receipts of the faculties, or those assigned for the expenses of general administration, should prove inadequate, the councils of the universities will make a distinct requisition, and will state the sums required to replace each deficiency.

77. This requisition will be addressed to our Royal Council of Public Instruction, who will transmit it, with suggestions, to our Minister the Secretary of State for the department of the Interior.

78. The expenses of the faculties and Universities, as settled by our Minister the Secretary of State for the department of the Interior, will be paid on his order from our Royal Treasury.

79. There will also be paid from our Royal Treasury, in like manner—1, the expenses of our Royal Council of Public Instruction; 2, those of the Normal School; 3, the Royal donations.

80. For these purposes the annual income of 400,000 francs, forming the appanage of the University of France, is placed at the disposal of our Minister the Secretary of State for the department of the Interior.

81. Further, and in provisional replacement of the tax abolished by Art. 68 of this present Decree, our Minister the Secretary of State for the department of the Interior, is authorized by us

for the promotion of public instruction in our kingdom, during the year 1815, to apply to the Minister of our Household, who will place at his disposal the sum of one million, to be deducted from the funds of our Civil List.

82. The funds proceeding from the reduction of one twenty-fifth of the appointments in the University of France, will be applied to retiring pensions; our Royal Council is charged to propose to us the most eligible mode of appropriating this fund, and also to suggest the means of securing a new one for the same purpose, in all the universities.

Title VI.

Temporary Arrangements.

83. The members of our Royal Council of Public Instruction, who are to be selected in conformity with Art. 52, the inspectors-general of studies, the rectors and inspectors of universities, will be appointed by us, in the first instance, from amongst all those who have been or are now actually employed in the different educational establishments.

The conditions of eligibility settled by that Article, as also by Articles 10, 16, and 58, apply to situations which may hereafter become vacant.

84. The members of suppressed universities and societies, who have taken degrees as professors in the old faculties, or who have filled the posts of superiors and principals of colleges, or chairs of philosophy or rhetoric, as also councillors, inspectors-general, rectors and inspectors of academies, and professors of faculties in the University of France, who may find themselves out of employment by the effect of the present decree, are eligible to all places whatever.

85. The fixed salaries of the deans and professors of faculties, and those of the provosts, inspectors of studies, and professors in the Royal colleges are not to be altered.

86. The deans and professors of the faculties that will be continued, the provosts and doctors of faculty of the district colleges at present in office, are to retain the same rights and privileges, and will be subject to the same regulations of repeal, as if they had been appointed in pursuance of the present decree.

We hereby inform and command our courts, tribunals, prefects, and administrative bodies to publish and register these presents wherever they may deem it necessary to do so. Moreover we direct our attorneys-general and prefects to see that this is done, and to certify the same; that is to say, the courts and tribunals to our Chancellor, and the prefects to our Minister the Secretary of State for the department of the Interior.

Given at Paris, in our Castle of the Tuileries, February 17, in the year of grace 1815, and in the twentieth of our reign.

(Signed) Louis.

By the King; the Minister Secretary of State for the Interior.

(Signed) The Abbé de Montesquiou.

No. VII.

Note drawn up and laid before the King and Council August 1816, on the question of dissolving the Chamber of 1815; by M. Lainé, Minister of the Interior.

It being considered probable that the King may be obliged to dissolve the Chamber after its assembly, let us consider what will be the consequences.

Dissolution during the session is an extreme measure. It is a sort of appeal made in the midst of passions in full conflict. The causes which lead to it, the feelings of resentment to which it will give rise, will spread throughout France.

The convocation of a new Chamber will require much time, and will render it almost impossible to introduce a budget this year. To hold back the budget until the first month of the year ensuing, is to run the risk of seeing the deficit increase and the available resources disappear.

This would in all probability render us incapable of paying the foreigners.

After such an unusual dissolution, justified by the danger which the Chamber may threaten, it is difficult to suppose that the electoral assemblies would be tranquil. And if agitation should exhibit itself, the return of the foreigners is to be apprehended from that cause. The dread of this consequence, in either case, will induce the King to hesitate; and whatever attempts may be made to disturb the public peace or to assail the Royal authority, his Majesty's heart, in the hope that such evils would be merely transitory, will decide with reluctance on such an extreme remedy as dissolution.

If then, the necessity of dissolving the Chamber becomes pressing, will it not be better, before it meets, to adopt means of preserving us from this menacing disaster?

The renewal of one-fifth of the members, which, under any circumstances, seems to me indispensable to carry out the Charter, and which I regret to say we too much neglected in the month of July 1815, will scarcely diminish the probable necessity of dissolution.

The members returned for the fourth series are, with a few exceptions, moderate; they have no disposition whatever to disturb public repose, or interfere with the Royal prerogative, which alone can maintain order by giving confidence to all classes. The other four-fifths remain unchanged; the apprehended dangers are consequently as imminent.

This consideration induces me to recommend the adoption of a measure which might facilitate a complete return to the Charter, by recalling the decree of the 13th of July, which infringed it in the articles of age and number, and has also reduced to problems many more of its conditions.

This measure would be to summon, by royal letters, only such deputies as have reached the age of forty, and according to the number stipulated in the Charter.

To effect this, we should choose the deputies who have been first named in each electoral college. We should thus pay a compliment to the electors by summoning those who appear to hold the most distinguished places in their confidence.

It is true it will be said that the Chamber not being dissolved, the present deputies have a kind of legal possession.

But the electors and the deputies they have chosen, only hold their power from the Decree. The same authority which conferred that power can recall it by revoking the Decree.

The King in his opening speech appeared to say that it was only owing to an extraordinary circumstance that he had assembled round the throne a greater number of deputies. That extraordinary circumstance has passed away. Peace is made, order is re-established, the Allies have retired from the heart of France and from the Capital.

This idea furnishes an answer to the objection that the operations of the Chamber are nullified. The King had the power of making it what it is, in consequence of existing circumstances.

The Chamber of Deputies does not alone make the laws. The Chamber of Peers, and the King, who in France is the chief branch of the legislative body, have co-operated in that enactment.

If this objection could hold good in the present case, it would equally hold good in all the rest. In fact, either after the dissolution, or under any other circumstances, the King will return to the Charter, in regard to age and number. On this hypothesis, it might be said that the operations of the existing Chamber are nullified. Article 14 of the Charter could always be explained by the extraordinary circumstances, and its complete re-establishment by the most sacred motives. To return to the Charter without dissolution is not then to nullify the operations of the Chamber more than to return to the Charter after dissolution.

Will it be said that the King is not more certain of a majority after the proposed reduction than at present? I reply that the probability is greatly increased.

An assembly less numerous will be more easily managed; reason will be more readily attended to. The Royal authority which is exercised in the reduction will be increased and secured.

Again, in the event of a dissolution, would the King be more certain of a majority? How many chances are against this! On one side the ultras, whose objection to transfer a portion of the Royal authority to what they call the aristocracy, occupy nearly all the posts which influence the operations of the electoral assemblies. On the other, they will be vehemently opposed by the partisans of a popular liberty not less hostile to the Kingly power. The struggles which will take place at the electoral assemblies, will be repeated in the Chamber, and what description of majority will emanate from such a contest?

If the plan of reduction appears inadmissible;—if on the other hand, it should be decided that the hostile spirit of the Chamber compels the dissolution after convocation;—I should not hesitate to prefer immediate dissolution to the danger which seems so likely to arise from dissolution after assembly.

But if immediate dissolution were to lead to the forming of a new Chamber animated by the same spirit and views, it would then become necessary to find remedies, to preserve the Royal authority, and to save France from the presence of foreigners.

The first method would be to sacrifice the Ministers, who are ready to lay down their places and their lives to preserve the King and France.

The above notes are exclusively founded on the probable necessity of dissolution after the Chamber is convoked.

This measure will become necessary if, under the pretext of amendments, the King's wishes are trifled with; if the budget should be thrown out, or too long delayed; or if the amendments or propositions are of a nature to alarm the country, and in consequence to call in the foreigners.

The customs adopted during the last session, the bills announced, the acrimony exhibited, the evidences we have thence derived, the hostility already prepared by ambitious disturbers, the determination evinced to weaken the Kingly authority by declaiming against the modified centralization of government, all supply powerful reasons for expecting the probable occurrences which will necessitate the dissolution of the Chamber.

Taking another view, it ought not to be easily believed that a few misguided Frenchmen, compromising the fortune of their country by continuing to oppose the Royal authority, may go the length of exposing themselves to the double scourge of foreign invasion and civil war, or that they be content with the loss of certain provinces through imprudent propositions, legally unjust, or....

Are we permitted to hope that in presenting such bills as religion and devotion to the King and the country may inspire us to frame, these bills will not be rejected?

Shall we be enabled to draw up these bills in such a manner as to convince the Session and the world that malevolent opposition alone can defeat them?

Notwithstanding the great probabilities that the dissolution may become necessary, the danger would be less formidable, if the King, at the opening of the session, were to express his wishes energetically; if he were to issue previous decrees, revoking all that has not been yet carried out in the Decrees of July 1815; if, above all, after having declared his will by solemn acts, his Majesty would firmly repeat those acts in the the immediate vicinity of the throne, by removing from his person all those who might be inclined to misrepresent or oppose his wishes.

To avoid resistance and contest, would the following plan be available?

When the bills, the decrees, and the other regulations are ready, would it be suitable for the King to hold an Extraordinary Council, to which he should summon the Princes of the Royal family, the Archbishop of Rheims, etc. Let all the bills to be brought forward be discussed and settled in that Council, and let the Princes and the chief Bishops declare which of these are to be adopted by unanimous consent. If, after this Council, all the great and influential personages summoned by his Majesty were to announce that such was the common wish of the King and the whole of the Royal family, France would perhaps be saved.

But the great remedy lies in the King's pleasure. Let that once be manifested, and let its execution be recommended by his Majesty to all who surround him, and the danger disappears.

"Domine dic tantum verbum, et sanabitur Gallia tua!"

No. VIII.

Correspondence between the Viscount de Châteaubriand, the Count Decazes, Minister of General Police, and M. Dambray, Chancellor of France, on occasion of the seizure of 'Monarchy according to the Charter,' in consequence of an infraction of the laws and regulations relative to printing. September, 1816.

1. Official Report of the Seizure.

October 19th, 1816.

On the 18th of September, in execution of the warrant of his Excellency, dated on that day, authorizing the seizure of a work entitled, 'Of Monarchy according to the Charter,' by M. de Châteaubriand, printed by Le Normant, Rue de Seine, No. 8, and which work had been on sale without the deposit of five copies having been made at the office for the general regulation of the book-trade, I went, with Messrs. Joly and Dussiriez, peace-officers and inspectors, to the house of the abovenamed M. Le Normant, where we arrived before ten o'clock in the morning.

M. Le Normant admitted to us that he had given notice of the work of M. de Châteaubriand, but that he had not yet deposited the five copies. He affirmed that on the same morning, at nine o'clock, he had sent to the office for the general regulation of bookselling, but that he was told that the office was not open. Of this he produced no proof.

He admitted that he had printed two thousand copies of this work, intending to make a fresh declaration, the first having only been for fifteen hundred copies; that he had delivered several hundreds copies to the author; that, finally, he had transmitted others on sale to the principal booksellers of the Palais-Royal, Delaunay, Petit, and Fabre.

While I was drawing up a report of these facts and statements, M. de Wilminet, peace-officer, came in with an individual in whose hands he had seen, near the Bridge of the Arts, the work now in question, at the moment when the person, who says his name is Derosne, was looking over the title. M. Derosne has admitted that he bought it for four francs, on the same day, the 18th, at about nine and a half in the morning. This copy has been deposited in our hands, and M. Le Normant has reimbursed the cost to M. Derosne.

We seized, in the second warehouse on the first floor, thirty stitched copies which we added to that of M. Derosne. In the workshops on the ground-floor, I seized a considerable quantity of printed sheets of the same work, which M. Le Normant estimates at nine thousand sheets; and thirty-one printing-forms which had been used for printing these sheets.

As it was sufficiently proved, both by facts and the admissions of the printer, that the work had been offered for sale before the five copies were deposited, we took possession of the stitched copies, the sheets, and the forms. The sheets were subsequently piled up in a carriage in the courtyard, and the stitched volumes made into a parcel, were deposited at the foot of the staircase at the entrance of the house. The forms, to the number of thirty-one, were placed under the steps of the garden, tied together with cord. Our seal had been already placed on the top, and M. de Wilminet prepared to affix it also on the lower parts. All this was done without the slightest disturbance or opposition, and with a perfect respect for the authorities.

Suddenly tumultuous cries were heard at the bottom of the entrance court.
M. de Châteaubriand arrived at that moment, and questioned some workmen who surrounded him. His words were interrupted by cries of "Here is M. de Châteaubriand!" The workshops resounded with his name; all the labouring men came out in a crowd and ran towards the court, exclaiming, "Here is M. de Châteaubriand! M. de Châteaubriand!" I myself distinctly heard the cry of "Long live M. de Châteaubriand!"

At the same instant a dozen infuriated workmen arrived at the gate of the garden, where I then was with M. de Wilminet and two inspectors, engaged in finishing the seals on the forms. They broke the seals and prepared to carry off the forms; they cried loudly and with a threatening air, "Long live the liberty of the press! Long live the King!" We took advantage of a moment of silence to ask if any order had arrived to suspend our work. "Yes, yes, here is our order. Long live the liberty of the press!" cried they with violent insolence: "Long live the King!" They approached close to us to utter these cries. "Well" said I to them, "if there is such an order, so much the better; let it be produced;" and we all said together, "You shall not touch these forms, until we have seen the order." "Yes, yes," cried they again, "there is an order; it comes from M. de Châteaubriand, he is a Peer of France. An order from M. de Châteaubriand is worth more than one from the Minister." Then they repeated violently the cries of "Long live the liberty of the press! Long live the King!"

In the meantime, the peace-officers and inspectors continued to guard the articles seized or sequestered, and prevented their being carried off. They took the parcel of stitched copies from the hands of a workman who was bearing it away.

The peace-officer who was affixing the seals, being compelled by violence to suspend the operation, addressed M. de Châteaubriand, and asked him if he had an order from the Minister. He replied, with passion, that an order from the Minister was nothing to him; he came to oppose what was going on; he was a Peer of France, the defender of the Charter, and particularly forbade anything to be taken away. "Moreover," he added, "this proceeding is useless and without object; I have distributed fifteen thousand copies of this work through all the different departments." The workmen then repeated that the order of M. de Châteaubriand was worth more than that of the Minister, and renewed, more violently than before, their cries of "Long live the liberty of the press! M. de Châteaubriand for ever! Long live the King!"

The peace-officer was surrounded. A man of colour, appearing much excited, said to him violently, "The order of M. de Châteaubriand is worth more than that of the Minister." Tumultuous cries were renewed round the peace-officer. I left the garden, leaving the forms in charge of the inspectors, to advance towards that side. During my passage, several workmen shouted violently, "Long live the King!" I held out my hand as a sign of peace, to keep at a respectful distance those who were disposed to come too near; and replied by the loyal cry of "Long live the King!" to the same shout uttered in a seditious spirit by the bewildered workmen.

M. de Châteaubriand was at this time in the entrance court, apparently intent on preventing the carriage laden with the sheets of his work from departing for its destination. I ascended the staircase for the purpose of signifying to M. Le Normant that it would be better for him to second my orders by using whatever influence he might possess over his workmen, so as to induce them to return to their workshops; and to let him know before them that he would be held responsible for what might happen. M. de Châteaubriand appeared at the foot of the staircase, and uttered, in a very impassioned tone, with his voice vehemently raised, in the midst of the workmen, who appeared to second him enthusiastically, nearly the following words:—

"I am a Peer of France. I do not acknowledge the order of the Ministry; I oppose it in the name of the Charter, of which I am the defender, and the protection of which every citizen may claim. I oppose the removal of my work. I forbid the transport of these sheets. I will only yield to force, and when I see the gendarmes."

Immediately, raising my voice to a loud tone, and extending my arm from the first landing-place of the staircase on which I then stood, I replied to him who had just manifested to myself formally and personally his determined resistance to the execution of the orders of his Majesty's minister, and had thereby shown that he was the real exciter of the movements that had taken place; I said—

"And I, in the name and on the part of the King, in my quality of Commissary of Police, appointed by his Majesty, and acting under the orders of his Excellency the Minister of General Police, demand respect for constituted authority. Let everything remain untouched; let all tumult cease, until the arrival of fresh orders which I expect from his Excellency."

While I uttered these words, profound silence was maintained. Calm had succeeded to tumult. Soon after, the gendarmes arrived. I then ordered the workmen to return to their workshops. M. de Châteaubriand, as soon as the gendarmes entered, retired into the apartments of M. Le Normant, and appeared no more. We then finished our work and prepared the report of all that had occurred, after having despatched to the Ministry of Police the articles seized, and committed the forms to the guard, and under the responsibility of M. Le Normant.

At the moment of the disturbance one of the stitched copies disappeared. Subsequently we seized, at the house of M. Le Marchand, a book-stitcher, and formerly a bookseller, in the Rue de la Parcheminerie, seven parcels of copies of the same work; and at No. 17, Rue des Prêtres, in a wareroom belonging to M. Le Normant, we placed eight forms under seal, and seized four thousand sheets of the same work.

I have forwarded to the Ministry of Police reports of these different operations, with the sheets and copies seized of the work of M. de Châteaubriand.

M. Le Normant appeared to me to conduct himself without blame during these transactions, which were carried into effect at his dwelling-place, and during the tumult which M. de Châteaubriand promoted on the occasion of the seizure of his work. But it is sufficiently proved by his own admission and by facts, that he has issued for sale to various booksellers, and has sold himself copies of this work before he had deposited the five as required by the laws.

As to M. de Châteaubriand, I am astonished that he should have so scandalously compromised the dignity of the titles with which he is decorated, by exhibiting himself under these circumstances, as if he had been nothing more than the leader of a troop of workmen, whom he had stirred up to commotion.

He was the cause of the workmen profaning the sacred cry of "Long live the King!" by using it in an act of rebellion against the authority of the Government, which is the same as that of the King.

He has excited these misguided men against a Commissary of Police, a public functionary appointed by his Majesty, and against three peace-officers in the execution of their duty, and without arms against a multitude.

He has committed an offence against the Royal government, by saying that he would acknowledge force alone, in a system based upon quite a different force from that of bayonets, and which only uses such coercive measures against persons who are strangers to every sentiment of honour.

Finally, this scene might have led to serious consequences if, imitating the conduct of M. de Châteaubriand, we had forgotten for a moment that we were acting by the orders of a Government as moderate as firm, and as strong in its wisdom as in its legitimacy.

2. The Viscount de Châteaubriand to the Count Decazes.

Paris, September 18th, 1816.

My Lord Count,

I called at your residence this morning to express my surprise. At twelve this day, I found at the house of M. Le Normant, my bookseller, some men who said they were sent by you to seize my new work, entitled 'Of Monarchy according to the Charter.'

Not seeing any written order, I declared that I would not allow the removal of my property unless gendarmes seized it by force. Some gendarmes arrived, and I then ordered my bookseller to allow the work to be carried away.

This act of deference to authority has not allowed me to forget what I owe to my rank as a Peer. If I had only considered my personal interests, I should not have interfered; but the privileges of the Peerage having been compromised, I have thought it right to enter a protest, a copy of which I have now the honour of forwarding to you. I demand, in the name of justice, the restitution of my work; and I candidly add, that if I do not receive it back, I shall employ every possible means that the political and civil laws place within my reach.

I have the honour to be, etc. etc.,

(Signed) Count de Châteaubriand.

3. The Count Decazes to the Viscount de Châteaubriand.

Paris, September 18th, 1816.

My Lord Viscount,

The Commissary of Police and the peace-officers, against whom you have thought proper to excite the rebellion of M. Le Normant's workmen, were the bearers of an order signed by one of the King's ministers, and in accordance with a law. That order was shown to the printer named, who read it several times, and felt that he had no right to oppose its execution, demanded in the King's name. Undoubtedly it never occurred to him that your rank as a Peer could place you above the operation of the laws, release you from the respect due by all citizens to public functionaries in the execution of their duty, and, above all, justify a revolt of his work-people against a Commissary of Police, and officers appointed by the King, invested with the distinctive symbols of their office, and acting under legal instructions.

I have seen with regret that you have thought otherwise, and that you have preferred, as you now require of me, to yield to force rather than to obey the law. That law, which M. Le Normant had infringed, is extremely distinct; it requires that no work whatever shall be published clandestinely, and that no publication or sale shall take place before the necessary deposit has been made at the office for the regulation of printing. None of these conditions have been fulfilled by M. Le Normant. If he has given notice, it was informal; for he has himself signed the Report drawn up by the Commissary of Police, to the effect that he proposed to strike off 1500 copies, and that he had already printed 2000.

From another quarter I have been informed that, although no deposit has been made at the office for the regulation of printing, several hundred copies have been despatched this morning before nine o'clock, from the residence of M. Le Normant, and sent to you, and to various booksellers; that other copies have been sold by M. Le Normant at his own house, for the price of four francs; and two of these last copies were in my hands this morning by half-past eight o'clock.

I have considered it my duty not to allow this infraction of the law, and to interdict the sale of a work thus clandestinely and illegally published; I have therefore ordered its seizure, in conformity with Articles 14 and 15 of the Law of the 21st of October, 1814.

No one in France, my Lord Viscount, is above the law; the Peers would be offended, on just grounds, if I thought they could set up such a pretension. Still less would they assume that the works which they feel disposed to publish and sell as private individuals and men of letters, when they wish to honour the literary profession with their labours, should enjoy exclusive privileges; and if these works are submitted to public criticism in common with those of other writers, they are not in any respect liberated from the control of justice, or the supervision of the Police, whose duty it is to take care that the laws, which are equally binding upon all classes of society, should be executed with equal impartiality.

I must also observe, in addition, that it was at the residence and printing-office of M. Le Normant, who is not a Peer of France, that the order constitutionally issued for the seizure of a work published by him in contravention to the law, was carried into effect; that the execution of the order had been completed when you presented yourself; and upon your declaration that you would not suffer your work to be taken away, the workmen broke the seals that had been affixed on some articles, and placed themselves in open rebellion against the King's authority. It can scarcely have escaped you, that by invoking that august name they have been guilty of a crime of which, no doubt, they did not perceive the extent; and to which they could not have been led, had they been more impressed with the respect due to the act of the King and his representatives, and if it could so happen that they did not read what they print.

I have felt these explanations due to your character; they will, I trust, convince you that if the dignity of the Peerage has been compromised in this matter, it has not been through me.

I have the honour to be,

My Lord Viscount,

Your very humble and very obedient Servant,

(Signed) The Count Decazes.

4. The Viscount de Châteaubriand to the Count Decazes.

Paris, September 19th, 1816.

My Lord Count,

I have received the letter which you have done me the honour to address to me on the 18th of this month. It contains no answer to mine of the same day.

You speak to me of works clandestinely published (in the face of the sun, with my name and titles). You speak of revolt and rebellion, when there has been neither revolt nor rebellion. You say that there were cries of "Long live the King!" That cry has not yet been included in the law of seditious exclamations, unless the Police are empowered to decree in opposition to the Chambers. For the rest, all will appear in due time and place. There will be no longer a pretence to confound the cause of the bookseller with mine; we shall soon know whether, under a free government, a police order, which I have not even seen, is binding on a Peer of France; we shall learn whether, in my case, all the rights secured to me by the charter, have not been violated, both as a Citizen and a Peer. We shall learn, through the laws themselves, which you have the extreme kindness to quote for me (a little incorrectly, it may be observed), whether I have not the right to publish my opinions; we shall learn, finally, whether France is henceforward to be governed by the Police or by the Constitution.

On the subject of my respect and loyalty to the King, my Lord Count, I require no lessons, and I might supply an example. With respect to my rank as a Peer, I shall endeavour to make it respected, equally with my dignity as a man; and I perfectly well knew, before you took the trouble to inform me, that it will never be compromised either by you or any one else. I have demanded at your hands the restitution of my work: am I to hope that it will be restored? This is the immediate question.

I have the honour to be,

My Lord Count,

Your very humble and very obedient Servant,

(Signed) The Viscount de Châteaubriand.

5. The Viscount de Châteaubriand to the Chancellor Dambray.

Paris, September 18th, 1816.

My Lord Chancellor,

I have the honour to forward to you a copy of the protest I have entered, and the letter I have just written to the Minister of Police.

Is it not strange, my Lord Chancellor, that in open day, by force, and in defiance of my remonstrances, the work of a Peer of France, to which my name is attached, and printed publicly in Paris, should have been carried off by the Police, as if it were a seditious or clandestine publication, such as the 'Yellow Dwarf,' or the 'Tri-coloured Dwarf'? Beyond what was due to my prerogative as a Peer of France, I may venture to say that I deserved personally a little more respect. If my work were objectionable, I might have been summoned before the competent tribunals: I should have answered the appeal.

I have protested for the honour of the Peerage, and I am determined to follow up this matter to the last extremity. I call for your support as President of the Chamber of Peers, and for your interference as the head of justice.

I am, with profound respect, etc. etc.,

(Signed) The Viscount Châteaubriand.

6. The Chancellor Dambray to the Count Decazes.

Paris, September, 19th, 1816.

I send you confidentially, my dear colleague, a letter which I received yesterday from M. de Châteaubriand, with the informal Protest of which he has made me the depository. I beg you will return these documents, which ought not to be made public. I enclose also a copy of my answer, which I also request you to return after reading; for I have kept no other. I hope it will meet your approbation.

I repeat the expression of my friendly sentiments.

Dambray.

7. The Chancellor Dambray to the Viscount de Châteaubriand.

Paris, September 19th, 1816.

My Lord Viscount,

I have received with the letter you have addressed to me, the declaration relative to the seizure which took place at the residence of your bookseller; I find it difficult to understand the use you propose to make of this document, which cannot extenuate in any manner the infraction of law committed by M. Le Normant. The Law of the 21st of October, 1814, is precise on this point. No printer can publish or offer for sale any work, in any manner whatever, before having deposited the prescribed number of copies. There is ground for seizure, the Article adds, and for sequestrating a work, if the printer does not produce the receipts of the deposit ordered by the preceding Article.

All infractions of this law (Art. 20) will be proved by the reports of the inspectors of the book-trade, and the Commissaries of Police.

You were probably unacquainted with these enactments when you fancied that your quality as a Peer of France gave you the right of personally opposing an act of the Police, ordered and sanctioned by the law, which all Frenchmen, whatever may be their rank, are equally bound to respect.

I am too much attached to you, Viscount, not to feel deep regret at the part you have taken in the scandalous scene which seems to have occurred with reference to this matter, and I regret sincerely that you have added errors of form to the real mistake of a publication which you could not but feel must be unpleasant to his Majesty. I know nothing of your work beyond the dissatisfaction which the King has publicly expressed with it; but I am grieved to notice the impression it has made upon a monarch who, on every occasion, has condescended to evince as much esteem for your person as admiration for your talents.

Receive, Viscount, the assurance of my high consideration, and of my inviolable attachment.
The Chancellor of France,
Dambray.

No. IX.

Table of the principal Reforms effected in the Administration of France from 1816 to 1820. Ministry of the Interior (M. Lainé).

From May, 1816, to December, 1818.

Sept. 4th, 1816.—Decree for the reorganization of the Polytechnic School.

Sept. 25th, 1816.—Decree to authorize the Society of French Missions.

Dec. 11th, 1816.—Decree for the organization of the National Guards of the Department of the Seine.

Dec. 23rd, 1816.—Decree for the institution of the Royal Chapter of St. Denis.

Feb. 26th, 1817.—Decree relative to the administration of the Public Works of Paris.

Ditto, ditto.—Decree for the organization of the Schools of Arts and Trades at Châlons and Angers.

March 12th, 1817.—Decree on the administration and funds of the Royal Colleges.

March 26th, 1817.—Decree authorizing the presence of the Prefects and Sub-Prefects at the General Councils of the Department or District.

April 2nd, 1817.—Decree to regulate Central Houses of Confinement.

Ditto, ditto.—Decree to regulate the conditions and mode of carrying out the royal authority for legacies or donations to Religious Establishments.

April 9th, 1817.—Decree for the assessment of 3,900,000 francs, destined to improve the condition of the Catholic Clergy.

Ditto, ditto.—Decree for the suppression of the Secretaries-General of the Prefectures, except only for the Department of the Seine.

April 16th, 1817.—Three Decrees to regulate the organization of, and persons employed in the Conservatory of Arts and Trades.

Sept. 10th, 1817.—Decree upon the system of the Port of Marseilles, with regard to Custom-house Duties and Storehouses.

Nov. 6th, 1817.—Decree to regulate the progressive reduction of the number of Councillors in each Prefecture.

May 20th, 1818.—Decree to increase Ecclesiastical Salaries, particularly those of the Curates.

June 9th, 1818.—Decree on the discontinuance of Compositions for Taxes payable at the Entrance of Towns.

July 29th, 1818.—Decree for the establishment of Savings Banks, and Provident Banks, in Paris.

Sept. 30th, 1818.—Decree which removes from his Royal Highness Monsieur, while leaving him the honorary privileges, the actual command of the National Guard of the Kingdom, to give it back to the Minister of the Interior, and the Municipal Authorities.

Oct. 7th, 1818.—Decree respecting the use and administration of Commons, or Town property.

Oct. 21st, 1818.—Decree respecting the premiums for the encouragement of the Maritime Fisheries.

Dec. 17th, 1818.—Decree relative to the organization and administration of the Educational Establishments called Britannic.

Count Decazes.

From December, 1818, to February, 1820.

Jan. 13th, 1819.—Decree to arrange public exhibitions of products of industry.—The first, to take place on the 25th of August, 1819.

Jan. 27th, 1819.—Decree for creating a Council of Agriculture.

Feb. 14th, 1819.—Decree for the encouragement of the Whale Fishery.

March 24th, 1819.—Decree introducing various reforms and improvements in the School of Law, at Paris.

April 9th, 1819.—Decree appointing a Jury of Manufacturers to select for reward the artists who have made the greatest progress in their respective trades.

April 10th, 1819.—Decree relative to the institution of the Council-General of Prisons.

April 19th, 1819.—Decree to facilitate the public sale of merchandise by auction.

June 23rd, 1819.—Decree to reduce the period of service of the National Guard of Paris.

June 29th, 1819.—Decree relative to holding Jewish Consistories.

Aug. 23rd, 1819.—Two Decrees upon the organization and privileges of the General Council of Commerce and Manufacture.

Aug. 25th, 1819.—Decree relative to the erection of 500 new Chapels of Ease.

Nov. 25th, 1819.—Decree relative to the organization and system of teaching of the Conservatory of Arts and Trades.

Dec. 22nd, 1819.—Decree relative to the organization and system of the Public Treasury of Poissy.

Dec. 25th, 1819.—Decree relative to the mode of Collation, and the system of public Bursaries in the Royal Colleges.

Dec. 29th, 1819.—Decree authorizing the foundation of a permanent asylum for old men and invalids, in the Quartier du gros Caillon.

Feb. 4th, 1820.—Decree for the regulation of public carriages throughout the Kingdom.

Ministry of War (Marshal Gouvion St. Cyr).

From September, 1817, to November, 1819.

Oct. 22nd, 1817.—Decree for the organization of the Corps of Geographic Engineers of War.

Nov. 6th, 1817.—Decree for the organization of the Staff of the military division of the Royal Guard.

Dec. 10th, 1817.—Decree respecting the system of administration of military supplies.

Dec. 17th. 1817.—Decree relative to the organization of the Staff of the Corps of Engineers.

Dec. 17th, 1817.—Decree relative to the organization of the Staff of the Corps of Artillery.

Dec. 24th, 1817.—Decree upon the organization of Military Schools.

March 25th, 1818.—Decree relative to the system and sale of gunpowder for purposes of war, mining, or the chase.

March 25th, 1818.—Decree relative to the system and organization of the Companies of

Discipline.

April 8th, 1818.—Decree for the formation of Departmental Legions in three battalions.

May 6th, 1818.—Decree relative to the organization of the Corps and School of the Staff.

May 20th, 1818.—Decree relative to the position and allowances of those not in active service, or on half-pay.

May 20th, 1818.—Instructions approved by the King relative to voluntary engagements.

June 10th, 1818.—Decree relative to the organization, system, and teaching of the Military Schools.

July 8th, 1818.—Decree relative to the organization and system of Regimental Schools in the Artillery.

July 15th, 1818.—Decree relative to the supply of gunpowder and saltpetre.

July 23rd, 1818.—Decree respecting the selection of the General Staff of the Army.

Aug. 3rd, 1818.—Decree relative to the military hierarchy, and the order of promotion, in conformity with the Law of the 10th of March, 1818.

Aug. 5th, 1818.—Decree relative to the allowances of Staff Officers.

Aug. 5th, 1818.—Decree relative to the system and expenses of Barracks.

Sept. 2nd, 1818.—Decree relative to the Corps of Gendarmes of Paris.

Dec. 30th, 1818.—Decree regulating the organization and system of the Body-guard of the King.

Dec. 30th, 1818.—Decree regulating the allowances to Governors of Military Divisions.

Feb. 17th, 1819.—Decree on the composition and strength of the eighty-six regiments of Infantry.

No. X.

M. Guizot to M. de Serre.
Paris, April 12th, 1820.
My dear Friend,

I have not written to you in all our troubles. I knew that you would hear from this place a hundred different opinions, and a hundred opposite statements on the position of affairs; and, although I had not entire confidence in any of those who addressed you, as you are not called upon, according to my judgment, to form any important resolution, I abstained from useless words. Today all has become clearer and more mature; the situation assumes externally the character it had until now concealed; I feel the necessity of telling you what I think of it, for the advantage of our future proceedings in general, and yours in particular.

The provisional bills have passed:—you have seen how: fatal to those who have gained them, and with immense profit to the Opposition. The debate has produced this result in the Chamber, that the right-hand party has extinguished itself, to follow in the suite of the right-centre; while the left-centre has consented to assume the same position with respect to the extreme left, from which, however, it has begun to separate within the last fifteen days. So much for the interior of the Chamber.

Without, you may be assured that the effect of these two debates upon the popular masses has been to cause the right-hand party to be looked upon as less haughty and exacting; the left, as more firm and more evenly regulated than was supposed: so that, at present, in the estimation of many worthy citizens, the fear of the right and the suspicion of the left are diminished in equal proportions. A great evil is comprised in this double fact. Last year we gained triumphs over the left, without and within the Chamber; at present the left triumphs over us! Last year we still remained, and were considered, as ever since 1815, a necessary and safe rampart against the Ultras, who were greatly dreaded, and whose rule seemed possible; today the Ultras are less feared, because their arrival at power is scarcely believed. The conclusion is, that we are less wanted than formerly.

Let us look to the future. The election bill, which Decazes presented eight days before his fall, is about to be withdrawn. This is certain. It is well known that it could never pass; that the discussions on its forty-eight articles would be interminable; the Ultras are very mistrustful of this its probable results; it is condemned; they will frame, and are already framing, another. What will this new bill be? I cannot tell. What appears to me certain is, that, if no change takes place in the present position, it will have for object, not to complete our institutions, not to correct the vices of the bill of the 5th of February, 1817, but to bring back exceptional elections; to restore, as is loudly proclaimed, something analogous to the Chamber of 1815. This is the avowed object, and, what is more, the natural and necessary end. This end will be pursued without accomplishment; such a bill will either fail in the debate, or in the application. If it passes, and after the debate which it cannot fail to provoke, the fundamental question, the question of the future, will escape from the Chamber, and seek its solution without, in the intervention of the masses. If the bill is rejected, the question may be confined within the Chamber; but it will no longer be the Ministry in office who will have the power and mission of solving it. If a choice is left to us, which I am far from despairing of, it will lie between a lamentable external revolution and a ministerial revolution of the most complete character. And this last chance, which is our only one, will vanish if we do not so manage as to offer the country, for the future, a ministry boldly constitutional.

In this position of affairs, what it is indispensable that you should be made acquainted with, and what you would discover in five minutes if you could pass five minutes here, is, that you are no longer a Minister, and that you form no portion of the Ministry in office. It would be impossible to induce you to speak with them as they speak, or as they are compelled to speak. The situation to which they are reduced has been imposed by necessity; they could only escape from it by completely changing their ground and their friends, by recovering eighty votes from the one hundred and fifteen of the actual Opposition, or by an appeal to a new Chamber. This last measure it will never adopt; and by the side of the powerlessness of the existing Cabinet, stands the impossibility of escaping from it by the aid of the right-hand party. An ultra ministry is impossible. The events in Spain, whatever they may ultimately lead to, have mortally wounded the governments of coups d'état and ordinances.

I have looked closely into all this, my dear friend; I have thought much on the subject when alone, more than I have communicated to others. You cannot remain indefinitely in a situation so critical and weak, so destitute of power for immediate government, and so hopeless for the future. I see but one thing to do at present; and that is, to prepare and hold back those who may save the Monarchy. I cannot see, in the existing state of affairs, any possibility of labouring effectively for its preservation. You can only drag yourselves timidly along the precipice which leads to its ruin. You may possibly not lose in the struggle your reputation for honest intentions and good-faith; but this is the maximum of hope which the present Cabinet can reasonably expect to preserve. Do not deceive yourself on this point; of all the plans of reform, at once monarchical and liberal, which you contemplated last year, nothing now remains. It is no longer a bold remedy which is sought for against the old revolutionary spirit; it is a miserable expedient which is adopted without confidence. It is not fit for you, my dear friend, to remain garotted under this system. Thank Heaven! you were accounted of some importance in the exceptional laws. As to the constitutional projects emanating from you, there are several—the integral renewing of the Chamber, for example—which have rather gained than lost ground, and which have become possible in another direction and with other men. I know that nothing happens either so decisively or completely as has been calculated, and that everything is, with time, an affair of arrangement and treaty. But as power is situated at present, you can do nothing, you are nothing; or rather, at this moment, you have not an inch of ground on which you can either hold yourself erect, or fall with honour. If you were here, either you would emerge, within a week, from this impotent position, or you would be lost with the rest, which Heaven forbid!

You see, my dear friend, that I speak to you with the most unmeasured frankness. It is because I have a profound conviction of the present evil and of the possibility of future safety. In this possibility you are a necessary instrument. Do not suffer yourself, while at a distance, to be compromised in what is neither your opinion nor your desire. Regulate your own destiny, or at least your position in the common destiny of all; and if you must fall, let it be for your own cause, and in accordance with your own convictions.

I add to this letter the Bill prepared by M. de Serre in November, 1819, and which he intended to present to the Chambers, to complete the Charter, and at the same time to reform the electoral law. It will be seen how much this Bill differed from that introduced in April, 1820, with reference to the law of elections alone, and which M. de Serre supported as a member of the second Cabinet of the Duke de Richelieu.

BILL FOR THE ORGANIZATION OF THE LEGISLATURE.

Art. 1. The Legislature assumes the name of Parliament of France.

Art. 2. The King convokes the Parliament every year.

Parliament will be convoked extraordinarily, at the latest, within two months after the King attains his majority, or succeeds to the throne; or under any event which may cause the establishment of a Regency.

Of the Peerage.

Art. 3. The Peerage can only be conferred on a Frenchman who has attained his majority, and is in the exercise of political and civil rights.

Art. 4. The character of Peer is indelible; it can neither be lost nor abdicated, from the moment when it has been conferred by the King.

Art. 5. The exercise of the rights and privileges of Peer can only be suspended under two conditions:—1. Condemnation to corporal punishment; 2. Interdiction pronounced according to the forms prescribed by the Civil Code. In either case, by the Chamber of Peers alone.

Art. 6. The Peers are admissible to the Chamber at the age of twenty-one, and can vote when they have completed their twenty-fifth year.

Art. 7. In case of the death of a Peer, his successor in the Peerage will be admitted as soon as he has attained the required age, on fulfilling the forms prescribed by the decree of the 23rd of March, 1816, which decree will be annexed to the present law.

Art. 8. A Peerage created by the King cannot henceforward, during the life of the titulary, be declared transmissible, except to the real and legitimate male children of the created Peer.

Art. 9. The inheritance of the Peerage cannot henceforward be conferred until a Majorat of the net revenue of twenty thousand francs, at least, shall be attached to the Peerage.

Dotation of the Peerage.

Art. 10. The Peerage will be endowed—1, With three five hundred thousand francs of rent, entered upon the great-book of the public debt, which sum will be unalienable, and exclusively applied to the formation of Majorats; 2, With eight hundred thousand francs of rent, equally entered and inalienable, to be applied to the expenses of the Chamber of Peers.

By means of this dotation, these expenses cease to be charged to the Budget of the State, and the domains, rents, and property of every kind, proceeding from the dotation of the former Senate, except the Palace of the Luxembourg and its dependencies, are reunited to the property of the State.

Art. 11. Three millions five francs of rent, intended for the formation of Majorats, are divided into fifty majorats of thirty thousand francs, and one hundred majorats of twenty thousand francs each, attached to the same number of peerages.

Art. 12. These Majorats will be conferred by the King exclusively upon lay Peers; they will be transmissible with the Peerage from male to male, in order of primogeniture, and in the real, direct, and legitimate line only.

Art. 13. A Peer cannot unite in his own person several of these Majorats.

Art. 14. Immediately on the endowment of a Majorat, and on the production of letters-patent, the titulary will be entered in the great-book of the public debt, for an unalienable revenue, according to the amount of his majorat.

Art. 15. In case of the extinction of the successors to any one of these Majorats, it reverts to the King's gift, who can confer it again, according to the above-named regulations.

Art. 16. The King can permit the titulary possessor of a Majorat to convert it into real property producing the same revenue, and which will be subject to the same reversion.

Art. 17. The dotation of the Peerage is inalienable, and cannot under any pretext whatever, be applied to any other purpose than that prescribed by the present law. This dotation remains charged, even to extinction, with the pensions at present enjoyed by the former Senators, as also with those which have been or may hereafter be granted to their widows.

Of the Chamber of Deputies.

Art. 18. The Chamber of Deputies to Parliament is composed of four hundred and fifty-six members.

Art. 19. The Deputies to Parliament are elected for seven years.

Art. 20. The Chamber is renewed integrally, either in case of dissolution, or at the expiration of the time for which the Deputies are elected.

Art. 21. The President of the Chamber of Deputies is elected according to the ordinary forms for the entire duration of the Parliament.

Art. 22. The rates which must be paid by an elector, or one eligible for an elector, consist of the principal of the direct taxes without regard to the additional hundredths. To this effect, the taxes for doors and windows will be separated from the the principal and additional hundredths, in such manner that two-thirds of the entire tax may be entered as principal and the remaining third as additional hundredths. For the future this plan will be permanent; the augmentations or diminutions of these two taxes will be made by the addition or reduction of the additional hundredths: the same rule will apply to the taxes on land, moveables, and other personal property, as soon as the principal of each is definitely settled. The tax on land and that on doors and windows will only be charged to the proprietor or temporary possessor, notwithstanding any contrary arrangement.

Art. 23. A son is liable for the taxes of his father, and a son-in-law whose wife is alive, or who has children by her, for the taxes of his father-in-law, in all cases where the father or father-in-law have transferred to them their respective rights.

The taxes of a widow, not re-married, are chargeable to whichever of her sons, or, in default of sons, to whichever of her sons-in-law, she may designate.

Art. 24. To constitute the eligibility of an elector, these taxes must have been paid one year at least before the day of the election. The heir or legatee on the general title, is considered responsible for the taxes payable by the parties from whom he derives.

Art. 25. Every elector and Deputy is bound to make affidavit, if required, that they pay really and personally, or that those whose rights they exercise pay really and personally, the rates required by the law; that they, or those whose rights they exercise, are the true and legitimate owners of the property on account of which the taxes are paid, or that they truly exercise the trade for the license of which the taxes are imposed.

This affidavit is received by the Chamber, for the Deputies, and at the electoral offices for the electors. It is signed by them, without prejudice to contradictory evidence.

Art. 26. Every Frenchman who has completed the age of thirty on the day of election, who is in the enjoyment of civil and political rights, and who pays a direct tax amounting to six hundred francs in principal, is eligible to the Chamber of Deputies.

Art. 27. The Deputies to Parliament are named partly by the electors of the department, and partly by the electors of the divisions into which each department is divided, in conformity with the table annexed to the present law.

The electors of each electoral divisions nominate directly the number of Deputies fixed by the same table.

This rule applies to the electors of each department.

Art. 28. All Frenchmen who have completed the age of thirty years, who exercise political and civil rights, who have their residence in the department, and who pay a direct tax of four hundred francs in principal, are electors for the department.

Art. 29. When the electors for the department are less than fifty in the department of Corsica, less than one hundred in the departments in the higher and lower Alps, of the Ardèche, of the Ariège, or the Corrèze, of the Creuse, of the Lozère, of the higher Marne, of the higher Pyrenees, of Vaucluse, of the Vosges; less than two hundred in the departments of the Ain, of the Ardennes, of the Aube, of the Aveyron, of the Central, of the Coasts of the North, of the Doubs, of the Drôme, of the Jura, of the Landes, of the Lot, of the Meuse, of the lower Pyrenees, of the lower and upper Rhine, of the upper Saône; and less than three hundred in the other departments; these numbers are to be completed by calling on those who are next in the ratio of taxation.

Art. 30. All Frenchmen aged thirty years complete, who exercise political and civil rights, who dwell in the electoral division, and who pay a direct tax of two hundred francs in principal, are electors for the division.

Art. 31. The electors of departments exercise their rights as electors of division, each in the division in which he dwells. To this effect, the elections for the departments will not take place till after those for the division.

Art. 32. The Deputies to Parliament named by the electors of division ought to be domiciled in the department, or at least to be proprietors there for more than a year, of a property paying six hundred francs in principal, or to have exercised public functions there for three years at the least.

The Deputies nominated by the electors of departments may be selected from all who are eligible throughout the kingdom.

Forms of Election.

Art. 33. At the hour and on the day fixed for the election, the Board will repair to the hall selected for its sittings. The Board is to be composed of a President appointed by the King, of the Mayor, of the senior Justice of the Peace, and of the two chief Municipal Councillors of the head-towns in which the election is held. At Paris, the senior Mayor and Justice of the Peace of the electoral division, and two members of the general Council of the Department, taken according to the order of their appointment, are to co-operate with the President in the formation of the Board.

The duties of secretary will be fulfilled by the Mayor's secretary.

Art. 34. The votes are given publicly by the inscription which each elector makes himself, or dictates to a member of the Board, of the names of the candidates upon an open register. The elector inscribes the names of as many candidates as there are Deputies to elect.

Art. 35. In order that any eligible person may become a candidate, and that the register may be opened in his favour, it is necessary that he should have been proposed to the Board by twenty electors at least, who inscribe his name upon the register.

At Paris, no one can be proposed, at the same election, as a candidate in more than two electoral districts at the same time.

Art. 36. At the opening of each sitting, the President announces the names of the candidates proposed, and the number of votes that each has obtained. The same announcement is printed and posted in the town after every sitting.

Art. 37. The register for the first series of votes remains open for three days at least, and for six hours every day.

No Deputy can be elected by the first series of votes, except by an absolute majority of the electors of the district and department, who have voted during the three days.

Art. 38. The third day and the hour appointed for voting having expired, the register is declared closed; the votes are summed up; the total number and the number given to each candidate are published, and the candidates who have obtained an absolute majority are announced.

If all the Deputies have not been elected by the first scrutiny of votes, the result is published and posted immediately; and after an interval of three days, a second series of votes is taken during the following days, in the same manner and under the same formalities and delays. The candidates who obtain a relative majority at the second voting are elected.

Art. 39. Before closing the registers at each voting, the President demands publicly whether there is any appeal against the manner in which the votes have been inscribed. If objections are made, they are to be entered on the official report of the election, and the registers, closed and sealed, are forwarded to the Chamber of Deputies, who will decide.

If there are no appeals, the registers are destroyed on the instant, and the official report alone is forwarded to the Chamber.

The official report and registers are signed by all the members of the Board.

If there are grounds for a provisional decision, the Board has the power of pronouncing it.

Art. 40. The President is invested with full power to maintain the freedom of the elections. The civil and military authorities are bound to obey his requisitions. The President maintains silence in the hall in which the election is held, and will not allow any individual to be present who is not an elector or a member of the Board.

Arrangements common to the two Chambers.

Art. 41. No proposition can be sent to a committee until it has been previously decided on in the Chamber. The Chamber, on all occasions, appoints the number of the members of the committee, and selects them, either by a single ballot from the entire list, or on the proposition of their own board.

Every motion coming from a Peer or Deputy must be announced at least eight days beforehand, in the Chamber to which he belongs.

Art. 42. No motion can be passed by the Chamber until after three separate readings, each with an interval between them of eight days at the least. The debate follows after each reading. When the debate has concluded, the Chamber votes on a new reading. After the last debate, it votes on the definitive adoption of the measure.

Art. 43. Every amendment must be proposed before the second reading. An amendment decided on after the second reading will of necessity demand another reading after the same interval.

Art. 44. Every amendment that may be discussed and voted separately from the motion under debate, will be considered as a new motion, and will have to undergo the same forms.

Art. 45. Written speeches, except the reports of committees and the first opening of a motion, are interdicted.

Art. 46. The Chamber of Peers cannot vote unless fifty Peers, at least, are present; the Chamber of Deputies cannot vote unless one hundred Members, at least, are present.

Art. 47. The vote in both Chambers is always public.

Fifteen Members can call for a division.

The division is made with closed doors.

Art. 48. The Chamber of Peers can admit the public to its sittings. On the demand of five Peers, or on that of the proposer of the motion, the sitting becomes private.

Art. 49. The Chamber of Deputies can only form itself into a secret committee to hear and discuss the propositions of one of its Members, when a secret committee is asked by the proposer of the motion, or by five Members at least.

Art. 50. The arrangements of the laws now in operation, and particularly those of the law of 17th February, 1817, and which are not affected by the present law, will continue to be carried on according to their form and tenour.

Temporary Arrangements.

Art. 51. The Chamber of Deputies, from this date until the Session of 1820, will be carried to the full number of 456 Members.

To this effect, the departments of the fourth series will each name the number of Deputies assigned to them by the present law; the other departments will also complete the number of Deputies, in the same manner assigned to them. The Deputies appointed in execution of the present article will be for seven years.

Art. 52. If the number of Deputies to be named to complete the deputation of any department, does not exceed that which the electors of the department ought to elect, they will all be elected by these electors. Should the case be otherwise, each Deputy exceeding this number will be chosen by the electors of one of the electoral divisions of the department, in the order hereinafter named:—

1. By such of the electoral divisions as have the right of naming more than one Deputy, unless one at least of the actual Deputies has his political residence in this division.

2. By the first of the electoral divisions in which no actual Deputy has his political residence.

3. By the first of the electoral divisions in which one or more of the actual Deputies have their political residence, in such manner that no single division shall name more Deputies than those assigned to it by the present law.

Art. 53. At the expiration of the powers of the present Deputies of the 5th, 1st, 2nd and 3rd series, a new election will be proceeded with for the election of an equal number of Deputies for each respective department, by such of the electoral divisions as have not, in execution of the preceding article, elected the full number of Deputies which are assigned to them by the present law.

Art. 54. The Deputies to be named in execution of the preceding article will be; those of the 5th series, for six years;—those of the 1st, for five years; those of the 2nd, for four years; and those of the 3rd, for three years.

Art. 55. The regulations prescribed by the above articles will be observed, if, between the present date and the integral renewing of the Chamber, a necessity should arise for replacing a Deputy.

Art. 56. All the elections that may take place under these temporary regulations, must be in accordance with the forms and conditions prescribed by the present law.

Art. 57. In case of a dissolution of the Chamber of Deputies, it must be integrally renewed within the term fixed by Article 50 of the Charter, and in conformity with the present law.

No. XI.

Letters relative to my Dismissal from the Council of State, on the 17th July, 1820.

M. de Serre (Keeper of the Great Seal) to M. Guizot.

Paris, July 17th, 1820.

I regret being compelled to announce to you that you have ceased to belong to the Council of State. The violent hostility in which you have lately indulged, without the shadow of a pretext, against the King's government, has rendered this measure inevitable. You will readily understand how much it is personally distressing to myself. My friendly feelings towards you induce me to express a hope that you may reserve yourself for the future, and that you will not compromise by false steps the talents which may still advantageously serve the King and the country.

You enjoy at present a pension of six thousand francs chargeable on the department of Foreign Affairs. This allowance will be continued. Rest assured that I shall be happy, in all that is compatible with my duty, to afford you proofs of my sincere attachment.

De Serre.

M. Guizot to M. de Serre.

July 17th, 1820.

I expected your letter; I had reason to foresee it, and I did foresee it when I so loudly declared my disapprobation of the acts and speeches of the Ministers. I congratulate myself that I have nothing to change in my conduct. Tomorrow, as today, I shall belong to myself, and to myself alone.

I have not and I never had any pension or allowance chargeable on the department of Foreign Affairs. I am therefore not necessitated to decline keeping it. I cannot comprehend how your mistake has arisen. I request you to rectify it, as regards yourself and the other Ministers, for I cannot suffer such an error to be propagated.

Accept, I entreat you, the assurance of my respectful consideration.

Guizot.

M. Guizot to the Baron Pasquier, Minister for Foreign Affairs.

Paris, July 17th, 1820.

Baron,

The Keeper of the Seals, on announcing to me that, in common with several of my friends, I am removed from the Council of State, writes to me thus: "You enjoy at present a pension of six thousand francs, chargeable on the department of Foreign Affairs; this allowance will be continued." I have been extremely astonished by this mistake; I am completely ignorant of the cause. I have not and I never had any pension or allowance of any description chargeable on the department of Foreign Affairs. Consequently I am not called upon to refuse its continuance. It will be very easy for you, Baron, to verify this fact, and I request you to do so, as well for the Keeper of the Seals as for yourself, for I cannot suffer the slightest doubt to exist on this subject.

Accept, etc.

Guizot.

The Baron Pasquier to M. Guizot.

Paris, July 18th, 1820.

Sir,

I have just discovered the cause of the mistake against which you protest, and into which I myself led the Keeper of the Seals.

Your name, in fact, appears in the list of expenses chargeable on my department, for a sum of 6000 francs. In notifying this charge to me, an error was committed in marking it as annual: I therefore considered it from that time in the light of a pension.

I have now ascertained that it does not assume that character, and that it related only to a specified sum which had been allowed to you, to assist in the establishment of a Journal. It was supposed that this assistance was to be continued, in the form of an annuity, towards covering the expenses.

I shall immediately undeceive the Keeper of the Seals by giving him the correct explanation.

Receive, I pray you, the assurance of my high consideration.

Pasquier.

No. XII.

M. Béranger to M. Guizot, Minister for Public Instruction.

M. Minister,

Excuse the liberty I take in recommending to your notice the widow and children of Emile Debraux. You will undoubtedly ask who was this Emile Debraux. I can inform you, for I have written his panegyric in verse and in prose. He was a writer of songs. You are too polite to ask me at present what a writer of songs is; and I am not sorry, for I should be considerably embarrassed in answering the question. What I can tell you is, that Debraux was a good Frenchman, who sang against the old Government until his voice was extinguished, and that he died six months after the Revolution of July, leaving his family in the most abject poverty. He was influential with the inferior classes; and you may rest assured that, as he was not quite as particular as I am in regard to rhyme and its consequences, he would have sung the new Government, for his only directing compass was the tricoloured flag.

For myself, I have always disavowed the title of a man of letters, as being too ambitious for a mere sonneteer; nevertheless, I am most anxious that you should consider the widow of Emile Debraux as the widow of a literary man, for it seems to me that it is only under that title she could have any claim to the relief distributed by your department.

I have already petitioned the Commission of Indemnity for Political Criminals, in favour of this family. But under the Restoration, Debraux underwent a very slight sentence, which gives but a small claim to his widow. From that quarter I therefore obtained only a trifle.

If I could be fortunate enough to interest you in the fate of these unfortunate people, I should applaud myself for the liberty I have taken in advocating their cause. I have been encouraged by the tokens of kindness you have sometimes bestowed on me.

I embrace this opportunity of renewing my thanks, and I beg you to receive the assurance of the high consideration with which I have the honour to remain,

Your very humble Servant,

Béranger.

Passy, Feb. 13th, 1834.

END OF VOLUME I.

JOHN EDWARD TAYLOR, PRINTER,
LITTLE QUEEN STREET, LINCOLN'S INN FIELDS.

Printed in Great Britain
by Amazon

21470166R00129